Eagle One

Raising Bald Eagles ~ A Wildlife Memoir

Dec 2013

To Scott,

To a fellow eagle Lover!

Best Regards,

Dianne

Eagle One

 CHANDLER HOUSE PRESS

WORCESTER, MASSACHUSETTS

Book design by Robin Wrighton

Edited by Margaret LeRoux and Gloria Abramoff

ISBN: 978-1886284-80-7

Library of Congress Card Number: 2013936574

Library of Congress Catalog Cataloging-in-Publication Data

Davis, Dianne Benson
Eagle One: Raising Bald Eagles, A Wildlife Memoir

First Edition

ABCDEFGHIJKL

1. Bald eagles—Behavior. 2. Wildlife—Massachusetts.
3. Quabbin Reservoir. 4. Human-animal relationships—Letters, journals.
5. Wildlife veterinary care. 6. Zoo care.

Printed in Lowell, Massachusetts by King Printing Company

Published by

Chandler House Press, Inc.
P. O. Box 20126
West Side Station
Worcester, MA 01602 USA

508 753-7419

Chandlerhousebooks.com

For information on publishing with Chandler House Press,
or for special purchases contact: chandlerhousepress@yahoo.com

Dedication

This book is dedicated to the people whose faith, love and support enabled me to write this book, and especially to

Billy, Becky and Ben ~ The Three Bs!

Table of Contents

Foreword

There are animal people, and there are animal people, and then there is Dianne Davis. Television and the Internet are full of animal people: programs, video clips and "reality" shows whose hosts specialize in everything from sharks and giant snakes to crocodiles, grizzly bears and Big Foot. While these glimpses into the world of certain kinds of wildlife are often entertaining, they aren't always reflective of the natural world. Wildlife is often misrepresented and opportunities for the viewer/reader to gain true insight into animals and animal behavior are lost.

Dianne Davis brings a refreshing, honest and personal perspective to animals, wildlife and to a lifetime devoted to their care and conservation. The list of animals Dianne has cared for and worked to conserve is likely longer than the list of animals she hasn't. In her capacity as naturalist, conservationist, educator, zoo keeper and veterinary technician, Dianne has touched upon virtually every aspect of human/animal interactions. In this, her first book, Dianne shares the variety of animal-related experiences she has enjoyed over her lifetime and the knowledge she has gained from them. Animals have truly defined Dianne's life from early childhood to now a proud grandmother, still currently caring for bald eagles, river otters, foxes, and owls in a zoo environment. She has seemingly developed a sixth sense, a sense that allows her to better understand an animal, whether it be a medical condition, a change in behavior or an action she can take to enhance an animal's well-being.

Perhaps the time that best defines Dianne's dedication to animals is the summer she spent raising and observing eight bald eagle chicks that were brought to her home state of Massachusetts as part of an ambitious project to restore our National Bird to the

Bay State. For the better part of four months, Dianne lived with the eagles, documented their growth, interactions and behaviors and watched them take their first flights, flights that would eventually return the bald eagle to its rightful place in the skies over southern New England. The time spent living in the wild with the eagles, learning about herself and interacting with her colleagues, friends and family would define her as a person and set the foundation for the rest of her life.

Throughout the book, Dianne shares insights about personal growth, hopes, fears, joys and sorrows. She freely shares her feelings about the end of a marriage, concerns for a young daughter, striving for an education and persevering toward her goals. From chapter to chapter the common thread that has shaped Dianne's life and held it together is animals. Add to her summer with the eagles, experiences like a twenty year relationship with a red-tailed hawk, tagging sea turtles, caring for a polar bear and educating thousands of students about the true wonders of nature and you have a clearer understanding of what being a real "animal person" is all about.

Bill Davis

INTRODUCTION

"No, I Don't Want to be a Veterinarian," was going to be the title if I ever wrote a book about animals. This was my standard response every time one of my parents' friends would comment, "You work with animals—you must want to be a veterinarian!" In reality, I always considered myself the right-hand person of the wildlife manager, the zoo director or the veterinarian. Rather than being the boss, I would be the one who fed the animal, held or restrained the animal, talked about the animal and trained people about the care of the animal.

When I said I worked with wildlife, I would get the same questions from animal lovers: How can they get involved with wildlife? How can they get experience working with wildlife? How can they get a job working with wildlife?

My goal is to give people ideas and avenues to help them follow their dreams, whether they are very young students, adults or even retirees. A zoo often provides the first look at exotic animals from around the world (and native animals from close to home) for most people. People ask if I like animals in captivity. Of course I would rather see them in the wild, but the words "species of special concern," "threatened species," "endangered species," and the ultimate word "extinction," are often first learned and understood at zoos. I wanted to work with other people who are dedicated to the daily lives of the animals in our care.

Volunteering is one great way of acquiring the experience and knowledge it takes to get ahead in the animal world. I've always embraced the idea of "See it, do it, teach it." By sharing my experiences with animals, as well as important life experiences, I hope to provide inspiration to others so that they may pursue their dreams, or take a chance when an opportunity knocks.

Finally, I gave a talk and brought some raptors to a college for an ornithology class. I had lunch with the professor before-hand and he commented that he thought that birds didn't have individual personalities. I smiled because I knew the slides I brought were going to change his opinion about that. The next year, he asked if I thought that birds had the ability to recognize different people. I smiled again, knowing someday I would give him a copy of this book.

1

Taking The Plunge

 THIS IS A STORY OF MY EXPERIENCE OF living alone for four glorious months in the most remote area of Massachusetts, the Quabbin Reservoir, with eight baby eagles as my companions. I was part of an ambitious effort to bring the bald eagle back to the state. The eagles would become an important chapter in my life, adding insights and skills that would change me forever.

Now that more than twenty-five years have passed since my time with the eagles, I thought I could reflect back and perhaps take some poetic license describing that long ago summer. However, the journal I kept at Quabbin brought me back to the reality of living each day as it happened and experiencing the earth as it spun. I learned that we are no different from other living creatures. We have behavioral and instinctive qualities that have evolved along with everything else on this planet. Living in the wilderness taught me to take the time to look closely both at animals and humans, their movements, gestures, and mannerisms. I learned the true importance of patient observation that summer.

Bald Eagle Restoration Project

I came to Quabbin when I was thirty-two years old to be a part of the Bald Eagle Restoration Project. This conservation effort by the Massachusetts Division of Fisheries and Wildlife originated in 1982. That year happened to be the bicentennial year of the eagle being named our national symbol. I really didn't know much about the Quabbin Reservoir, even though I had hiked and birded there a few times. The remote reservoir forms a huge "V" in the middle of Massachusetts. The Prescott Peninsula separates the "V" into the east and west valleys. It was said to be a good birding area because of the combination of forest edge and the water itself.

The bald eagle, with its white head and tail, had not nested in Massachusetts since the turn of the twentieth century. At that time, seventy-five percent of the land had been cleared for agricultural purposes, taking eagle habitat with it. Indiscriminate shooting also took its toll, contributing to the eagles' decline. Their seven-foot wing span made it easy for ill-informed people to think of the bald eagle as a threat to their livestock.

A ground-breaking book, *The Birds of Massachusetts and Other New England States* was written by Edward Howe Forbush, the state ornithologist in 1925. "It is only a question of time when [bald] eagles will disappear unless a wildlife reservation can be established in this region," he wrote. Eagles are primarily fish eaters and stay close to water, becoming opportunistic scavengers when need be. The last-known eagle nest in Massachusetts was found in Sandwich on Cape Cod, and the eagles disappeared from the state in 1905.

With a growing human population, undisturbed habitats where bald eagles could set up a territory, successfully raise their young, and find quality feeding grounds were at a premium. The Bald Eagle Protection Act of 1940 was enacted to give the eagles a little breathing room to reoccupy previously lost habitat. Records indicate that the first reported sighting of a bald eagle after the creation of Quabbin was in 1948. They used the locality regularly as a summering and wintering area, but there was no evidence that nesting occurred. During the 1950s and 1960s, the overuse of pesticides poisoned the environment and nearly sealed the fate of the bald eagle in the lower forty-eight states. DDT (dichloro-diphenyl trichloroethane) was welcomed then as a miracle chemical for man's agricultural demands, but spelled disaster for the environment. This chemical worked its way up the food chain and became increasingly concentrated in the tissues of higher predators. Organochlorines like DDT had been found to interfere with the eagles' calcium metabolism, resulting in thinner eggshells that often broke during incubation. Rachel Carson's book, *Silent Spring*, brought the problem to the nation's attention and helped spur a public outcry against the use of DDT.

In December of 1972, the use of DDT was banned in the United States. That landmark decision helped pave the way for restoring the bald eagle as a breeding bird in Massachusetts and the rest of the continental United States. With the passing of the Endangered Species Act in 1973, federal funds became available to further eagle research and protection.

As the remnant eagle population slowly rebounded in Maine, the Quabbin proved to be an ideal wintering location for these birds. Eagles learned to take advantage of the vast open water—which remained ice-free—as places to the north became icebound.

The reservation was uninhabited by humans and recreational activities were limited to specific fishing and hiking areas. This created large, undisturbed areas where the wintering bald eagles and other reclusive animals like the eastern coyote and bobcat could thrive. Porcupines enjoyed browsing the hemlock canopy, much to the dismay of state foresters, while beavers took up residence along every waterway and on many sections of inviting shoreline. There were no reported signs of thousand-pound moose or curious black bear on the Prescott Peninsula in 1985 (otherwise, the chances of a woman being chosen to live at the Quabbin during the restoration project would have been slim to none.)

With watershed areas protected and human access restricted, a prime opportunity to restore the bald eagle in Massachusetts was created. The problem, however, was that no eagles naturally called

Massachusetts home. Maine was the nearest area where a few dozen pairs of eagles were still nesting.

Beginning in 1976, the state of New York successfully pioneered the use of a falconry technique for restoring the bald eagle to their state by modifying the centuries-old method of "hacking" birds. The traditional method was to raise baby raptors, or birds of prey, up to flying age and then train them to hunt with a person in the field. The bird had complete freedom of flight, could sharpen its flying skills, build strong muscles and good lung capacity. All the while, the bird was dependent on humans for food. When the birds developed their ability to hunt by themselves, it was time to begin working together as a hunting team.

The New York and Massachusetts eagle project modified the falconry technique by acquiring five-week-old baby eagles from wild nests in Alaska, the Great Lakes region and Canada, areas where the birds were not endangered. The adopted birds were developing body feathers at that age over a warm downy coat, which protected them from the cold. To prevent the birds from imprinting on their human caretakers, they were fed remotely through a trap door and observed through one-way glass for six weeks while their feathers grew in. Then they released the eagles to the wild in their twelfth week of life. By that age they were full-sized birds and quite capable of flight.

Animals of many species seem to imprint on their surroundings and eventually return to the general area where they grew up to produce their young. Examples include ospreys, which migrate south but return to within twenty miles of where they were raised to nest themselves. Similarly, Atlantic salmon return to spawn in the same tributary where they were hatched years before.

The goal of the eagle project was to allow the natural parents to raise an eaglet for the first five weeks in a wild nest. This allowed the impressionable chick time to fully imprint on its white-headed parents. It also allowed feather growth to be advanced enough so that the babies did not have to be" brooded" or kept warm by their parents. By five weeks of age, the babies had learned to feed themselves.

In 1985, eight different Nova Scotia nests were visited and only one chick was taken from each nest. The other young eagle was left for the parents to raise, eliminating sibling rivalry. The remaining chick would have no competition for the food the parents provided and we would feed the fostered baby all the food he or she needed while under our custodial care.

Each eaglet was placed with another baby at the Quabbin Reservoir on a "hack tower," a thirty-foot tall, man-made structure overlooking their newly adopted habitat. This would allow them to grow up in a seemingly natural, but safe and controlled environment. We hoped that the young eagles would imprint on

their new surroundings in Massachusetts as they began to adjust to life in their artificial eagle nests.

Each eagle was fitted with a United States Fish and Wildlife Service aluminum leg band for identification purposes (sort of like a Social Security number without the benefits!) Each bird also bore a blue numbered tag to distinguish it from the others.

Eating, preening, exercising, and interacting with their nest mate for the next six weeks would be the order of business. They remained on the tower until twelve weeks of age when they attained their full adult size. At that age their plumage was all brown, which even fooled John James Audubon back in the 1800s. He didn't know a juvenile bald eagle looked different from an adult "white-headed" eagle and thought there was an additional species of eagle in America.

When they were eleven weeks old, the now-grown youngsters were caught in their cages so radio transmitters could be attached to the middle tail feather. That way they could be tracked for several months after they left the immediate area in case they ran into trouble. At twelve weeks the babies were strong, antsy, and wanted out. The barred doors opened and the eagles were given their long-awaited freedom. Food was still provided near the tower and along the shores for the eagles to find while they honed their ability to forage and hunt on their own. Over the following months, they gradually dispersed from the Quabbin region. This, in a nutshell, was my task as the "hack site attendant" for the summer of 1985.

Jack Swedberg And Brad Blodget

I need to mention two people who came into my life who were instrumental in both inspiring and helping me to eventually take my place in the eagle restoration project.

I was an impressionable high school teenager when I first met Jack Swedberg. At that time Jack, the senior wildlife photographer for the Massachusetts Division of Fisheries and Wildlife, headed up the restoration project in cooperation with the United States Fish and Wildlife Service and the Metropolitan District Commission (MDC).

At age fifty-six, he dreamed of restoring the bald eagle as a nesting bird in Massachusetts. As a boy, Jack had fished in the Swift River Valley and was himself imprinted on the land that surrounded the reservoir. He gave me the chance of a lifetime to live alone in the wilderness and care for eight baby bald eagles.

Jack was presenting a lecture and film on "Wildlife in Massachusetts" in downtown Worcester. I had been reading passages from *Walden* in English class and was drawn to its nature theme. I obtained a ticket at the school office and went after school by myself. I was totally engrossed in the lecture and film about Jack's wildlife adventures. He observed and photographed wildlife while sitting in a blind.

Sometimes he camouflaged himself in a man-made beaver lodge, and then floated the lodge around a pond with cameras poking out through holes in between the sticks. He joked about the time a father was canoeing with his child and she happened to see the "beaver lodge." "What's that, Daddy?" she asked.

"Why it's a beaver lodge and I bet there is a beaver family in there right now." Jack was tempted to say something from inside the blind but thought better of it. He didn't want to be responsible for a capsized canoe.

I have always subconsciously compiled goals I hoped to accomplish in my life. That day, at the age of sixteen, I added to the list: "Spend a day in the field watching wildlife with Jack Swedberg."

When I was a senior in high school I volunteered as a junior naturalist at the Worcester Science Center. My job there involved working with polar bears, mountain lions, wolves, birds of prey and exotic animals. Jack Swedberg, along with his co-worker, Bill Byrne, a photographer with Mass Fish and Wildlife, came for a tour of the museum. I felt honored to shake Jack's hand and let him know how much I had enjoyed his wonderful nature film.

Brad Blodget

Another naturalist who was influential in my life was a birder, Brad Blodget. As a member of the Forbush Bird Club, he and the other birders often wandered through our backyard on their way to see the good array of warblers in our adjoining woods. Brad, with his lanky 6′5″ frame and blond hair, always stood out among the group of much older die-hard birders. He must have been in his early twenties at the time.

It seemed odd to me to see a young man walking along, peering into the woods looking for a pileated woodpecker that he had heard from the road. I was intrigued and began to believe that it was okay to be seen being actively engaged with nature, and still be "normal."

I got to know Brad better when he was hired at the Worcester Science Center as an educational associate. He greeted the public and did wonderful educational programs. He seemed out of his element, though, with crowds of noisy school children.

I saw a different person when we sometimes went birding together. He would call in warblers by "pishing," making soft noises like "chit-chit-chit." At the sound of his vocalization, birds flew out of the woods and up in the tree above our heads. Pishing captivated warblers, chickadees and the chatty tufted titmouse. He taught me so much about birds and made the learning fun.

One day we left a birding area in the town of Petersham and headed to an Audubon sanctuary to continue looking for birds. We chuckled at the different bird calls that sounded like human phrases. For instance, the secretive barred owl hoots, "Who cooks for you, who cooks for you all," and the song sparrow sings out, "Madge, Madge, Madge, please put on your tea kettle." The cute-sounding yellow warbler sings, "Sweet, sweet, sweeter than sweet." Brad would follow up with, "Quick—three beers," by the olive-sided flycatcher. Then came the ever pleasant, "Please, please, please to meet you," by the chestnut-sided warbler. How about, "Old Sam Peabody, Peabody, Peabody, poor Sam Peabody, Peabody, Peabody," by the white-throated sparrow? I started to doubt him when he came up with, "Here I am, where are you, way up high," by the red-eyed vireo. He had fun sharing them and we laughed as we pulled into the Audubon parking lot.

Suddenly Brad shouted, "Women unite! Fight for the night!"

I said, "Wow, what bird says that?"

He answered, "Huh? Oh, that's a bumper sticker on that car in front of us."

Brad sure knew his birds. Eventually he decided to leave the museum and go back to school and pursue a master's degree in biology. It was a smart move; years later he became the state ornithologist for Massachusetts Fish and Wildlife.

2

Childhood Connections

 MY FIRST RECOLLECTION OF AN INTEREST in wildlife came when I was six years old. My older brother Ronnie and his neighborhood friends were chasing a baby bunny around our yard. The scared rabbit sought shelter under our neighbor's small porch. Being quite small myself, I was hurriedly escorted over to the cramped crawl space and told to go under and get that prized bunny! I was half

squeezed and half shoved into the tight quarters. Although it was quite dark, the sun's rays filtered through the latticework on the side. The small brown creature that I was to capture and surrender to my brother was at the other end of the narrow crawl space under the porch. He remained motionless with his ears back against his neck and a blank stare on his face. I inched my way slowly on my stomach with head low and arms out to my sides. My sneakers dug into the dusty dirt just enough to propel me forward at a snail's pace in the cramped space. I was going to be a hero in my big brother's eyes, I hoped.

As I approached to within arm's reach of my quarry, my now dirty face brushed up against an awful sticky, invisible wall. In the dim light I couldn't identify this sudden roadblock, but the tacky material gave as I pulled back. Ahhh, a spider's web—and it had been on my face! I panicked as I tried to scramble back out, but in my fright I filled my lungs with the dusty air and wedged myself against the supporting framework of the porch.

My brother asked what was taking so long. I squeaked, "Spider web!" I could see the bunny still quietly positioned in the far corner. Now I was trapped and scared like him.

My brother instructed me not to move. I thought he was going to rescue me. A minute later a bristly object was pushed up beside me. It was a broom. "Hit the web with the broom," Ronnie said. They didn't care about me! As I hit the web I thought of the spider that lived in that web. It now had to be on the ground with me. As I advanced, the bunny darted out another exit, and I was stuck with the possibility that the spider was on me. Just as I started to panic again, my brother dragged me out backwards by my feet. The rest of the kids had run off after the bunny. I came out of that experience with a sore back, scraped stomach, sympathy for the bunny and a fear of spiders in tight areas that lasts to this day.

Turning Points

I grew up in Worcester, Massachusetts, but when I was seven and eight years old I spent two impressionable years in the nearby town of Sudbury. The Sudbury River was just down the street and I spent a fair amount of time there catching bullfrogs. If I approached slowly and talked in a soft voice, they just sat there and let me grab them. I loved catching the big ones, but I always let them go. There was nothing quite like the eye of a bullfrog for its beauty. I caught and brought home painted turtles to show my brother. Sometimes my turtle container wasn't reliable and the turtles escaped. Once, as I ran for the school bus, I passed one of the turtles on its way back to the river. I never kept them more than a few days, especially after one left me with a bloody bite mark on my index finger.

Ronnie and I often went to the river to search for snakes. I always looked for the elusive ones and grabbed them by the tail. They tried to bite, but I eventually rode my bike home with a snake in my bicycle basket.

Ronnie told me that Mom was afraid of snakes, but she never let me know. She always seemed proud of my ability to bring home yet another animal because she understood how happy it made me.

My Nature Instructor

In grammar school I had the good fortune of having a nature instructor from Audubon come into my fifth grade class. Her name was Miss Marjorie Smith, and she was tall and thin with glasses. Her most-used word was the mispronunciation of the word *interesting*. Everything was "very inneresting" and so, of course, that's what we called her, "Miss Inneresting."

Her first nature lesson was about the migration of monarch butterflies. It just so happened that I spent the previous weekend visiting my grandparents' house in New Hampshire. I captured many monarch butterflies in the field across the street from their house and brought them home. My father and I fashioned an old clothes hamper into a large cage with screening on the front. Now I knew why there were so many of them in the field that day. They were migrating!

I raised my hand so that I could tell Miss Smith I had captured seven monarchs the day before. She seemed genuinely thrilled and suggested we band the butterflies at lunch time. She asked for directions to my house and met me there.

I caught the butterflies one at a time and she banded the right wing with a little piece of sticky paper which had a number and an address where whoever found the butterfly could write in and report it. We let each one go separately and watched them fly away.

During the next class, "Miss Inneresting" gave us a sheet of paper on birds of prey. The lesson taught us all about the different kinds of hawks in Massachusetts: the buteos, accipiters and falcons. I was mesmerized by the whole topic and listened intently. (I have kept and copied that paper for over thirty-five years and have shared it with others interested in hawks.) Miss Smith's attention and enthusiasm were instrumental in shaping my future, especially my work with birds of prey.

In grammar school I recall having trouble with reading books. One teacher told me I garbled the English language. I had a hard time concentrating and I spent most of my time staring out the window. Consequently, I was held back in the fourth grade.

In junior high school one of my English teachers took pity on me and brought me to the library. She asked me what I was interested in, and I said I had kept a pet squirrel in grammar school and that I liked falcons. We looked in the index catalog under falcons and found a book called, *The Summer of the Falcon*, by Jean Craighead George. That book was another turning point in my life. It was about a girl my age who raised a young falcon. She had to decide whether to act like a young lady or to go outdoors and be with her falcon. I loved that story and wanted to read more.

Mickey And Thunder

I've kept animals ever since I was in grammar school and they all contributed something that helped shape my future. I had in my care: two Dutch rabbits, two hamsters, anoles (lizards), the cats, Thunder and Samantha and a gray squirrel named Mickey that I had found on my paper route. She had fallen out of her nest on top of a telephone pole. Her nose was bleeding, so I took her home. I fed her with an eye dropper that she latched onto with her long, thin fingers. She made a cute suckling noise as she drank, followed me around the house, and slept in a drawer next to my bed. I did my sixth grade school project on her. I drew pictures of her eating out of the cat bowl and chasing me around the yard like a little madman, while Thunder, the cat, looked on. I still have that poster.

Pete

I have been sort of a loner all my life. My best friends in junior high school were my dog, Pete, my cat, Samantha, and my Muscovy duck, Chuck, with whom I whiled away the lazy summer months.

Pete was a border collie-shepherd mix. He and I would get up early in the morning and take off into the adjacent woods. We traveled miles up and down the power lines, followed streams to their origin and explored old paths we found in the deep woods. We ate lunch from food that I stuffed in my coat pockets.

Pete showed me that animals communicate with one another. He once ran up to another dog, barked twice and then they both tore up the street together. Who knows what they were after? If they could communicate through barking then I could communicate with Pete. It was a great relationship. When I was home sick from school he would curl up by my side until I got better. He walked by my side and every few steps looked up at me for attention and approval. Every once in a great while, he got out of line and I found myself hissing backwards through my teeth. Then he would obediently sit by my side and look up with questioning eyes. We all loved Pete, but Ronnie always said there was no question that Pete was "Dianne's dog."

Samantha

Samantha, our black cat, was very independent. She loved being outside and was a fixture on our side porch. Our house was two hundred and fifty years old and had many holes in the foundation where she found intruding mice. My parents were glad to have her. If Pete was by my side, Samantha was always in my lap.

One late night while I brushed my teeth and got ready for bed, Samantha called to me with an unsettling "meow." She was quite pregnant at the time. When I came out she led me to my room and jumped up on the bed. I gently crawled under the covers and Samantha settled down on my lap. I called to my family and they came in and watched as Samantha pushed against my hands with each contraction. She gave birth to four black kittens. She cared for them diligently and was a good mother. She was very comfortable with me doting over them. I loved her dearly too, and she and Pete helped me through my long, teenage years.

Chuck

And then there was Chuck. When I was fifteen, our family visited our uncle's farm in rural Michigan for a reunion. We had lots of cousins, some we knew and some we really didn't know at all. Everybody got along fine, playing and sleeping in the hay barn. I felt uncomfortable with so many kids, so I tagged along with my cousin, Jerry, who worked on a dairy farm down the dirt road. We milked cows, sprayed milk into the barn kittens' mouths, spread manure and drank cold raw milk out of the cooling tanks. I spent the whole week traveling back and forth from the farm. I loved being up close with the big cows. I think I spent more time petting them than milking them. I learned to drive for the first time in a beat-up old farm truck. I only ran into the electric fence once! When the week was up, Jerry surprised me with a duckling to take home with me. I couldn't believe my parents let me keep it. We headed home in the family station wagon with my entire family and one duck.

We had to cross into Canada on our way home to Massachusetts and we weren't certain that pet ducks were welcome. At the border my mother was so nervous that she put her hand over her heart and kept repeating, "1926, 1926," when the guards asked *where* she was born. I thought we were goners. The duck was hidden in a box with a blanket and some magazines over it. We snuck him into the hotel and up the elevator. There were other people with us and he didn't peep once until the other people got off at their floor. Then he gave a series of soft peeps and we laughed all the way to our floor. He slept in the bathtub so he wouldn't leave "packages" on the rug.

I named him "Chuck" and my father purchased another duckling at the feed store to keep him company. Both turned out to be South American Muscovy ducks. I named the second one Little One because he was so small. We had a stream running alongside our property, so my father and I built a little dam and let the water fill up to become a swirling pool. We built a duck house and fenced in the surrounding area. There they lived happily and I started high school that fall.

The Elvidge Farm

There was a feature story in the local newspaper about an older couple who owned a dairy farm in Grafton, Massachusetts. I wrote them a detailed letter about my summer farming experience and they invited me to visit them and their cows. My mom drove me there and after a tour of their farm they asked me if I wanted to work there on weekends. They didn't have to ask me twice.

My parents dropped me off on Friday nights and Mr. Elvidge and I got up before the crack of dawn on Saturdays and wandered, bleary-eyed, to the old barn. There were over fifty cows to milk twice a day. We worked our tails off and at noontime Mrs. Elvidge had a huge lunch waiting for us. I couldn't believe how much food I ate. Soon we went back to work and cleaned up the barn before the afternoon's milking. Wesley and Eleanor Elvidge were the nicest, friendliest, people I had ever met.

Learning From My Ducks

Between milking cows and spending time with Pete, Samantha and Chuck, my life was great. Chuck, who I was sure was a female, matured to feathers of greens and browns and could fly, but her mate, Little One, became too heavy to get off the ground. I guess his name didn't fit him too well. For exercise, Chuck would fly circles around our acre of land at tree level. She and Little One watched the sky frequently and if they saw a hawk they would keep an eye on it until it moved out of sight. It seemed every day they practiced "how to avoid getting picked off by a hawk." One duck started making noises, since they really didn't quack, followed by the other duck doing the same thing while in the water. They moved their wings in and out and quickly worked themselves into a frenzy, and then dived under the water, came to the surface, and then dived with much fanfare again and again.

At the time, I often watched the television program, "Wild Kingdom." On one show a wild duck was swimming in the water when a falcon dived down and latched onto it. The duck used that same tactic of diving again and again and the falcon finally had to let go or be drowned. I learned so much from my ducks at the time!

In the winter I chopped a large hole in the ice so they could swim. In the spring, Chuck left a surprise in the duck box where they slept at night. A beautiful egg! She laid a whole clutch and sat on them dutifully. Upon hatching, the ducklings followed their parents onto the grass in search of bugs and tender shoots. We found homes for all of them at the feed store where I had acquired Little One.

Little One and his mate enjoyed the summer and Chuck learned to fly to the hickory tree outside my second-story window. From there she would fly into my bedroom. One day Little One disappeared. With Pete by my side, I desperately searched everywhere. I followed the quiet stream up and down and all through the adjacent woods. We spent a miserable week looking for Little

One but without success. Chuck started to come to my window more often and slept in the hickory tree at night.

I was walking home one day when a young girl from up the street told me she was sorry that her dog had killed my duck. I ran home and told my mom and she said she knew. "Why didn't you tell me?" I cried. She said she didn't want to break my heart.

High School

High school was the most intense time of my life, or so I thought. I attended Burncoat Senior High School in Worcester instead of Doherty High School, the neighborhood high school where my brother and sisters went, because Burncoat offered agricultural courses. I am grateful to my junior high school guidance counselor for noticing my interest in wildlife and nature. He alerted me when an agricultural teacher from Burncoat came to our school to speak to anyone interested in the plant and animal sciences.

My parents were very supportive, considering my enrollment meant that I had to take a bus that traveled past the school my twin sister, Linda, attended. Then I had to transfer downtown at city hall and head out across town, to the Burncoat area. I was the only female in the dual programs.

The ecology movement was in its infancy and I celebrated the first Earth Day in 1970, collecting trash along the shores of Lake Quinsigamond in Worcester. I remember taking a bus across town and being handed a plastic trash bag. I was then taken to a secluded section of the lake and left by myself. Trash was everywhere. It seemed to me that there must be a better way of dealing with the environment than dropping concerned citizens off to clean up after inconsiderate people. There were tires, a washing machine and a grocery carriage sticking out of the shallow water. I remember thinking that I should write a letter to the local newspaper to remind people that it was a waste of energy and resources to pick up what shouldn't be there in the first place. I hoped Earth

Day would work its way into schools so the environmental movement could expand in the future.

In tenth grade I took an English literature course that helped me find the words to describe my bond with nature. I felt a deep personal connection reading Thoreau and Emerson. One of our assignments was to read passages from *Walden* that described the importance of living "deliberately" and learning to "simplify, simplify." These were ideals I could identify with. Knowing that others shared the notion of "loving to be alone" allowed me to do just that. Before, I had always thought there was something wrong with me. Emerson in "Self-Reliance" wrote, "Insist on yourself; never imitate. Your own gifts you can present every moment." In Emerson's book, *Nature*, he wrote, "Nature satisfies the soul purely by its loveliness." I knew for the first time there were others who had the same passion for living a life in tune with the natural world. School seemed more bearable and I felt secure in the authors' words.

I wrote my term paper in health class on pollution. At the time, the Blackstone River in Massachusetts was one of the most polluted rivers in America. At home I created a floor-to-ceiling collage for my bedroom wall on environmental pollution and wildlife in trouble. I showed smokestacks pouring filth into the atmosphere, peregrine falcons' eggshells thinning because of the misuse of pesticides and a bald eagle that had been shot. The poster also showed multi-colored contaminants flowing from factories and spilling into major rivers.

I covered my bedroom walls with *Life* and *Look* magazine photos of animals and scenic landscapes from around the globe. My mother was quite tolerant of my artistic taste, considering all the thumbtack holes. I also displayed a poster of Earth taken from one of the Apollo space flights to the moon. It was the one where you could see the earth rising up behind the moon that dominated the foreground. It made me aware that the earth was all we had. It's just an ancient ball, completely self-contained. There were no replacement parts, so we all have to work commonly as one unit for its protection.

3

Gaining Experience

Zookeeper

 AFTER VOLUNTEERING AT THE SCIENCE Center in Worcester during high school, I was offered a job as a fulltime zookeeper when I graduated. I decided not to attend Colorado State University to study zoology even though I had been accepted as a freshman. I stayed at the Science Center for six years and married my co-worker, Paul, who was also a zookeeper. We were inseparable. He first asked me out one night while I was putting new paint on the walls of the gila monster's exhibit and he was painting the kestrel's (sparrow hawk) enclosure. When we went on a date, it was to a pet shop to learn all about the different reptiles and exotics they sold. You could buy anything back then, including endangered species like the indigo snake from Florida or a burrowing owl from out west. We went canoeing on our days off to isolated ponds to catch and release turtles.

Sheba And Wolf

One day we received two wolves at the center that had been raised as pets. The female, Sheba, had been kept in a dirty backyard and bred with a domestic dog to produce wolf/dog hybrids to be sold as "wild" pets. She was somewhat tame and Paul developed a bonding relationship with her. The male wolf was brought to us by animal control officers. The cautious men had him chained to the inside wall of the van. When they opened the door, there he was with the fur on his back raised and his teeth bared. He was one scary animal. They removed him with a long rabies pole and led him to the enclosed exhibit where Sheba was. We respectfully named him Wolf. The two of them got along fine and Paul and I were allowed to be a part of their pack. Daily cleaning and feeding went along smoothly.

Everything went well and everyone got along fine until the next spring when coy Sheba came into heat. Sheba, who loved Paul's attention, started to act a little friskier around him. She lowered her head and put her long tail between her legs and had love in her eyes. Paul, in turn, gave her lots of attention and belly rubs. Wolf, up to this time, accepted Paul too. Paul was still the Alpha male, but everything was about to change. Paul entered the exhibit one day and Wolf walked slowly up to him and put his large front paws on Paul's shoulders. They looked into each other's eyes and Wolf gave a low guttural growl. Sheba was now Wolf's mate and Paul knew his new place in the pack. At that same time, Sheba raised her hackles to me and paced the entrance door with teeth bared when I arrived to clean. I decided not to enter the exhibit anymore.

Paul was still able to work with the wolves every day. Sheba and Wolf dug a deep den in the hill and raised four black-colored pups. Paul was allowed to go down in the dark den and check on the litter. One day he came up with two dead pups. It seemed that Sheba neglected or killed them and stuffed them in a corner of the den. Maybe she knew the exhibit was not big enough to have four young pups. When the remaining pups were old enough to come to the den entrance, Wolf trotted down to the feeding area and gobbled up the food as fast as he could. Then he trotted back up to the cozy den and whined until the wobbly pups appeared at the entrance. They licked his large face until he regurgitated the tasty food from his stomach. The pups grew quickly and knew their place in the pack.

At work we raised all kinds of orphaned, native birds and mammals, including owls, hawks, songbirds, baby raccoons, cottontails, gray squirrels, woodchucks and assorted other creatures. All that practical experience in native animal husbandry helped us acquire skills necessary to raise a neglected wolf pup from Sheba and Wolf one spring.

Nahani

We named the pup Nahani and Paul became her guardian. Every morning, even as a young pup, she made a little high-pitched howling noise for her breakfast of milk formula. She downed a bottle in no time at all and then curled up in a ball in her cozy towels and fell asleep. We learned a lot about nutrition and formulas because she developed a calcium deficiency that had to be corrected.

We walked Nahani around the property and occasionally led her beside the wolf enclosure that held her mother, father and older siblings from the previous year. The pack ran back and forth along the fence, eyeing her with close attention. Nahani pranced back and forth, wagging her tail and jumping up and down as in

NAHANI THE WOLF CUB

play. When she grew older, Paul tried to reintroduce her to the wolf pack. She walked in with her tail held high and a bounce in her step. To our horror, Nahani was immediately attacked. Paul ran in and tried desperately to separate the group and grab Nahani out of there. She suffered multiple puncture wounds and lacerations that required stitches.

She had entered a wolf pack that had an established order and discipline. Each animal knew its place based on a hierarchy. Wolf reigned supreme. His mate was second and last year's pups were old enough to know where they stood. There never were any battles among them. Nahani walked into their territory with a playful approach. She should have entered the exhibit with her head and tail down in a submissive posture. She was lucky they didn't kill her and it was clear that we still had a lot to learn about animal behavior. We had to find her a new home away from the Science Center because we had nowhere else to keep her.

Red-Tailed Hawk

Another time we acquired a juvenile, red-tailed hawk. I decided to work with him, remembering the book I read in junior high school, *The Summer of the Falcon*. I started to call him to the fist with a piece of meat on a thick glove. I didn't remember how to make the fastening straps called jesses for the legs so I worked without them. I practiced with him only in the exhibit and remembered reading that you should not look directly at a wild hawk when you first start working with one. They don't like it.

While I was in the exhibit one day, a visitor asked me a question and I mistakenly looked right into the eyes of this wild creature. He immediately glared at me, opened his mouth in rage and flew at my unprotected face. He attached his talons to my skin and battered me with his wings. I remember one talon was stuck and I had to pry it out quickly. I could feel blood running down my face like tears. That encounter convinced me that I needed to research the art of falconry. Since the bird was wild enough, we decided to let him go.

The Fire

Paul was a herpetologist and kept many venomous snakes that I never handled. The director of the museum let us live in an old house on the property that had plenty of room for Paul's rattlesnakes, vipers and non-venomous snakes. We were newly married and moved in after replacing all the wallpaper and getting all new appliances. One night after we went out for dinner at a coworker's house, some kids set a couple of fires in the neighborhood for kicks. They set a garage on fire down the hill and while fighting that fire, one of the firemen looked up over the trees and noticed a second, larger fire; it was our house! When we returned home to the blaze and the firemen arrived, Paul yelled that there were venomous snakes in the house. They stopped dead in their tracks. After the fire was just about out, they put a fireman's coat on Paul, attached a rope to him, and sent him into the smoldering house to get the snakes out.

All the snakes were dead from the smoke and heat. One fireman came over to me with his up-turned hat in his hand. It held a black kitten that I had received a week earlier; she didn't make it either. It was a very sad day; the house was a complete loss.

Ursa The Polar Bear

Our biggest challenge as zookeepers came in 1976 when the Science Center's female polar bear, Ursa, carried one of her day-old twin cubs out of the protected den and into the open exhibit area. Major, her thousand-pound mate, had been removed and sent to another zoo during her pregnancy. He would harm the baby if left in the exhibit.

A local reporter covering the story on the birth of the twin cubs was with us when this happened. That was a special event as the twins were the first polar bear cubs to be born in captivity on the East Coast.

We ran outside and watched in bewilderment as Ursa cautiously carried the screaming baby in her mouth. She dangled the delicate cub upside down by a tiny hind foot. Ursa weighed over six hundred pounds, while her hairless infant weighed just twenty-two ounces! The neonate's eyes and ears were still closed because of its young age. The cold December air was still, broken only by the clicking of the reporter's camera and the human-like screams of the tiny helpless cub. It was an eerie and frightening sound. Ursa tried to abandon the helpless baby in some moist leaves, but hurried back and picked up the infant with the next wail. She paced back and forth and walked over to the exhibit pool and dunked the baby in the frigid water. She quickly lifted it back out as the cub squirmed from the cold. It was so disheartening watching Ursa. She seemed driven

to abandon the baby but was unable to follow through because of the cub's stimulating cries. Ursa appeared frustrated and began carelessly swinging the baby, allowing it to forcefully hit the rough concrete walls. We felt helpless because we couldn't safely approach Ursa. We decided to close the heavy steel door while she was in the outside exhibit area and go in the den and retrieve the other baby. We had no idea why she had taken the first cub out of her den and we didn't want her to return to hurt or kill the second baby.

We raised the inside door to the den and entered nervously, not knowing what to expect. The vulnerable cub was lying in a bed of straw and seemed so small, barely the size of a dog pup. Her black skin was easily noticeable through a crew cut of white fur. The tiny paws were the size of a dime. Paul scooped her up in a towel and rushed her into the museum, where we nestled her in an empty aquarium with a soft towel under a heat lamp. We were certainly not expecting this turn of events, for Ursa had been taking care of them for a day.

We returned to the exhibit and were eventually able to retrieve the other critically wounded cub from Ursa, only to see it die from its injuries the next day. A necropsy revealed a ruptured duodenum or small intestine, which was probably why she was trying to abandon it. Ursa instinctively knew there was something wrong with the cub.

The news coverage was nonstop from that moment on. The local reporter who had witnessed the drama made it front page news. The plight of the surviving cub traveled swiftly around the world. The media attention became overwhelming. Four television news stations converged on us the second morning and some asked me to persuade the tiny cub to cry on camera. Through my facemask I made eye contact with the museum director who nodded his agreement when I gave him a "back me up when I politely refuse the request" look.

Sasha

Paul and I lived at the zoo for the next two months, caring for the healthy cub that we named Sasha. We spent Christmas of 1975 and the New Year, toasting the continuing success of the growing baby. The junior naturalists, teenage volunteers, bought us a small live evergreen to be planted in the spring in Sasha's honor.

We wore facemasks and scrubbed our hands thoroughly to minimize the threat to the tiny cub's immune system. We slept on the museum's rugged floor and ate on an irregular schedule. I lost more than twenty pounds from the combination of poor diet, lack of sleep and constant bouts with winter colds that passed easily through the staff.

I left after two months of caring for Sasha because

I became dangerously thin. A chest X-ray revealed spots on my lungs, the onset of pneumonia. It was clear that I needed to go home and recuperate. Sasha, who seemed to be doing great, walking and moving around, suddenly died on her eightieth day while I was home. It was a devastating loss. The physical and emotional stress of the entire situation led me to leave the zoo. I needed to distance myself and completely recover from the whole ordeal. Paul left the Science Center soon after.

That experience would prove valuable; when I raised the baby eagles, the lessons learned from the tiny polar bear cub became evident. I conditioned myself to eat three square meals a day, sleep eight hours each night and just take better care of myself. I knew I couldn't allow myself to get that rundown again.

4

Habiba

 IN 1978, WHEN I WAS TWENTY-FIVE YEARS old, I became a licensed falconer and wildlife rehabilitator. I flew a two-year-old red-tailed hawk named Habiba, which means "sweetheart" in Arabic.

She had been hand-raised at a nature facility. She was too tame to be released back to the wild, but I could give her an opportunity to fly free and let her hunt her natural prey of small mammals. At that time I was the only female falconer in Massachusetts, but made lasting friends with the other falconers when I went to annual falconry meets.

Habiba and I had a great relationship. She probably had been found as a downy chick at a few weeks of age and her behavior pattern was altered by the hand-rearing technique used in those days. She was fed and raised by people, so she imprinted, or recognized herself as a pint-sized human being and developed a "chirping" vocabulary. Because of this misguided upbringing, she chased after her own species instead of coexisting with them when we passed through fields. She was a mixed-up bird, now stuck in a human world. Her only hope for a halfway normal life was to be given to a falconer who could let her fly free to hunt during the winter months. (We had to abide by hunting laws and hunting seasons.) Because of her "vocal" habits my sponsor in falconry

DIANNE AND HABIBA HUNTING IN A WINTER FIELD

gave her to me. He said we both talked a lot and should make a good team. He felt she would be a good bird for me to start off with as an apprentice in the sport.

Her voice was soft and friendly yet changed with the passing seasons. When upset or territorial she let out a loud ear-piercing scream. With a cold stare and arched back she looked quite menacing to any rival red-tailed hawk in the area. In her brown eyes, so true and clear, I could sense her predatory way of life. Her fixed brow gave her a look of intensity known throughout her species. Each smooth feather revealed a multitude of patterns and an array of colors. Between the teardrop-like streaks adorning her breast and splashes of white on her brown back, she was perfectly camouflaged in the natural environment. If hot or upset, Habiba pulled her feathers tightly against her body, which made her look like she was wearing long baggy feather pants. When relaxed, she looked twice her natural size. Each feather stood out to give her an appearance of a fluffy, warm, and contented bird. Lastly, her black talons were long, sharp, and menacing. Potential animal traps and defense mechanisms, they also were used for precise landings and accurate head scratching, even around her eyes. Her talons, used in conjunction with her beak, equipped her with permanent utensils. Nature did right by her.

After a season of unity and partnership in the field, our relationship evolved. As the gentle breezes and warm spring came, her internal biological clock sensed a time to find a mate and raise a family. As a human, I was her unnatural, but only choice. One day she flew to a corner of her mews and crouched down. She stared straight ahead and wouldn't look at me. Dipping and swaying with her bronze wings and dark orange tail, she lowered her body down flat as a pancake. What was this new behavior? Well, I'd watched enough nature shows on television to know she was playing hard to get and wanted me to play along. On a daily basis, she displayed exaggerated body language, hoping to entice me to breed with her. I finally put my hands firmly on her back and her tail instantly moved to the side. Hmmm, interesting! A pat under her tail convinced her that we had mated and her instinct took over.

Nesting

I scattered piles of sticks randomly in her living quarters. Meticulously and methodically, she looked each one over and decided which stick was perfect for the framework of her nest. One by one she took long twigs in her talons or reached down and picked them up in her beak. The weight of the twig sent her head swaying from side to side. She laid the sticks down to form a perfect natural nest. Pine boughs I provided lined the inside, forming a warm and soft barrier between her and the uncomfortable sticks. After some years of observing this behavior, I noticed that she did not lay eggs until the green boughs appeared. She then laid a single, splotched egg and a few days later, another: this time a solid pale green-colored egg. They were things of beauty, round and smooth but unfortunately not fertile.

HABIBA LINING HER NEST WITH PINE BOUGHS AND FEATHERS

HABIBA ATTEMPTING TO FEED THE BABY CHICKEN

Brooding Eggs

I called Tom Ricardi, a good falconry friend of mine who had raised and bred rare peregrine falcons successfully. He suggested I give her some fertile chicken eggs to see if she could brood them and hatch them out. I acquired two duck eggs and although I shined a bright light on them every few days and watched the shadows develop, they never hatched. Tom said if the temperature drops below a certain threshold, the embryo stops developing. I also read that the female red-tail sits on the nest sixty percent of the time, with her mate incubating the eggs in between. I wasn't doing my part!

Rooster

One season, after "mating" with Habiba and providing sticks and greenery to line her nest, I acquired a fertile chicken egg to replace her clutch. This time I relieved her of her duties so she could eat, exercise, and take an extended bath. I kept the developing egg in my pocket with a hot water bottle. This time it hatched. The downy yellow chick was tiny. Habiba was a good mother and cared for it diligently, thinking it was her own. After all, she watched it hatch from an egg that she was sitting on. She doted

over the fluff ball and tried to feed it dead mice. Habiba tore off tiny pieces and offered it to her baby. "Mom" was getting frustrated because her chick was not stationary or looking up for food. Habiba started feeding the top of the baby's head and matted the feathers down. The chick just wandered around the nest and looked for grain to eat. I obliged by providing chicken scratch on the side until it got used to looking up to accept the tasty morsels of meat from its foster mom. It took both of them a while to work out the kinks but before too long, the chick started to look up and accept Habiba's increasingly generous portions of meat.

The chick grew to be a full-grown white rooster and was actually taller than Habiba. While Habiba sat on her high perch outside in the sun, the rooster perched right beside her. Even though the process of hatching and raising young was a success, the experience was still frustrating to me because Habiba was not naturally raising her own species.

Baby Hawk

Years later a downy hawk was brought to me, an orphan from a felled tree. The siblings had been killed. I introduced the frightened chick to Habiba, but she wanted nothing to do with it. She was sitting on eggs at the time. I fed the baby repeatedly in front of her and she stood there and watched. All of a sudden Habiba stepped in front of me and took the food I was offering the hungry chick. Habiba took over the feedings and proceeded to raise the nestling. As the chick grew I realized it was a broad-winged hawk, which is in the same family of hawks but not as large as a red-tail. The fledgling baby eventually flew away as Habiba watched with indifference. I vowed not to cross-foster a different species again because the broad-winged imprinted on the red-tail. Wait until it tried to mate as an adult with a red-tail hawk: dinner would be served. I was still learning. There was always next year.

Love Triangle

When Habiba and I went out hunting in the cold winter months, I usually let her fly up to a tall tree the minute we were away from the car. I noticed that when my husband Paul came, Habiba would fly at him and brush him on the shoulder with her outstretched wings. Sometimes she even landed on his back and hunched over, giving her ear-piercing scream. Habiba asserted her dominance and showed Paul his place in this bizarre love triangle.

Hunting Rabbits

When we hunted, I started walking and worked the low bushes with my foot until I found a handy poking stick. As I walked I turned and said, "Are you coming?" Habiba flew out of the tree and sailed past me up into a lofty tree far beyond. If I saw a bunny first I shouted, "Ho...Ho...Ho!" If she was paying attention she would turn and look my way. If she saw the quarry darting through the underbrush she catapulted off her branch and gave chase. Of course the quick bunnies weren't stupid. They knew where their dens were and either made a beeline for one of them or started a long run that took them on a very large circular route covering a great distance.

Most of the time the watchful bunny was too well adapted to its territory and Habiba was no match. Sometimes Habiba surprised one and crashed through the bushes or along a rabbit trail. I ran to the spot and saw Habiba mantling over bunny fur, peeping and grabbing it as if to say, "I almost got it, see?"

I was out one cold but calm day at our favorite hunting ground when I heard some rustling to the side of me. Habiba and I were both on the alert. Out between some brush stepped a young boy of about twelve. I introduced myself and pointed to Habiba in the tree. I don't think he knew what to make of us. I called Habiba down to my fist so that the boy could get a closer look. I let him pat her and then I let her fly back into another tree. I put the glove on the boy's fist with a piece of meat and

DIANNE OFFERS A TREAT FOR HABIBA'S LANDING

called Habiba back down. As she came swiftly to the glove I told the boy she wouldn't hurt him and to hold the glove up firmly. Habiba landed lightly on the glove to receive the morsel of food and the expression on the boy's face was enlightening. He was speechless but elated that he was holding a red-tailed hawk on his fist. We went our separate ways, believing that this would be a one-time encounter.

Habiba And The Red Fox

Once Habiba was out in front of me and quickly flew down to the middle of an old hay field. I gave chase and as I rounded a large black walnut tree, there was Habiba standing in the open with wings outstretched. What was she doing now? Something was jumping up in front of her but my view was blocked by Habiba's body. As I approached, there stood a beautiful red fox, with his front paw caught in a steel leg-hold trap. He was scared to death and paid more attention to me than the annoying hawk that kept chest-punching him. Habiba kept up the attack by whipping her wings in the fox's face. He just eyed me as he backed up as far as the chain on the trap would let him and winced at Habiba's mock assaults. I quickly pushed Habiba aside, for the terrified fox could have had her for a snack if he wasn't caught. I stood there and told him it was okay, using a soft soothing voice. I slowly took my heavy winter jacket off and inched my way forward, gently putting it over the fox. Habiba kept trying to interfere and I told her to leave him alone.

Once the trembling fox was covered I tried to open the trap. I found I couldn't hold the fox to avoid getting bitten and spring the release on the trap at the same time. I realized I needed help so I wrapped the fox up in my coat, trap and all. The problem was how was I going to get the large fox and Habiba back to the car? Since I was wearing a ski hat I decided to put Habiba up on my head and use the hat for protection from her piercing talons. Then I tucked the fox under my arm like a football. Habiba cooperated nicely. She stood on my head and occasionally put a wing out to help balance herself because of my uneven gait through the brushy areas. I reached an old cart road and prayed nobody saw us. My only obstacle now was to retrieve my car keys from my jacket. It took me a while but I managed to fish them out of the pocket without getting bitten. Habiba sat in the backseat on her perch while I drove with one hand on the wheel and the other cradling the wrapped-up fox in my lap.

At home I beeped the horn and Paul came to the rescue. He carefully removed the trap. Luckily the fox was caught only by two of his toes and they were pinched but not damaged. I brought him back to the same spot and let him go later that night. I called the local environmental police officer the next day and told him about the illegally set trap.

Hunting Experiences With Habiba

Years later Habiba and I accidentally chased prey with a wild red-tail. I pushed a bunny out in front of me and heard the crash of a red-tail. I assumed it was Habiba and wondered why I hadn't heard the falconry bells on her legs. When I ran over to see if she had connected, I found a wild juvenile red-tail hawk with yellow eyes and a brown striped tail. (Habiba had brown eyes and the red tail of an adult.) It flew up to a branch and stared at me for a moment and then took off. I whistled and Habiba, who was around the corner in another tree, flew over. If only I could have told her the action she missed. I had been actually hunting with a wild hawk.

Another time Habiba chased a bunny that ran right past me. Just as she attempted to lock talons with her prey, the agile bunny stopped dead in his tracks, crouched down and let Habiba fly over it and hit the ground. Then the strangest thing happened.

THE LICENSE ATTACHED TO DIANNE'S BELT
IS REQUIRED BY LAW FOR FALCONRY

The bold rabbit jumped right over Habiba and raced up the hill like a bullet. Habiba leaped in the air and pumped her wings with powerful strokes, disappearing up over the hill. As I approached the crest I looked and saw no chase and no Habiba. Where could they have possibly gone? The air was quiet. I called Habiba with no response. I blew my whistle and swung my lure, a piece of leather with meat attached at one end. She never missed an opportunity to practice her skills by attacking the lure. No Habiba.

I searched the leafless trees, looked in bushes, and knew she couldn't possibly have gone beyond the horizon because it was simply too far away. I became worried and shouted her name again and again.

Finally I heard a faint muffled chirp. I desperately called her name as my heart pounded, "HABIBA!" I walked in circles and tried to key in on the persistent chirps. There, under a brush-covered log, were the tips of Habiba's tail feathers sticking out of a hole in the ground. She was buried alive! I collapsed in a heap at the hole and feverishly tried to work my hands around her body to pull her out backwards. The ground was frozen and wouldn't budge. I took off my gloves and shimmied my hands in alongside her body. She had somehow jammed herself in there and her wings were preventing me from pulling her back out. I folded them in and inched her out while she objected with rapid chirps. What was she complaining about? I was saving her life. As her ruffled head popped out I still had trouble breaking her free. I lifted her up and noticed that she was extra heavy. I looked underneath and saw that clutched in her talons was her long-legged prize.

She ate well that night, for mice paled by comparison to wild rabbit. She had worked hard for her dinner, and it had almost cost her life.

A year after working with Habiba, I was interviewed for a magazine article called "Falcon Lady." When the writer arrived with the photographer who should step out of the car but Jack Swedberg. I was honored to have Jack take photographs of Habiba flying free over the fields and through the woods. Jack seemed quite surprised at the way Habiba didn't seem to want to lose sight of me instead of vice-versa. He was very patient and took some beautiful pictures.

"It's An Animal's World"

In the late 1970s, Paul and I founded, "It's an Animal's World," animal programs we did for scouts and civic groups around central Massachusetts. Paul had gone back to school during the day to finish his degree in biology. He had quit college when he was hired at the Science Center full-time.

We built a very functional heated room for the critters in our basement. It housed two claw-footed bathtubs with running water and drains for a mammoth snapping turtle named Rutherford in one bathtub and a three-and-a-half-foot South American caiman that resembles a small alligator in the other.

On one whole wall was a long snake cage with the front made of sliding glass doors. There we kept an eighteen-foot reticulated python named Crusher and a nine-foot boa constrictor named Baby Bertha. Crusher was always the hit of the program because we would ask six or seven kids to stand up in front of the rest of the audience and we would drape Crusher across their outstretched arms.

We also had many turtles, including box turtles, wood turtles and a pancake tortoise, which, as the name suggests, was flat as a pancake. For mammals we had a de-scented skunk and an opossum and for birds we had a blind barred owl, and of course, Habiba.

DIANNE AND BABY BERTHA, THE BOA CONSTRICTOR

5

Job Offer

 IN 1981, WITH ZOO, WILDLIFE AND falconry experience, I was invited to sit in on a meeting at Fish and Wildlife to discuss the possibility of reintroducing the bald eagle to Massachusetts. It was good to see Brad, Jack and Bill Byrne there among all the Fish and Wildlife personnel. I felt privileged to be included for such an important undertaking.

The Quabbin Reservoir was suggested as a location for the restoration project. The actual hack site that was selected was on the Prescott Peninsula in the tiny town of New Salem. This area was closed to the general public by a series of locked gates to minimize human disturbance to the wildlife there. The eight-mile dirt road to the secluded site was the only access by land, and the waters around the hack site were off limits to fishermen.

A few people, usually master's degree candidates, would monitor the eagle chicks. We wrote down suggestions on the logistics that day, and I went home wondering if I would ever be given a chance beyond the planning stage, since I had chosen not to go to college. At the time I was working mornings in a restaurant and flying Habiba in the afternoons while Paul was finishing up college credits.

Later that year Brad Blodget came into the restaurant for a cup of coffee. He seemed quite eager to talk to me. He usually dropped by to bring an injured owl or hawk. (There were not many veterinarians in the state that would look at injured wildlife back in the late 1970s.) He asked me if I was ready to help with the eagle project. I remember turning sideways and saying, "Brad, look at me! I'm about to have a child!"

I was disappointed to know that I couldn't be a part of the project when it started in 1982. Two eagles, Betsy and Ross, were hacked out successfully that first year while I had a beautiful baby girl named Becky.

Upon graduation from Worcester State College, Paul got a job with the MSPCA in Boston and then transferred to Methuen where he was the shelter manager working with unwanted dogs and cats. We lived in a large house right on the property. It also was a home for old retired horses. There was a large barn and even a chicken coop. Paul and I still rehabilitated wildlife. There was a large fenced-in area that housed a seventeen-year-old female white-tailed deer named Patches. She was very friendly and ate out of my hand. Two sheep rounded out the animal population.

In the spring of 1984, Brad again recommended me to work for Fish and Wildlife and hack the first peregrine falcons in downtown Boston. Since the eastern peregrine was lost as a breeding bird east of the Mississippi River, another victim of pesticides, Boston's skyscrapers would serve as a substitute for natural cliff faces.

Young peregrine chicks were hatched in captivity by Cornell University with the help of falconers and distributed throughout the country to reestablish the falcons. I again reluctantly refused. I was toilet-training Becky and once I started, I couldn't stop.

The peregrine chicks took three weeks to fledge (take their first flight), and would be fed regularly and monitored closely. I knew I had missed two opportunities to raise endangered raptors, but I also knew that I had made the right decision to stay home with

Becky. Besides, I would have had to commute to Boston every day to feed the growing birds.

In July of that same year, 1984, Brad was going to look in on the eagle project and asked if I would like to go along. We arrived the day the birds were being released.

That was my first trip inside the locked gates of Quabbin. I felt so privileged to be able to observe wildlife in a natural setting. The dirt roads twisted and turned and deer trails led off everywhere into the woods. There were many areas where towering red pines grew in stately rows, planted when the reservoir was created.

With Brad as my guide, I looked closely at the vast park-like acres of red pine with an understory of ferns. It was once thought that red pines would hold the soil intact, but the foresters soon realized that they used more ground water than a mixed forest would. Also, winter snows became trapped and lingered in the pine boughs and evaporated rather than reaching the ground and ultimately the reservoir. Further, if there were a devastating hurricane like the one that hit the valley in 1938, whole areas of red pine would be blown down, exposing loose soils to rapid erosion. Forest diversity with different aged trees and species of plants was the key to effective watershed management. It's all about habitat.

Brad gave me a biology lesson in deer overpopulation. It seemed that the deer were eating any new tender shoots that tried to emerge and grow. This allowed for no new oak, maples, poplars or woody shrubs. With most natural predators eliminated and no hunting allowed inside the reservation, the deer population ran rampant and was having a serious impact on the fragile habitat. Fish and Wildlife staff estimated the deer at sixty deer per square mile. For the forest to be healthy and regenerate, the deer population needed to be closer to ten to twelve deer per square mile.

As an experiment, the Metropolitan District Commission sectioned off large areas of land with electric fences to keep the deer out. The difference was remarkable as far as the diversity and growth of plant life. Outside the enclosures were the park-like red pine and ferns, and inside the fenced area it was like a jungle where tender sprouts were protected. I found that I had a lot to learn about the management of a northern forest.

One more locked gate to go through and we had two more miles to go. We seemed to be heading down off the slope of the peninsula and followed Prescott Brook as it meandered through the protected woods. When we finally reached the hack site, we found others who also had come to view the eagle release. As I exited the car the warm breezes that swirled around in the cove blew up onshore and mixed with the scented pines. The sky was a brilliant blue and the limited scenery around the narrow cove was quite beautiful. A small island jutted out of the water near the distant shore and the reservoir was framed on three sides by grass and trees.

Everyone who was there had something to do with the eagle project. People exchanged greetings and I stood in Brad's shadow as everyone got organized. Jack Swedberg greeted me with a warm handshake and then hurried off to attend to other guests. Some people took positions in boats out on the bay, ready to retrieve any birds that didn't pass their first flight test. The rest of us were ferried over to an observation area. That way we could view the flight of the twelve-week-old eagles from a distance and not interfere with their release. The actual eagle hack tower looked like a gigantic wooden erector set: an 8 x 8 x 5 foot tall double box positioned on thirty foot stilts with a ladder leading up to a back platform. Conduit bars created the top, front and sides of the eagle cages to allow for maximum visibility and ventilation.

I watched as the hack site attendant, Dave Nelson, remotely pulled open the doors with ropes. Some of the twelve-week-old babies bolted through the open doors and flew spectacularly. It was amazing that this was the first flight of their lives as they flew strong and high. I was thrilled to be there and felt my heart pounding as another bird flew by. The large wingspan and broad tail mesmerized me. The eaglets seemed to be thinking, "All right, we've got this flying down, but how do we land?" Each of the eagles took off in a different direction and some seemed more determined to get free fast. Some stayed on the tower in the security of their home and watched the others leave. Finally we were ferried back from the observation area. One eaglet still hadn't flown away. I guess he was content where he was. What the heck, there was free food and shelter!

As we reached land, Jack Swedberg helped us ashore. I was all smiles. I couldn't believe that I had been able to witness the release. Jack turned to me in front of the people gathered and said, "So Dianne, are you ready to do this next year?" Shyly I said, "Sure!" I assumed he was joking. He turned and introduced me to two gentlemen who were also there to watch the release. Dick Dyer and Paul Nickerson were with the United States Fish and Wildlife Service. Paul was the regional director overseeing all work with endangered species in the northeastern states.

As part of his introduction, Jack said that I was a wildlife rehabilitator and a master falconer. "A falconer, eh?" Paul said suspiciously. I began talking to him about why I was a falconer as well as a rehabilitator. "Flying a bird in the wild gives me an opportunity to see her hunt and at the same time study her behavior," I said with the confidence that comes from experience. I went on to explain that some of the handful of falconers in Massachusetts were licensed rehabilitators who use their knowledge and skills to get injured hawks and owls back into the wild.

I tried to speak quickly, for this was probably my only chance to make a favorable impression as a falconer on a federal official. I explained that being in the field with a free-flying hawk and witnessing her hunt was an incredible experience. I was able to observe how gracefully she flew, what strategy she used to find and take prey, and also what means the prey used to escape.

I described how much I had learned from Habiba, my partner in the field for seven years. By observing how difficult it was for

any wild hawk to acquire its next meal, I gained insight into reha-
bilitating injured hawks. With that knowledge I could better
judge whether a bird of prey was ready to be released. The prey
isn't just sitting there waiting to be caught. They have their dens,
escape routes, camouflage, senses and physical abilities to elude
winged predators.

"You can't just let a rehabilitated bird go after a little R&R at
your facilities. You have to get them back into flying shape or
they're going to starve before they can strengthen flight muscles
on their own. So that's why I am a falconer." I hope he understood. He smiled, which to me was a good sign. When I got home
I told my husband that Jack had jokingly offered me the chance
to care for the baby eagles next summer.

That fall I applied for a special purpose permit to work with a
non-releasable eagle. I had been doing "It's an Animal's World"
with my husband for six years. I called Jack Swedberg and said I
would like to meet with him at his office at Fish and Wildlife and
discuss a proposal with him. He said he had a feeling he knew
what this was about, but I said I didn't think so. I was not even
going to broach the subject of his offer the summer before. I didn't
want him to feel uncomfortable for offering me the chance to be
the hack site attendant in jest. I knew the job would have to go
to a graduate student.

At our informal meeting I asked, "If I were to train a non-
releasable bald eagle, would you like to incorporate the bird in
some of your lectures?" I guess he was receptive to the idea but
I don't really remember his response. All I could remember him
saying at one point was, "You're still interested in hacking the
eaglets next summer, aren't you?" I told him quite frankly that I
thought he was only kidding. I was a housewife with a high
school education, not a biologist doing a master's thesis. He told
me to go home and think about it. I went home and told my
husband that the unbelievable offer was real. He said with
enthusiasm, "Go for it!"

The first thing I did was to go out and buy an expensive Nikon camera and take a photography class in order to use it properly.

Mid-Winter Bald Eagle Survey

I was invited to be part of the mid-winter bald eagle survey in January of 1985. People all over the United States were spending a designated day doing a census on wintering eagles. Jack Swedberg headed up the Massachusetts count. We observed eagles and kept track of where they were, how many adults and juveniles, which way they were flying and at what time they were seen so that we wouldn't record duplicate sightings. Observation teams were typically made up of groups of three and stationed at prime wintering eagle areas around the state. These included Quabbin, the Connecticut River, the coast of Cape Cod, Assawompsett Pond, and along the Merrimack River where birds were seen each year.

It was an enjoyable day but very cold. The lettuce on my Italian grinder froze. Our group was made up of Jack's best friend, Roy Lindstrom, and Bill Easte, a fisheries biologist for Fish and Wildlife. We saw many birds through our scopes and had a wonderful time. Jack did an official count by helicopter and checked the ground notes later to see if he had missed any. I would love to have been up in the helicopter flying over the reservoir. What a feeling to observe eagles perched below and to see the immense reservoir from the air. The sky was overcast but crisp and my heart raced as the chopper hovered over our observation site.

We were tucked in the woods in a blind and out of sight of the eagles flying by. We punched through the snow to a small clearing to let Jack know we were at our station. Besides, eagles in the vicinity sometimes flew out of their perched areas as the helicopter flew by and we wanted to record them in our notes. Jack sat in the co-pilot seat and waved before they turned to move on.

That year one group saw an immature golden eagle in the west valley of the Quabbin. Jack said he spotted the bird by air and the golden eagle twisted its head up to stare at the helicopter with indifference. Goldens are larger than bald eagles, weighing in at approximately fifteen pounds. They tend to hunt live prey for their food rather than scavenge, so few animals bother them. Twenty-eight bald eagles and three golden eagles were tallied in the state during the winter survey of 1985.

DIANNE WITH ROY LINDSTROM, LEFT, AND BILL EASTE, RIGHT,
AT BALD EAGLE MID-WINTER SURVEY FROM A BLIND

6

Quabbin: My Home In The Wilderness

 ON APRIL 12, 1985, I JOINED UP WITH BILL Davis of the State Division of Fisheries and Wildlife and Dave Nelson, a student at UMass. We met in New Salem at the entrance to the Quabbin reservation.

Brad Blodget had introduced me to Bill when I was visiting the Westborough Fish and Wildlife headquarters a few months earlier. I brought an injured barred owl to the Tufts Veterinary School in Grafton and, since I was in the area, I thought I would pop in on Brad who shared an office with Bill. Brad had assigned him to work with ospreys as one of his tasks. The "fish hawk," as they are often called, had low numbers in the 1960s. There were only eleven pairs in the state due to the use of pesticides. Exclusively fish eaters, the osprey were at the top of the food chain and suffered greatly. Once DDT was banned in 1972, numbers started growing. There were forty-one pairs in the state in 1981 when Bill began installing over a hundred nesting poles throughout southeastern Massachusetts. Bill was very courteous and well-mannered, as I remember. He seemed young with clean-cut brown hair and a boyish look.

Dave Nelson had been the hack site attendant for the previous three summers and was working on his master's degree at UMass. He met me to answer any questions I had about spending my summer alone with baby eagles. Dave was very helpful, friendly and shared his experiences willingly. I tried not to show him I was nervous about working on the project. I was actually terrified at times when I really thought about it. I was afraid to even mention my concerns to my husband Paul.

I traveled to Quabbin one or two days a week during the spring of 1985 to help renovate the eagle tower to accommodate the extra birds I was to raise. I learned how to start, run, and maintain the motorboat so I could set nets to catch fish for the baby eagles to eat. It took me a few tries before I could land the boat without bumping into the dock.

We unlocked the first gate to the property of the Metropolitan District Commission (MDC), which managed the land surrounding the Quabbin Reservoir. Traveling the well-worn, hard-packed dirt road leading into the area was always a special treat. There were patches of dense woods close to the gate. From there the forest

WHITE TAILED DEER AT QUABBIN

opened up and was interspersed with grassy fields where bluebird houses were positioned on poles. I always searched for a splash of blue and had my binoculars handy for a closer look.

White-tailed deer were another attraction along the eight-mile journey. If you were lucky, you could see deer at the back edge of the fields. They would snap their heads up out of the tall grass, then turn and run at a healthy gait among the ferns and red pine. Sometimes deer would run alongside the road and dart across in front of us. I was reminded frequently by biologists who traveled the road regularly that if a deer crosses in front of you, slow down. One or more deer usually follow it and they are the ones you will likely hit.

The topography of the reservation was varied, with level areas giving way to uneven land that pitched downward toward the reservoir. There were many ancient, massive sugar maples lining what once was the main street of one of those long-since disappeared towns. Most of the trees had seen better days, with giant fallen limbs decomposing beneath them.

Six miles into the reservation is the Five College Radio Astronomy Observatory, better known as the "Astronomy Site." The domed building sat in the middle of a field bordered by red pines and looked like a large two-story golf ball. Once, while admiring the shape of the building, I saw a red-shouldered hawk circling above. At the time, I had only seen one other red-shouldered hawk in my life, so that was a treat. At the turn of the twentieth century, red-shouldered hawks were plentiful and red-tailed hawks were rare. Now the opposite is true because of the change in habitat.

For the last two miles of the journey we could put the car in neutral and coast almost the whole way because of the drop in elevation. I loved looking through the woods at some neglected stone walls that bordered former farmlands. Four towns made up the Swift River Valley until the early twentieth century. Now all that remains are the stone cellar holes filled in with vegetation, reminders that there was human life and toil in these areas before

Boston demanded more water for its growing population. I would find occasional smooth colored glass fragments and even some bits and pieces of china along the water's edges during my visits to Quabbin, more testimony to the people who had lived there fifty years before.

History Of The Area

I visited the Quabbin Visitor's Center in Belchertown one day on one of my trips out to the hack site. I wanted to learn the reason why four towns were legislated out of existence to build the Quabbin Reservoir. What I found was a history lesson in books, brochures, and pamphlets. It seems that since 1652 European settlers in Boston had tried to secure a reliable water supply. By 1673, the city's population had reached 18,000 and increased only marginally for the next 122 years, but by 1817 the population had doubled. At the end of the nineteenth century the number of Bostonians had soared to over 500,000 and the entire metropolitan area topped one million inhabitants.

Over those two-and-a-half centuries following the Pilgrims' arrival on Massachusetts' shores, Boston's need for water grew along with its population. By the late 1700s it was clear that Boston would need to look to outlying towns for its water supply and began acquiring water rights and building reservoirs to the west in the towns of Natick, Sudbury, and Framingham. In 1895, the Wachusett Reservoir construction began at a cost of $11,000,000. When completed in 1908, it was the largest reservoir in the world with a sixty-five billion-gallon capacity. But even that huge project didn't solve Boston's water problem.

In 1922, the Metropolitan District Water Supply Commission (MDWSC) and the Department of Public Health filed a joint report. The report recommended taking water from the Ware River and creating a massive reservoir further to the west in the Swift River Valley. This, the MDWSC predicted, could meet the water demand for an ever-growing population in the Boston area.

THREE VIEWS OF QUABBIN TAKEN FROM THE SAME LOCATION.
TOP: WITH TOWNS STILL VISIBLE (1927)
CENTER: THE VALLEY CLEARED OF STRUCTURES (1939)
BELOW: THE RESERVOIR CREATED IN THE FLOODED VALLEY (1989)

In 1926, the Ware River Act was passed, making funds available for a twelve-mile-long aqueduct from the Ware River to the Wachusett Reservoir. One year later funds were allocated for the construction of a reservoir in the Swift River Valley.

The reservoir was created in the 1930s by flooding the four valley towns of Dana, Greenwich, Prescott, and Enfield. Each town was close to the banks of the Swift River, a connection that would prove fatal for them, and forced their residents to relocate. In 1932 the MDWSC oversaw all activities and protected the new reservation. The commission voted to call the immense reservoir "Quabbin," a Nipmuck Indian word for "the place for the meeting of many waters." Once flooded, Quabbin became Boston's drinking water. It eventually supplied two and a half-million people in forty-six Massachusetts communities more than sixty-five miles to the east.

The increasingly immense project had a price tag of $53,000,000, but the twenty-three men who lost their lives during construction paid a much higher price. There were 2,500 people who once called the Swift River Valley home who were forced to leave, and 7,613 gravesites were moved from the valley and placed in the newly created Quabbin Park cemetery. Six hundred and fifty houses were relocated and thirty-six miles of railroad track removed.

In 1936, all remaining trees were cut down and the ground vegetation burned. The area had been virtually wiped clean of all signs of human occupancy. Nature was allowed to reclaim the valley through rising water and the encroaching wilderness.

Beginning in 1939, the Swift River was dammed and the reservoir began to rise. Red pine was planted in tidy rows where farm fields were once worked. In 1941, the Prescott Peninsula was closed to the public. That same year, water was first sent through the 24.6-mile Quabbin Aqueduct to the Wachusett Reservoir. The twelve by eleven-foot underground tunnel could move 610 million gallons of water from Quabbin to Wachusett in a single day.

Seven years later the reservoir reached its capacity of 412 billion gallons, one of the largest manmade drinking water supplies in the world. Quabbin's surface area measures 25,000 acres, surrounded by 55,000 acres of watershed land. The average depth of the reservoir is fifty-one feet, but at the valley floor, depths go from one hundred ten feet to a maximum depth of one hundred fifty-one feet. As the area reverted from fields and fence rows to woodlands and wetlands, locals began referring to it as an "accidental wilderness."

Beaver

On one trip, Billy Davis and I saw a large beaver in the center of the old Prescott road. I asked if we could stop and observe him. I couldn't believe I was standing near this beautifully glistening brown mammal. I was so excited that I forgot to keep my distance. Before I could react, he slapped his tail on the dirt road with a loud startling noise. Within seconds he moved his heavy body down the road and off into the woods. I was embarrassed as I slowly climbed back in the Fish and Wildlife truck. I didn't observe him from the vehicle like I should have, but rather disturbed him when he was away from water and out of his protective element. I still had a lot to learn about being a part of the land instead of trying to dominate it.

Painted Turtle

On a later work trip, I noticed a painted turtle laying her eggs. This time I rolled down my window and inched in a wide path around her, leaving her alone to her maternal duties. She had left the safety of the water far down at the bottom of the hill and exposed herself to every predator that came along. It was fortunate that most animals that posed a threat to the turtle were out foraging only at night. I had already seen the tracks of raccoons and coyotes.

The road passed through additional woods and more wind-blown fields. This used to be the main road going from the town of Greenwich to the center of Prescott. Slow-running Prescott Brook crisscrossed under the road through aging stone culverts. Eventually the road ran along the free-flowing brook until it reached the reservoir. I found it hard to believe that residents of four entire towns were asked to pack up their lives and belongings and move.

Modifying The Tower

We were building an addition to the existing eagle hack tower during our weekly spring trips. The tall tower was positioned on a point of land overlooking the vast undisturbed water. The orig-inal tower could only support up to six birds on one level. We were adding a second floor to comfortably accommo-date eight birds. A blind equipped with one-way tinted glass for precise observation was placed in the middle of both the first and sec-ond floors. We built a trap door for fast and easy access to both decks and installed feeding chutes at the rear of the cages so food could be dropped into the nest without human contact with the birds.

The Eagle Tree

While hammering away one day, Jack Swedberg motioned to Billy Davis to look over at the "eagle tree." I stopped my nailing and swung my head around to see what they were talking about. Jack had seen a white head shining in the sun's rays. A wild bald eagle; it would be my first sighting on the project.

But where were they looking? What eagle tree? There were thousands of trees in sight. Why couldn't I pick the bird out? I wasn't familiar with the landscape. I was an untrained stranger. Would I become knowledgeable about the features of the landscape, the trees, the wildlife itself? All of a sudden I started to question what I was doing out here. These were professional wildlife biologists who had been coming here for years. Jack himself had been photographing eagles at Quabbin since the 1950s when hardly anyone even knew there were eagles in the state. I was a housewife with knowledge of birds of prey and falconry, but with no wilderness skills.

I started trembling high up on the second half-completed platform. Was I ready for this? I looked out over the shoreline with panicked, envious eyes and was directed to the "eagle tree" with pointed finger and a pair of binoculars. There he was! He was glancing back at us from a quarter mile away, a live bald eagle: a spring migrant and a magnificent bird. He was perched on an exposed branch of a dead tree, soaking up the sun's rays. His dark form was a black hole in the deep woods behind him. His head was fluffed out in contentment. His shadowed white tail dropped straight down behind the limb with smooth rounded edges.

The "eagle tree" that Jack directed us to was a massive, dead oak with inviting perches. Jack told me that in the summer and fall to come I would see several of my baby eagles use it as a community gathering area. It stood off a little from the rest of the forest and was an ideal lookout for the cautious birds. It offered a wide-angle view of a broad cove and the expansive reservoir in front. The eagles' backs were protected from the wind and any sneak attacks from other eagles entering the tree. Loon Island, a small ledge and gravel outcrop in front of the tower, was also a favorite area where the baby eagles of past years frequently perched on trees after they fledged.

Encouragement

Another spring day, Jack, his friend Roy, and I met at the restaurant in New Salem and drove down to the hack site together. We were finishing up the tower and were going to try to capture spawning fish, white suckers, in Prescott Brook. As Jack and I traveled down the foot path to the brook, I said that I was the luckiest person on earth to be entrusted with these birds' lives. Jack stopped abruptly and said with all sincerity, "You are a part of this project because of your skills with birds of prey and you've worked hard for it." He never realized how much that encouragement meant to me then and for the rest of my life.

We fenced the river upstream to create a pool and started to capture the large slippery fish with our hands. The fish splashed and squirmed their way between the moss-covered rocks that lined the bottom of the cold stream. I tried to balance myself between the banks and the slick rocks that protruded from the churning water. I was soaked and slimy by the time we finished. We eventually had a good supply in a penned area above our makeshift dam.

Preparing For Young Eagles

The time was approaching when the young eagles were going to be arriving. We had one more opportunity to put the final touches on the tower. I met up with Billy Davis and Billy Byrne, the wildlife photographer, which was always enjoyable, for as I got to know them better we became fast friends. We had worked on the tower that morning and then walked over to an abandoned beaver lodge in the cove to take cuttings from a high and dry part of the structure. We used the sticks for the eagle nests, since many wild nests are comprised of such "stolen" items. I could hear a northern water thrush calling from upstream and a house wren gave us constant, bubbling music as we worked.

The weather forecast predicted afternoon showers, so we took advantage of the lingering sun and sat in a sunny spot near the receding water to eat our lunch. The edges of my roast beef sandwich looked a little green in the sun, but I ate it anyway. We wanted to take the small boat out after lunch and throw a line over the side to get some fresh fish for the holding pen anchored in the cove. Also, Billy Byrne wanted our help to motor over to Gibbs Cove and retrieve a one-man popup blind that he used during the winter to observe and photograph the shy eagles.

White-Tailed Deer Fawn

As we laughed and joked, Billy Davis noticed an unfamiliar object swimming toward Loon Island. It was obviously a mammal but did not have the characteristic form of a swimming beaver, raccoon or muskrat. Since we were heading out in the boat anyway, we decided to check it out. As we approached the strange form, Billy identified it with his binoculars. It turned out to be a white-tailed deer fawn!

We cut the engine so as not to disturb the determined youngster by getting too close. We looked back at Gibbs Shore area where it had come from and saw "mom" at the water's edge. The large doe was looking right at us with her body erect and ears at full attention. As we drifted quietly along we watched the fawn swim to the Loon Island shore and effectively punch its delicate hooves in the soft sand up to firmer ground. There it shook the cold water from its spotted coat and daintily walked over next to a sun-warmed boulder and bedded down. We looked at each other for a logical explanation and then looked back to the doe, far away on the mainland. She watched for a few more seconds, turned, and then ambled back to the cover of the trees. It was as if she had told her fawn to go to the island where it would be safe while she went off on an errand. I was awestruck by the way animals communicate what seem to be complex ideas to one another.

A Storm Closes In

We started the outboard and moved on to our original task of securing some fish for the eagle project. We had some solid strikes and pulled up several two-pound smallmouth bass and put them in a large bucket to transport back to the holding pen. We kept one eye on the threatening clouds to the west. The wind quickly picked up and the storm closed in. We decided that it was time to head back in, but of course we were a little too late.

We made it back as far as Gibbs Cove where Billy Byrne's tent (blind) was still set up. The heavens opened up and the hard rain came down in buckets. Two of us jumped out and pulled the boat up on shore and ran to the tiny tent as fast as we could. Billy D. pulled the boat up further after all the human weight was out. The trees were swaying back and forth and we were drenched by the time we made it to the little tent.

Our cozy quarters consisted of one wooden chair that could accommodate two of us while one person crouched behind it. We jokingly complained to Billy B. about the cramped quarters, but he reminded us that a "one-man blind" means just that. The rain came down so hard that the tent shook from the fury of the storm. As I looked out the peepholes where cameras were usually positioned, I could see the swaying trees losing small branches and newly-formed leaf clusters. Up above, the clouds flew by and the reservoir was a bubbling cauldron of churning water. We weren't going anywhere!

There seemed no end to the storm as we sat cramped, wet and steamy for two hours. We were a little reluctant to venture outside and risk being electrocuted. The two Billys are quite witty when they get together and we passed the time with one-liners and lots of laughs. Every so often we switched positions taking turns crouching behind the chair and straightening our backs by sitting on half the chair. Every time we decided to make a break for the boat, the wind and the heavy rains held us back. I was beginning to feel under the weather myself; I thought that perhaps the roast beef sandwich from lunch had something to do with it. When we finally ran for the boat, I decided to walk the shoreline back to the hack site rather than get in the boat with the waves still running high.

Billy D. drove the boat back to the fish pen and added fish to the growing stock. The storm moved east. We gathered all our gear and headed home after a long and productive day. As we walked to the truck we could hear the roar of the rain-swollen brook. We traveled up the road and glanced over to the dam that Jack, Roy and I had created the previous week to keep the suckers upstream. In the short time we had spent in the tent, torrential rains raised the water level high enough to allow all the suckers to spill over the top of the dam and escape back to the reservoir. I was secretly happy that they were all freed, though it did mean that I had only the fish in my pen for reserves in case of emergencies. I would have to net at least sixteen pounds of fish a day from the reservoir.

Preparing For The Summer At Quabbin

The time was coming soon when I would travel the one-hour trip to Quabbin from my home and stay there for the summer, excluding some weekend days. I lived in a small tent trailer positioned on a point overlooking the Quabbin. If I crouched down outside the trailer, I could look through some green shrubbery and see the eagle hack tower. It looked like an extremely tall clubhouse on very long stilts, accessed by a thirty-foot ladder.

My tent-trailer was a metal-framed base on wheels, with blue canvas sides and an aluminum roof. The mesh screened windows provided adequate air circulation and I kept the rain out by zipping up plastic curtains. My dwelling was small but comfortable. It was eight by six feet with a bunk bed on one end overlooking the reservoir. I had a propane stove for cooking, a Formica-topped table to write on and some cramped cupboards to store my food. Because there were no human developments nearby, I had no source of electricity. There was no fresh water other than the reservoir itself, so I carried a large plastic jug that I replenished every other day, courtesy of the astronomy site.

I was fortunate to have access to the building that housed the astronomy site. It was two miles back up the dirt road through one locked gate; there was a phone there in case of an emergency and it was where I changed my ice packs, refilled my water jug, took showers and used the refrigerator for my perishables, including precious cream for my hot teas.

The observatory was a research facility operated jointly by five colleges in the Amherst area. I was told it received radio waves and other scientific data from outer space via a huge enclosed satellite dish. Fortunately the "heavens" had too much interference during the summer months so I could use their facility in peace each night.

I had a non-functioning little refrigerator in my tent that protected my boxed food items from the mice that scavenged my quarters at night. I learned that I would have to wash my utensils before every meal and open my cans from the bottom. I hid my limited wardrobe underneath the camper's hinged seats. I housed everything else like raincoats, telescope, books, jackets, extra blankets, and my pots and pans at the other end of the cozy trailer. My bed faced the water, giving me a fantastic view of some of the most beautiful and secluded scenery in Massachusetts.

Keeping A Journal

One day my mother sent me an informal letter, jotted on the back of a crossed-out grocery list:

```
Dear Dianne,
  Our best wishes go with you on your new
adventure. I'd say it takes loads of guts. I
hope you take a notebook and write a journal.
Just remember, we all love you and will be
thinking of you.
                          Love, Mom
```

Because of that note, when I started the eagle project I wrote letters to Paul, Becky, who was three at the time, my parents and friends. They all saved the letters for me and these accounts became my journal. Years later they helped me remember that summer, describing the details of my daily life and all the adventures and excitement of my season at the Quabbin.

I went home most weekends during the summer. I made meals ahead of time and froze them so Paul could get Becky from the babysitter, come home and put them in the oven. I was glad Paul was so supportive. He was interested in wildlife as much as I was. During previous summers he worked with the endangered Plymouth red-bellied turtle in Plymouth, Massachusetts. He helped trap and mark the shells of the turtles that comprised this isolated population; there were only two hundred of the adult turtles left in the wild in and around Plymouth.

Paul also had lived in a shack with no amenities, so he knew how exciting it would be for me to take on this summer project. He wasn't worried at all. I, on the other hand, took a self-defense class. I wanted to be in the right frame of mind. One night, just before I left for the Quabbin, I woke in the middle of the night and thought, "What am I doing? I'll be all alone in the woods far away from everyone!" A feeling of panic came over me and I felt as if my guts were turned inside out. I remember I eventually fell back to sleep and didn't mention my fears to Paul or anyone else.

7

Letters From Quabbin

You're Not Alone

As you lay in your tent under the stars,
So far away from home,
Quabbin is still, the water is calm,
But don't worry, you're not alone.

Outside the loons are calling,
To the eagle in the sky,
To warn him not to get too close,
To their humble home nearby.

The crickets chirp their steady tune,
To calm you from your loneliness;
Their chirping sound is full of joy,
Because you are their guest.

At night before you go to bed,
Just think of me at home.
You'll look out over Quabbin,
And know you're not alone.

[Becky, my daughter, wrote this poem ten years later, February 17, 1995, from her memory of Quabbin visits.]

Day 1

I moved the rest of my gear into my tent camper on June 21, 1985.

```
June 21, 1985 - 10:00 p.m.

Dear Mom, Dad, Scotty and Louise (my close fal-
conry friend and his wife)
```

I'm writing to you all so I can save time and repetition. Mom, can you share these letters with Scotty since he lives near you? I'm eating cold beef stew directly out of the tin can. No one is here so I don't have to watch my manners. It saves on dishes with my limited water supply.

The barred owls are hooting, "Who cooks for you, who cooks for youuuuuwaaa?" They began at 9:20 this evening. It's the first time I've ever heard wild barred owls. For the first half hour it seemed as if they were testing their voices because they were "hacking" back and forth to each other. I couldn't identify them by species because I had never heard that vocabulary before. Then the familiar, "Who cooks for youooo" call bellowed, back and forth.

The loons are calling their lonely "O loos" or "wail," as the scientific community calls it. The water is calm and the sound seems to be traveling far across the peaceful reservoir. Together they contribute to a tranquil evening. The crickets are out and provide soothing background music in the darkened wilderness.

I have four baby phoebes living on the spare tire of my stationary camper. The parents built a mud nest after the tent trailer was set up earlier this spring and stayed empty without human disturbances for a few weeks before I moved in. They were pink "blobs" last week but now appear moth-eaten because their feathers are coming in sparsely. They look like they're

crammed in a small jar,
one on top of the other,
because they're getting
considerably large for
the nest. I will avoid
that side of the camper
now that I live here,
to give them their
privacy. Come to think
of it, I could hear the
male's beautiful voice,
"Phoebe, Phoeblee,"
earlier in the spring
when we came up to modify
the tower. Now the male
is silent.

I'm using a flashlight to write this letter to
you because I couldn't get my brand new Fish &
Wildlife issued Coleman lantern to work. I first
forgot where I packed my stick matches. I know I
stuffed them in my gear at the last minute this
morning, but it's a mystery to me as to where
they are now. I finally found a lighter in the
car and still couldn't figure out how to ignite
that darn lantern. I knew my inexperience would
show up eventually, but I didn't think it would
be this early in the project. It's extremely
dark out here. Surprisingly, I'm not afraid to
be here alone. I'll let you know after tonight.
Good thing the batteries in my flashlight work!

Well, now that the small talk and my dinner
are over and the dishes washed, I'll prepare a
hot cup of tea. Thanks, Mom, for the Eagle mug
for a going-away gift. I just christened it.
What memories I'll have when I drink tea out of
it years from now. Now, let me tell you about
the babies' first day.

Earlier today, before the eagles came, I drove
down the long, sometimes dusty, road to the now-
familiar hack site. I got the rest of my gear
stored into the nooks and crannies of my

trailer. Besides my water jug for drinking and
washing up, I have a large cooler with ice
packs. I filled it with soda, hot dogs, milk,
butter, cream, and other miscellaneous items.

Bill Davis from Fish and Wildlife, and an
intern, came to meet me at the hack site to make
sure I was all settled in. We all drove together
at one o'clock to the town of Orange where they
have an airstrip. Jack Swedberg arrived by plane
with the eagles from Nova Scotia. He went up a
few days earlier to assist the Canadian Fish and
Wildlife in gathering eight eagle chicks from
eight different nests. They're not endangered up
in the pristine area around the Bras d'Or lakes
on Cape Breton Island.

When we arrived, the plane was early and
already on the runway. All the eagle crates
were cooling in the limited shade under the
aircraft's wing for it was very hot today.
Groups of curious people quietly milled around,
bending down to take a long peek at the enormous
babies. I was quite surprised at the eaglets'
large size. Jack was standing next to the birds
like a proud father. I was trembling while
trying to restrain my enthusiasm as I approached
the eagle crates, smelly as they were from their
fish breakfast. People were silently watching
my reaction to the birds as Jack introduced
me. They all just wandered around and smiled
at my elated expression. Cameras were clicking
everywhere and there was great excitement in
the air. Dick Dyer from the United States Fish
and Wildlife came over and we shook hands. I
met him last year at the hack site when the
1984 eagles were released. Just think, if I
hadn't been invited to the eagle release last
year, I probably wouldn't be here today.

Jack pointed out one bird while we were
loading the crates into the van. It was too
quiet and didn't look as alert as the others.

The downy chick appeared to be the smallest of the eight babies at five-and-a-half weeks old. The charcoal gray chick had a thick, wooly coat of down with little feathers poking through. I peered into the side of the crate and saw that she was slumped down and didn't respond to me visually or by my tapping on the door. Without hesitation I suggested we get her out immediately. It was an awesome but scary feeling to go ahead and pull her six-pound body out of the hot crate. I quickly prayed that she was all right. At that point I realized that there was no turning back and that I had better be ready for this endeavor.

   After I pulled the eaglet out, Jack grabbed the needle-sharp talons because, although she was still small, her feet and talons were adult-sized. We let some air circulate around her body by rubbing the trapped air out of her steamy down coat. She was hot and bulky. It was my first look and touch of a bald eagle. Her eyes were coal black, her tongue was a pale pink and pushed forward, panting, and her black talons and bright yellow feet seemed too big for her body. The number on her blue leg tag read #8. I had asked Billy D. to bring water and stale Coke. He was surprised by the second item until I explained; you had used it, Scotty, with very good success on newly-arrived sick hawks and owls that were brought to you. Sometimes there's just no substitute for experience. Thanks for sharing yours with me, Scotty. You've certainly gained enough of it through falconry and rehabbing.

   I opened the beak and we gave her your remedy. I cautioned Bill, who was squirting the liquid into the baby eagle's mouth, to be very careful not to get any down her windpipe. She slowly cooled down and perked up. What a relief. This was just ten minutes into the project and I had three months to go.

Dr. Pokras from Tufts Veterinary School's Wildlife Clinic in Grafton arrived just as I was putting the chick back into the crate. He said the baby was still warm but looked okay and suggested we move them into the van and head out. We said our good-byes to the Feds and made the ten-mile trip down to the Quabbin gate in no time at all.

After unlocking the entrance, we started our trip down the road. It led us into the heart of an area that was off-limits to the rest of the world. I was not going to leave this place at the end of the day as I had done in the past. I was going to stay for most of three months and enjoy some solitude while worrying all the time that my charges were going to stay healthy.

We passed deer galore as they bounded off into the thicker woods with their tails "flagging" from side to side. I was in a Massachusetts Fish and Wildlife van facing backwards, looking at the eagle crates. I checked on #8 many times to see if she was still with us. You can't look too many times when you're scared to death something might happen before the birds are even placed in the tower.

Following us was a van with Dr. Pokras and eager fourth-year veterinary students. They were to give each bird a thorough physical exam. Every time we saw a deer along the dirt road the Tufts van would slow down and all faces would be pressed against the windows. It brought me back to my first trip down the eight-mile stretch. I could see excitement in their body movements as I looked back at their van. The students were bobbing their heads back and forth to see anything that moved in the tantalizing woods. It's amazing to think that there is this much wildlife here in Massachusetts. I still can't believe it. It makes me feel like a kid with wide-eyed excitement when a deer looks up from feeding for a split second.

The Tufts van slowed down a few times to take a glimpse of a head or hind-end of a deer. A deer froze and peered back at the van from the protection of the red pines. It then leaped over an old stone wall and slipped deeper into the woods. We passed the Five College Observatory dome after six miles and then we started our descent to the reservoir and the hack site. After unlocking the second and final gate that consisted of a bar-way board going across the road between two posts, we started down the remaining two miles.

The babies were quiet and I was in kind of a daze. I was apprehensive about my next few months with these helpless feathery blobs in the backseat. The Tufts van caught up to us at this point, for no deer had been sighted for the last mile or two. I'll bet they were wondering what that big golf ball-shaped building was.

We arrived at the hack site, and car doors opened and closed as people started to gather their gear. I'm so used to associating this place with complete tranquility. Some of us carried one or two eagle crates while others carried the veterinary medical bags. We set up base camp under the tower itself and opened all the crates by taking the tops off the boxes. The birds stayed cool thanks to a breeze that came off the reservoir. Since they were only six weeks old, their wing feathers were not developed yet, so there was no chance that any of the chicks would get up and fly away, let alone walk. Dr. Pokras and his crew took blood and fecal samples. We took measurements of their wings and I kept reading the ruler wrong because it was in millimeters. I still wasn't sure if they picked the right person for the job if I couldn't even read a ruler!

The medical process took a long time because there were eight birds to examine. Most of the

chicks, however, just sat in their opened crates
in the shade of the hack tower. However, eagle
#7 did not like what was happening. He lunged at
the students as they worked on him and tried to
bite any finger that wandered too close. We then
paired them up by size in each of the four nest
boxes. By matching them in this manner, no chick
would totally dominate the other. We had only
one altercation between eagle #1 and eagle #4.
They were the two largest birds; #1 was the
aggressor and #4 tried desperately to defend
herself. All they could really do at this stage
of their lives was scamper around on their
ankles and attempt to intimidate each other with
awkward flaps of their gangly wings and
vocalizations made up of tentative grunts and
cackles. Number 1 earned her name right then:
Attila! They finally settled down in neutral
corners of the nest box we built into each cage.

Billy D. brought up some fresh fish and opened
up one side with a knife. We slid one fish down
each chute into the nest boxes and watched the

PLACING BABY EAGLES IN HACK TOWER NEST

birds through the one-way glass. The babies
stared at it. Some tried to eventually tear into
the fish, but it looked like they were
struggling to tear any pieces from it. We left
them to settle down and get comfortable with
their new bunkmates.

After all the babies were given a clean bill
of health, we all talked for a while over soft
drinks. The Tufts van made its way back out the
long road with their chilled blood samples
safely stored in a cooler. The rest of us
breathed a sigh of relief and settled down under
the tower to discuss strategy and logistics. We
scheduled some weekend coverage so I could go
home and see my family occasionally.

My most important responsibility was to pull
the thirty-foot ladder back from the tower at
sundown. This was done with a set of pulleys
because the wooden ladder was too heavy to work
by hand. This safeguards the babies from being
eaten by prowling raccoons that could easily
climb the ladder and have a defenseless eaglet
for a midnight snack. The support poles for the
tower have predator guards of aluminum flashing
to prevent raccoons from shimmying up them. Jack
looked me square in the eye and took a very
serious tone. He said he would hate to come down
to the hack site and find a raccoon had killed
one of my eagles. I decided that if I left the
hack site to pull nets or venture up to the
astronomy site, I would pull the ladder back.
It gave me added peace of mind.

Around five o'clock, both Billys and Jack said
their goodbyes and headed back up the dirt road
and were gone. I found myself totally alone for
the first time. I had been here so many times
now during the renovation of the tower that it
already felt like home. I turned slowly after
the vehicle sounds disappeared up the road. I
was left with the murmuring of Prescott Brook

beside me and the soft echoes it produced throughout the woods. I looked out over the reservoir and took a deep breath. I let it out slowly and sprinted back up the path to check on the babies.

I continued to watch the eagles from 5:30 to 7:00 p.m. I had a makeshift stool on each floor to sit on. I climbed the stout ladder inside the double-decker through a trap door I had requested during the construction phase. I could observe any altercation between two babies or monitor how much they all were eating. I didn't have to go outside and up through the outside ladder. It was like a little clubhouse, dark and cozy.

I am recording all feeding activities on one page of a notebook and individual activities on the chicks' own separate charts. They all looked so much alike. I had to wait until they moved to get a glimpse of their blue leg tag numbers 1 through 8 that were attached to aluminum federal bands.

I quickly found that the eagles needed their food cut up into bite-sized pieces. They quit trying to tear into a whole fish if there was no white meat exposed. Only one side of the fish was slit open and most of them were face down from the chicks struggling with them. They finally managed to gorge themselves by nightfall. I wanted to make sure they would eat regularly for their first few days to help them adjust to the change in their young lives. They can fill their crop, which is a dilation of the eaglet's esophagus, or more simply, a pouch in the neck area where extra food is stored when their stomachs are full.

I heard the loons at 7:00 p.m. while climbing down the ladder, so I leaned against it and peered through the rungs at the beautiful reservoir. I report the loons' activities to MDC Natural Resource Specialist, Paul Lyons,

by recording my observations on a notepad that
I keep in my back pocket. Seems the loon
population struggled with the pesticide DDT in
their bodies too. When the chemical was banned
in 1972, the loons started their comeback and
Loon Island in front of me was the first
documented nest at Quabbin.

A distant deer was walking toward the
reservoir and caught my attention. She looked
so sleek and peaceful, taking smooth small steps
in the soft sand along the shore. The sun had set
behind the trees so she was in the lengthening
forest shadows. I looked further down and there
was yet another deer and beyond that one was
another doe with a tiny fawn. None of the deer
could see each other due to the irregular
curvature of the shoreline. It was interesting
that they all arrived to drink and feed on the
shoreline vegetation at the same time. I watched
them for a while as the sun was going down and
continued to lean my tired body and cheek against
the ladder. I looked through the rungs again and
couldn't believe I was going to spend the next
two-and-a-half months here. The reservoir was
quiet and the scenery was so peaceful.

Small insects buzzed in circles above the
water and the crickets were beginning to softly
twitch their wings in unison. The shimmering
water mirrored the landscape that surrounded it.

By 8:30 p.m. the baby eagles were all asleep.
They each laid flat on their nests with wings
slightly out and legs tucked under them. Their
little backs moved up and down as they slept
soundly. Numbers 5 and 3 looked so peaceful
and compatible that I named them Dick and
Jane (after you, Mom and Dad.) I named #2,
Ernie, which meant #7, who was so nasty under
the tower, will be Bert. I remembered to pull
back the ladder and even secured a latch on my
trailer door. Just knowing I could latch my

door made me feel better, even though, if it
wanted to, anything could come right through
the canvas.

I learned to block that out of my mind and
instead I tried to get the lantern to light.
Little did I know that the lantern was not going
to work. I'm not too enthusiastic about walking
around outside in the dark. I pass so many small
animals during the day that scurry around in the
bushes and undergrowth as I go back and forth
from my tent to the hack tower, that I didn't
want them to scare me at night.

Well, it's 11:15 p.m. I wanted to go to bed at
9:00 p.m. so I won't get rundown.

I love you all. You're in my thoughts so I
never feel alone.

Love, Dianne

First Night Alone

Because I wrote my first notes and letters by flashlight, the
nighttime sounds filtered in through the canvas. A barred owl and
a whippoorwill serenaded me. A loon yodeled at midnight. I swear
I could hear human voices that first night. No one could possibly
be outside lurking around in the darkness, I told myself. I had my
flashlight on while writing my notes so anything could see me, yet
I wouldn't be able to see them. My heart became audible as the
noises continued and I didn't dare look out the plastic windows for
fear of seeing a scary face. As I listened more selectively, the sounds
seemed to be a chanting noise that made me hold my breath to
allow my ears to strain and try to decipher the faint syllables.

All at once I discovered they weren't human sounds at all but
the wind moving through the trees and the tumbling waters of
Prescott Brook in the distance. I could easily see how the early
Native Americans could sense the presence of spirits and feel that
they were one with the land. The sounds soon comforted me and

I was not afraid to be in this tiny tent under a towering pine tree on a point overlooking the Quabbin.

I read *People* magazines that my sister gave me to help me fall asleep. Rock Hudson was in the news because he had acquired a mysterious disease, later identified as AIDS. Michael Jackson had a new video debuting called "Thriller" that was making headlines. When my eyes got heavy I closed the magazine, turned off my flashlight and closed my eyes. I slept soundly.

First Morning

I arose the first morning of my summer adventure at 7:00 a.m. I walked down the winding path to the tower and unhooked the suspended ladder. I was supposed to lean it gently against the tower and climb up and check on the babies. At first the heavy wooden ladder was quite cumbersome and even got twisted sideways in midair. I obviously had to get used to the pulley system. All I could think was, "Oh noooo!" I strained to hold the rope to prevent the ladder from crashing to the ground. Only one foot-base of the cumbersome ladder was on the pine needles. The other was swinging back and forth because the ground sloped unevenly toward the water. I couldn't believe this was happening. There was no one to help me and I had to think fast to solve the problem. My arms were starting to shake and my muscles were cramping up. I knew I had to keep tension on the strong rope. I tried to walk backwards and pivot the top of the swinging ladder back over to catch the eagle tower. At the same time, I tried desperately to flip the base back toward me with the top of my right foot. I finally synchronized the two motions and the ladder straightened itself out. *Thank you God*, I thought. For a minute it looked like I was not going to be able to get up to the tower and the eaglets would not get their first breakfast on my watch.

Once up on the tower, I had marvelous opportunities to observe the newly-adopted chicks. Although their exact ages could not be determined, close observations of nesting behavior by research biologists suggested that young bald eagles were able to feed on their own at six weeks of age, although not very efficiently. Feather development of my birds indicated that Attila and her nest mate #4 (I named her Marjorie after Miss Smith, the Audubon teacher of so many years ago), were approximately seven weeks old, while Bert, Ernie, Dick, and Jane were six. The eaglet that was overheated at the airport was around five weeks old and is doing fine today. I've named her Woodstock because she is the smallest, cutest and a fighter. I named her nest mate Snoopy. He is the second smallest eaglet. Judging gender at this stage is inexact at best, but those who weigh more have bigger feet and heavier beaks are believed to be females.

They were all sitting quietly. I knew they had been up for quite a while because they had already eaten last night's leftovers. (They had full crops.) I climbed down the troublesome ladder, walked down the path to the tent and started my tea water. Then I visited my Port-a-Jon, inconveniently located way down the winding

DIANNE CLIMBING THE HACK SITE TOWER

path near my car. Then it was back up to the tent to get out of my warm sweatpants and sweatshirt and into my day clothes. I organized the cramped camper, swept out the pine needles, and got my hot tea and cold cereal. Then I climbed back up the ladder with my breakfast and sat down to watch the now settled-in babies.

I fed the birds fresh fish twice a day during the hot summer months. I sat there and took copious notes on food intake and behavior, taking great care to insure the health of the birds through careful observation. I checked eyes for brightness, inspected feces for enough content, and monitored the bird's overall appearance as much as possible through the one-way glass.

Next, it was back down from the tower and out to the small boat, a thirteen-foot Boston Whaler, to get some fresh fish from the holding pen. After cutting up the scaly fish it was back to the tower, feeding one nest box at a time. I recorded who was eating, how much, if they defecated, and any interactions between nest mates as they moved around the nest box. Afterwards I returned to the dock and washed out my fish buckets.

I never realized until that first day of "primitive living," that bare wood could cause me so much pain and discomfort. Slivers came from everything I touched, including rough-cut lumber that I used as a cutting board to cut up the babies' food. Slivers also came from the thirty-foot ladder I climbed, the tower, the fish

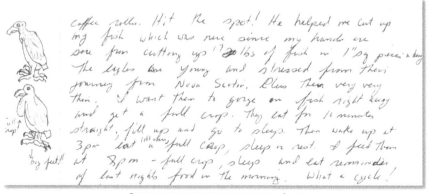

LETTER ILLUSTRATING BABY EAGLE'S CROP

holding pen, and even the dock where I tied my boat. Modern man has no idea how lucky he is with the invention of the wood sander, polyurethane and Formica! By the second day I found myself adding to my now sore fingers by stirring vitamins into the cut-up fish with my precious hands. YEEOOW! All those needle-sharp fins were quite an eye-opening, painful experience.

Knives presented another problem. I wore out my fingers by repeatedly pressing down on a dull knife to cut through ten pounds of fish, once in the morning and once in the early evening. Many times the shiny blade would slide off the side of the fish because it wasn't sharp enough to cut through the scales.

Day 2

Saturday, June 22, 1985 - 10:30 a.m.

Dear Paul and Becky,

I had my first guests today. The MDC police came to the hack site by boat. The loons warned me before I saw the boat by announcing the intrusion into their territory. I couldn't understand why they were calling until the boat appeared from around the point. I made a mental note of their vocal response. The inquisitive police were friendly folks, polite and courteous, and seemed to accept me all right, even though I was in "their" territory.

1:15 p.m.

Jack came to visit with his friend, Roy, my partner on the eagle count the previous winter. We sat in the warm sun under the tower. All eight birds were sound asleep thirty feet above.

My first makeshift bandage went on this morning at 9:00 a.m. because I tried to cut the fish into one-inch pieces and my knife slipped. Yeeow again! (Pressure bandages really work!) I thought for a while I would have to leave and

get stitches, but Jack looked at my finger and
said it should heal okay. He said he'd get me
a sharper knife so I don't struggle so much.

My first night here was fine. I was so geared
up I couldn't get to sleep until 1:30 a.m. It
was quite cold outside but with sweatpants and a
sweatshirt I was toasty warm. Bill Davis said he
was going to call you last night to let you know
everything went okay with the birds' arrival.
I'm sending you a copy of the local newspaper
Jack brought me today. There were pictures of
the birds and me.

Well, Jack is checking the fish in the long,
hooped-shaped fyke nets with Roy. Bill Easte, a
fisheries biologist at Fish and Wildlife went
with them. He is underwater at the moment, scuba
diving, to look at the smallmouth bass spawning
habitat. To each his own. I'm going to close now
and see how things are going down by the water.
Jack said he would mail this letter to you if I
finished it.

Say "Hi" to everyone in Methuen. I miss you
already. Kiss Becky and give her a big hug and
this piece of gum.

                    Love, Dianne

Late afternoon was the same routine as early morning; I cut
up more fish, fed and monitored the hungry babies, and then
cleaned up. By the time I finished my chores the sun was setting.
After washing up I checked on the babies one last time. With the
ladder pulled back for the night I gathered my duffel bag and
headed up to the astronomy site. I was too tired and nervous the
first night to leave the babies alone, not knowing what the night
would be like out there. By the second night, everything I touched
smelled like fish. I had to try out that shower.

I carried my towel, thawed ice packs, hair dryer, dop kit and
a change of clothes down the path to my car. It was tricky to

actually stay on the path because it followed the contour of the hill. I walked away from the reservoir and then through the over-grown shrubs. I had to then wind down the path, which had dips and rocks to jump over. Toward the end I had to take a left again and crash through more greens to the soft pine needles that made up the beginning of the road out. I brought my trusty flashlight too so that I could find my way back up through the labyrinth when it was darker.

I thoroughly enjoyed the hot shower. Warm air blowing on my short hair and cold face from the hair dryer will quickly become a luxury. I truly treasured the warmth and hot water at the astronomy site.

On my way back, an adult raccoon crossed the road in front of me, followed in the shadows by three little tykes. I stopped the car where they crossed and rolled down my window. Raising baby raccoons at the zoo years ago made me fluent in raccoon vocabu-lary. I communicated to the babies in their mother's voice. Two babies stopped in their tracks and turned around. I called again, "Oooooooo?" One obediently ran up to my car door completely bewildered. I looked down at his puzzled face. The mother had climbed a tree with the other two kits and now called to the baby. The juvenile twisted his ears to the back and pawed the ground with his delicate little fingers. One more call from the mother with no competition from me and the baby retreated into the woods to join its family.

Second Night

Back at my tent I settled down with a cup of hot tea and my scribbled notes. Jack taught me how to start the Coleman lantern. It served as my only company by providing me with welcomed background noise. My sore hands hurt to the point that even opening the locked gate to get to the astronomy site was a big challenge. My fingers were stiff, swollen, and almost non-func-tioning. I will learn to take great care of them once they heal.

Since the first two days had ended with a tremendous thunderstorm, it seemed that all the insects took shelter in my tent. When I turned off the light and pulled the covers up around my neck I inevitably heard a loud, high-pitched "eeeeeee" close to my ear. I was too tired, comfortable, and warm to get up. To sleep I had to completely hide under the blankets. I eventually had to get up, start the lantern, approach the pesky mosquitoes one by one, and systematically smack them before jumping back into bed. After that night I learned to methodically search the tent for all the awaiting mosquitoes. They hung out on the blue plastic walls and acted tough.

My other nocturnal companions were secretive mice. They came at 2:00 a.m. and nibbled on my perishables and urinated on all my canned goods. They had already attempted to nest in my utensil drawer, even before I moved in. The first item on my list of things to bring back from home would be an effective mousetrap!

Some of my longest and most arduous hours were spent in the rain those first few days. My tent, the tower, the boat dock and the Port-a-Jon were all in opposite directions. I lived in my rain gear for the first forty-eight hours of the project.

Day 3

The next day, to my relief, the welcoming sun came out. The blue sky was brilliant. I noticed right away how different the wilderness sounded. Life seemed to exist in sensory checks and balances. A background chorus of familiar insects and birds, such as the chickadees and red-eyed vireo, comforted and soothed my soul. I went to peek in on the phoebes and the nest was empty. I looked forward to seeing them each morning, and then today, they were gone—fledged—never to be enjoyed again.

I was happy to hear a truck rumbling down the road along the flowing brook. I could use some help cutting the fish up as my sore hands were still trying to heal and I would enjoy conversation with another human being. It was Billy D. He came to check on how everything was going and to see if I needed any supplies. Jack and the two Billys took turns checking in on me and being my relief, so I could go home on weekends. As he approached with a bag in his hand, I squeaked a greeting and grabbed my throat in disbelief. I think we were both surprised. When Billy asked why I didn't know I had laryngitis, I whispered, "How could I have known? There is no one here to talk to!" I had radioed the MDC earlier in the morning and had checked in with a raspy voice. We laughed and he handed me a juice and muffin from the New Salem Restaurant. Yum!

Billy did indeed help me cut up all the fish so that made my hands happy. I've learned that he is detail-oriented and a dedicated wildlife professional. He wanted to make sure I was used to the daily routine. As we walked over to the tower we noticed a few great horned owl feathers at a dusty part in the path. We had stumbled upon the private bathing area of the resident great horned owl. Cool! I've only heard him once and the sound had come from the Gibbs Bay area to the south. That made me a little concerned for the barred owls. Great horned owls would not think twice about having a barred owl for dinner.

We climbed up the ladder each carrying a bucket of fish. We observed the birds after all the rain over the past few days and agreed that they looked good. I needed a second vote of confidence on their development. We fed the inquisitive babies and had fun watching them eat in the warm sun. Their home was finally able to dry out, including the nesting platforms and the decks.

Billy brought two "gill nets" because I would need more fish than I had in my live fish pen. Remember, my suckers were washed back downstream during the storm. We jumped in my boat and motored out into the reservoir and he showed me how to set the nets. They were a hundred feet long, eight feet high and dropped into fifty to eighty feet of water. We set one south of the tower and one to the north that day.

Out on the reservoir past the restricted vantage from my bay, the Quabbin was spectacular, offering panoramic views in all directions. Looking north, the serpentine ridges of the Prescott Peninsula resembled an elongated sea monster. Turkey vultures nonchalantly rode invisible warm air currents along its irregular spine. The forest itself was a mixture of many species of trees that blended together in an uneven carpet. Far to the north in neighboring New Hampshire, Mount Monadnock teased me with its grandeur, particularly on this clear crisp day. The islands of Mount Pomeroy and Mount Lizzie resembled twin icebergs, jutting out of the water with very steep sides. Narrow Loon Island stood alone, seemingly an accident torn away from the mainland. It provided a few good eagle perch trees, some brushy areas, and a long sandbar. Loads of washed and polished pebbles along the shore proved that the water was still stealing soil and vegetation from the land. I felt fortunate living at Quabbin all by myself, surrounded by that beautiful scenery. I looked forward to my daily net-pulling chores because the view was my reward.

Now the live fish in my pen would only be used if my nets did not catch enough for my daily needs. I said goodbye to Billy and thanked him for his help. I had a good night's sleep, knowing that the growing babies were eating and appeared okay.

Day 4

The next day was interesting, to say the least. After feeding the babies their breakfast I decided to go out on the reservoir and haul the long gill nets in by myself. Billy had said to grab the orange buoy line and pull until the net came to the surface, then place the float and lead line into the net basket, always making sure I was balanced. When a section with a fish came to the surface, I was to step on the lead line. In this way I could work on untangling a fish and not have to worry about the long net escaping back to the depths of Quabbin. I quickly learned to respect the fish because many of them were still very much alive and kicking with sharp fins flailing.

I then took the slippery fish out, one by one, but they were not just caught by their gills as the name "gill net" implied. Most were halfway through the net. Grabbing the fish and trying to work them out was quite an experience. I learned that it was easier to pull the stiff fish through instead of backing them out. I knew I would soon build strong arms and legs from hauling in the nets, but that first night I was sore from using muscles I never knew I had.

Afternoon chores included repairing nets because they often tore when entangled on underwater stumps that I seem to find all too often. I guess they didn't burn all the stumps after cutting the trees back in the 1920s. I also waited until after dark to reset the nets because of the pair of loons that included my bay in their watery territory. They are uncommon in Massachusetts and are found only on a handful of quiet lakes. Knowing that loons dive for their food, I couldn't risk capturing them in the underwater nets. That was the main reason I put the nets well to the north and south of the heart of the loon territory. There were disadvantages, however. When the temperamental motor on my undersized boat occasionally conked out, I had to paddle all the way back, usually as my luck would have it, against the prevailing wind, rolling waves, and often in the rain.

Monday, June 24, 1985 - 4:00 p.m.

Dear Mom, Dad, Scotty and Louise,

I'm able to write you at this time because there is one heck of a thunder and lightning display going on outside! I was able to get my gill-netted fish out of the pen, get the boat inland out of the waves and tie it down before the storm. Then I checked on the babies. I was up on the tower when it began to pour and when the darkened blind lit up I mentally braced myself and "Boooooom!"

I decided that this was not the best location during an electrical storm and prepared to leave, but delayed my retreat until after the next flash of lightning. We have a lightning rod to safeguard the tower and eagles but that didn't quiet my childhood fears of thunder and lightning storms. Well, let me tell you, the flash was so bright and the "crack" came so fast and loud that the force shook the tower. I was watching one baby's response to the storm through the one-way glass at that instant. He must have been looking toward the glass when the lightning illuminated my blind area for he acted startled. I think he got a brief glimpse of my ghost-like appearance.

I didn't wait for any more scientific observations. I was out that door so fast and praying while practically sliding down the ladder. I raced up the path, past the tent, and started to push my way through the ferns to take a short cut down to the dock where I had left my binoculars. "Flash...Crack...Boom!" And then the heavens really opened up. I turned quickly with my arms folded over my head and scurried back to the safety of my small tent. I managed to cut my shin on a fallen log hidden among the wet ferns in my haste to get under cover. Ouch! So here I am with time to write to you.

Other than the storm, everything has gone well. The babies are wonderful although I worry and hope that they stay healthy. They're moderately thin so I cut all their food into tiny pieces like their parents would. I feed ten pounds of fish in the morning and another ten pounds in the afternoon. It takes an hour and a half to cut up the food for each feeding. I sliced the top of my finger very badly the first day, but it is okay today. I soak it two to three times a day and it is healing nicely. I'll have a lasting scar to remind me of the eagle project.

4:30 p.m.

The rain stopped so I went to the dock to retrieve my binoculars. While there I noticed how calm the waters had become. Then I looked at the lofty clouds in awe. The sky looked like something out of the Steven Spielberg movie, *Close Encounters*. The clouds were ominous so I decided to go back to the shelter of the tent and eat because it started raining again. The storms here at Quabbin appear to strike fast, continue south, and then swing back around to clobber me again.

The wildlife here is wonderful. Yesterday I saw a baby porcupine. He was small enough to fit in the palm of my hand, but I wisely left him alone when he quilled up his tiny hind end.

Two enterprising turkey vultures ate the fish heads I put out on a sandy point along the shore. The first day, I hid the fish guts, tails and heads because I didn't know what to do with them. A turkey vulture came over the trees into sight and must have hit a fragrant air current that was carrying the fish aroma. He immediately teeter-tottered back and forth on the warm breeze. Then he spiraled down and landed right next to the covered fish. Turkey vultures, unlike most birds, have a sense of smell. Tipping back and forth on those massive wings must help them zero in on the updrafts which advertise the rotted flesh that they call dinner.

They were tattling on my secret dumping site. I finally gave in and put the fish heads out on a point so they could come in each morning for a free breakfast. They look comical running back and forth, all hunched over with their featherless, red wrinkled heads. I look forward to their arrival each day.

Two days ago when I went to pull back the ladder for the night, a large deer was on the

path in front of me. She startled me because I
heard her stomp before I saw her. By the time I
looked up we were only ten feet away from each
other. We momentarily stared without moving. She
held her large ears up and positioned herself
forward. We had each other's undivided
attention. She was tall and sleek with her
summer coat red. I stood with my hands down to
my side and didn't move an inch. After thirty
seconds she stomped her foot, which made me
jump. Slowly she turned and bounded back up
through the woods with her tail flagging. Her
gait was heavy and deliberate with exaggerated
jumping and crashing to make herself appear
heavier than she was. Her large ears were
rotated back in my direction so even though she
was watching where she was going, I knew her
attention was on me.

   After that, I noticed a well-worn path from
the woods down to the water that must have been
used by her. My living there will probably cause
her to reroute her way and bypass my small
campsite. Now the mostly solitary deer come down
to the water less frequently to drink, as they
are keenly aware of my presence. Too bad,
because I enjoyed the chance encounters.

   Last night I saw another deer, or maybe it was
the same one of two nights ago. She was coming
down for her nightly drink from across Prescott
Brook. I happened to be in my outhouse where I
have befriended a spider in its web. Being by
myself, I prop the privy door open with a stick,
which allows me to tolerate the spider. I found
myself sitting a little longer at dusk, just
staring out the door, for the murmur of Prescott
Brook was soothing and the soft green scenery
was pleasing. Besides, the spider was good
company and I think it enjoyed the flies I
dropped into its web.

   All of a sudden I was alarmed by a high-
pitched noise and I couldn't imagine what made

it. I peered out the door and looked across the
brook and up the steep slope. A large doe was
making the sound by snorting air through her
nostrils. It was amazingly loud and shrill. Then
she followed up with the same loud, noisy,
intimidating gait that I had seen before. She
had to go up a steep banking to reach the cover
of the forest but did so effortlessly. Who needs
nature films?

One of my duties here is to monitor a pair
of loons. Conveniently, they have set up
housekeeping on a tiny island in front of the
eagle tower. The MDC biologist wanted to know
why they kept failing every time they attempted
to nest. (I write loon notes in between taking
eagle notes.) One loon yodeled thirty-eight
times last night at midnight. The disturbed
echoing call really traveled over the still
water. Something had his dander up: probably
an intruding loon. The barred owls immediately
reacted to the commotion and responded with a
series of hoots themselves. Then a whippoorwill
broke in with his very sharp and exacting,
"Whippoorwill... whippoorwill... whippoorwill!"
It is really noisy out here at night as nature's
second shift comes on duty.

5:00 p.m.

The nagging rain finally stopped and the water
is calm for the first time in two days. There is
even a promising break in the lingering cloud
cover. I am going to leave and take my hot chili
outside and watch the busy loons. I've been
eating ravenously over the last couple of days,
just like I did on the Elvidge dairy farm.
Remember?

Jack Swedberg came out Saturday morning and
brought me home-baked New Salem Restaurant
muffins and a coffee. He is so full of energy
and truly is the catalyst behind the eagle
project. A tanned, robust outdoorsman, he loves

a good laugh. He has faith in me and I don't
want to let him down.

Initially Jack gave me a CB radio to
communicate with the MDC police in case of
an emergency. I could pick up voices with a
southern twang that sounded like they came from
Tennessee or Georgia, but I couldn't communicate
with the police just six miles away by way of
the water. I have an MDC walkie-talkie instead.
I will change the battery pack every other day
and house the base charger at the astronomy
site. I have to call the MDC at 9:00 in the
morning and 9:00 at night for radio checks.
It lets them know I survived another day. My
handle is "Eagle One."

Billy Byrne was my only guest on Sunday.
We had a nice conversation about how he got
started with photography. He borrowed his
father's Kodak camera early on and went to the
University of Maine for his bachelor of science
in wildlife management and spent his summers
working with wildlife.

After college he spent two years as a sergeant
in the army in Vietnam, teaching infantrymen
rapid rope descent from Huey helicopters. He
said it became useful years later when banding
raven chicks on cliffs in Massachusetts.

Billy bought his first Nikon camera while on
R&R in Tokyo. After the army he was hired by the
Division of Fisheries and Wildlife. Then he
applied for and landed a photography position.
His beautiful, breathtaking pictures have
appeared in the *Massachusetts Wildlife magazine*,
National Wildlife, *Smithsonian*, *National Audubon*
and *Northern Woodlands*.

I don't believe this! The radio just announced
tornado warnings. What next? I really am having
fun! Well, I finished my chili. I had better cut
the fish up and feed the babies so I can be
finished by 9:00 p.m. Because there were so many

wet days in a row, I have made two trips up to
the astronomy site to take a hot shower. I can
take a quick shower, change the ice packs for my
cooler and be back down to the hack site within
an hour.

Take care all,

Love, Dianne

8

Eight Feathered Babies

 I SAT ON THE STOOL AND PEERED AT MY baby eagles through the one-way glass in the observation cubbyhole. They were a sight to see; everything interested them. A tuft of downy feather that the wind blew around had their undivided attention. Iridescent blue tree swallows zipped by the eagles' living quarters with their noisy chatter. All eyes would be on a wandering turkey vulture that drifted by on large, out-stretched wings, turned up slightly in a shallow "V" position.

Taking extensive notes on all eight babies allowed me the chance to pick out individual traits and personalities. I still had to double-check the birds' blue tag numbers to make sure I was recording information in their individual notebooks. During the day I recorded all my observations collectively, alternating between four eaglets on the top platform and the four on the bottom platform. Then at night I would rewrite the information on separate sections of a notebook, monitoring each bird as an individual. This way their health, weight, and appetite could be tracked and graphed.

Woodstock and Snoopy were in the lower right nest cage. That area was sheltered and received the least amount of sun and rain. That way they didn't overheat or get totally soaked. The other birds were older, could figure out how to get out of the sun and had plumage that could handle a downpour. We learned later that regardless of size, we should pair the chicks by feather development so that they are behaviorally the same age.

I learned that submissive birds tended to have very expressive actions. Woodstock, a female (big feet), tended to be submissive to Snoopy, the male, to the point that she was whining and whistling for food from her nest mate. Snoopy seemed gentle and caring and didn't show any aggression toward Woodstock, who held her head down and cowered if Snoopy even looked at her.

On their first morning on the tower, both birds were outside their nest, lying on the deck at the front bars, asleep. They could hardly move about on their uncoordinated legs. They were still too young to flap into the stick-filled nest, let alone scamper to it. I took it upon myself to sneak into the cage and quietly place them back into the nest where the food landed.

It had rained the night before and all their straw bedding had sifted through the tidy nest. I put more bedding in and lifted each bird separately back into the now cozy nest. There was no reaction from the sleepy babies and I quietly backed out of the cage and closed the door. I debated whether I was going to report my intervention in the records because I'm not supposed to have any contact with the birds once we place them in their new home. I did write it in my notes and even confessed to Jack when he arrived later that day. He said, "No problem."

On the bottom deck to the left were Dick and Jane. Jane was a very alert and energetic baby who liked to eat, walked around a lot, and was very strong. She looked menacing and had sparkling tips on her dark brown head feathers that resembled twinkling stars. (They don't acquire a white head until they're four or five years old.) When she turned, it seemed deliberate and the stars danced on her magnificent head. She liked to watch the passing swallows and could be very aggressive toward Dick, who would back right down and become submissive. I enjoyed watching her exercise her wings for she was very deliberate and took her workouts quite seriously, concentrating on every powerful stroke.

Dick was probably a male because he was so small. He was a very dark chocolate brown bird who tended to keep his feathers tight. His tiny tail, which was still growing, had the appearance of a juvenile golden eagle's with brown at the base and broad white areas forming a band like the feathers on an Indian headdress. Once he started walking around, he did so with absolute confidence.

Dick cowered sometimes if Jane even looked at him. Other times the two of them would sit or lie next to each other and play "beaks" by tapping each other's beaks in a curious manner. It was a somewhat mutual truce where no one won or lost. Dick sometimes would sneak a piece of fish from Jane but confident Jane would take it right back. Every now and then I would throw in a lake trout that had pink-colored flesh instead of white. Dick would get so excited he would forget his fear of Jane and ease his way in next to her and watch. Every time Jane picked up a piece of trout, Dick would grab it right out of her sharp beak, without a scuffle. For a little guy, he had guts!

I sometimes worried about Dick. He had a dry cough that persisted for twelve or more times at a sitting. He would violently shake his head and stick his tongue out, panting. (I often worried if he was going to make it to flying age.) Yet, he always got through his coughing spells and was fine.

Attila and Marjorie were in the top right cage. Attila quarreled with Marjorie just after we placed the two of them in their nest box that first day. I remember Jack Swedberg tapping on the one-way glass to distract them and get them to stop. I'll bet they were wondering where that noise came from because they stopped their bickering immediately and looked around. Attila was definitely dominant over Marjorie, even though they were about the same size. They were the biggest babies and were about a good week ahead of the other birds in development. Attila tended to be meticulous by carefully "muting" or defecating outside the nest box. She preened, moved the nest bedding around after eating fish, and was very adamant about who was in charge in their domicile.

The first morning, Attila somehow got out of the nest with Marjorie and both were at the front bars. Attila was nibbling on the bars and was even trying to poke her head through them. Afterwards she walked back over to the nest on her "ankles," took a giant leap and clambered back up into the nest box using her sparsely feathered wings. She was a very active seven-week-old baby. The other birds did not show that kind of strength. Sometimes Attila would make a nasty lunge at Marjorie. She really meant business if Marjorie got in her space. If she wanted the food Marjorie had, she would slowly reach under and grab it. If Marjorie protested with a nip, Attila would let her have it. Attila knew that the trap door was on top of their cage and would wait right underneath it for her meals. Sometimes she made it hard for me to get the food down to them without dropping a few pieces of cut-up fish on her back. She would respond with a high-pitched chirp.

As Attila grew even stronger and more coordinated, she threw her weight around. She would run over to Marjorie, push her aside with one bump of her developing wings, and gorge on the fish until her crop was full.

Marjorie became my favorite bird, probably because Attila picked on her early and often. She really took a licking. She learned quickly to be submissive and shrug her shoulders in a hunched position while bowing her head when Attila was in one of her moods.

Marjorie was a soft chocolate brown bird with a happy-go-lucky disposition and yellow "eyebrows." She broke her two "deck" feathers, which were the central tail feathers; so that when she fanned her tail I could readily tell her from Attila. Her magnificent head feathers fluffed up in contentment, particularly if she was out of Attila's reach. She always seemed especially interested in everything and everyone. She would often watch the two birds in the top left cage and was always first to reach every developmental milestone. She was the first one to deliberately half-leap, half-fall out of the nest. Later she used her new-found agility to jump on a scale with a perch on top where I could record her weight—9.1 pounds at seven weeks old. She even ventured out on a long perch stick by sliding her legs, side to side, with deliberate precision.

Marjorie liked to prance around once she acquired her sea legs. Within a week she could jump out of the nest with no problem and she really enjoyed shredding the ends of the scale perch with her hooked beak. Then suddenly she would snap at the air in mock battle, accompanied by a menacing look that I was not accustomed to. Sometimes she would chirp and squeal at the rain falling on her dark shoulders. The peeps seemed inappropriate coming from our national symbol, but they sounded wonderful to me, coming from the other side of the one-way glass. They seemed so social in their antics.

At seven to eight weeks of age I saw her "mantle" or droop her wings down around her food to conceal it from Attila. That was a new behavior for her, although it is quite normal among birds of prey.

Last, but not least, in the top left cage I had Bert and Ernie. Ernie, who seemed submissive to Bert, liked to vocalize at the passing swallows as well as any low-flying plane that ventured by. They were a series of whistles and chirps. It was a treat when the resident kingfisher landed on the outside perch and scolded all the babies. Ernie loved it! He would twist his head this way and that to focus better on the little "fisher bird."

Ernie was very hungry those first few days and was one of the birds that had difficulty tearing into the whole fish that we left them that first night. After I cut the fish up into smaller pieces, he did fine. One day I saw that he was out of the nest box and lying at the front bars. When I dropped the food in the nest from the trap door above, Ernie got up and walked over to the nest box. He just couldn't figure out how to get in. After watching Bert eating piece after piece, Ernie tried again. He bobbed his head back and forth and shifted his weight from one foot to the other. He was determined to get back in where he could eat.

Ernie stretched his neck and head close to Bert, who was busily eating near the edge and Bert lunged at him with a sharp nip. Ernie was getting desperate and stood on his toes and talons. He opened his wings to try and hoist himself into the nest but couldn't. I tried to remain patient and not go in their living quarters like I had for Woodstock and Snoopy. Finally I dropped some food past the nest so it would land on the deck where he was. He ate as much as he could of the bite-sized fish chunks and then settled down on the wooden deck and went to sleep.

At noon on the third day I checked on the babies and noticed Ernie still hadn't made it back up into the nest box. He looked dead lying out there on the deck. His body appeared flattened out and his eyes were closed. I was reassured that he was eating because I could see he had a crop full of fish. I was also confident he was alive because the feathers on his back were rising and falling ever so slightly, showing me the rhythm of his breathing. I was relieved as I watched him wake up, stretch a wing and leg at the same time, stand up and stare into the nest where Bert was fast asleep.

By 8:30 p.m., he still had not been able to clamber back in the nest. At dusk I sneaked in quietly while he slept and picked him up, cradled him by his feet and body and placed him back in the nest. Boy was he thin. I know he should be skinny because he had not developed his pectoral muscles, but it still was worrisome.

I kept a close eye on him. It wasn't until the twelfth day that I found him out of the nest again, but this time it was on purpose. However, he still had a hard time trying to pull himself back into the nest. Food was a great stimulus but it was still a struggle.

Finally he learned to take his growing wings and brace them against the side perch. He would then press down and as his body lifted, he could catch a sharp talon on the nest frame and swing up into the nest. It took him a lot longer to get back in but it was a great accomplishment, and food was his reward.

Bert, now he was a different bird. I am guessing he was a male based on his weight. He didn't like anyone. When we were giving him a physical exam and taking blood that first day, he displayed a nasty disposition. He didn't even like sitting in the open crate in the shade under the tower. He grunted defiantly at everyone. Most of the other birds hung their heads down to tune us out or watched us without concern.

Bert ruled his nest box. He wasn't as aggressive as Attila was to Marjorie, but he was definitely the boss over timid Ernie. He remained sensitive to any human contact. I had to be very quick and quiet when dropping fish through the trap door on top of the cage. He would utter an alarmed grunt, even if just my finger showed while dropping the fish in. He did not like humans at all. I respected his desire to be left alone.

The time I entered the cage to put Ernie quietly back in the nest, Bert became very upset. He flared his head feathers to look like a maned lion or hooded cobra. He was quite impressive and grunted with wings outstretched making himself appear as large as possible. I swear he watched the trap door at feeding time so that he could grunt at me. For Bert, noise suggested a possible look at a human body part. Ernie, on the other hand, waited anxiously when he heard the slightest noise behind the wall. Noise meant food to him.

9

Voice On The Water

Loons

 THE MYSTERIOUS LOONS WERE VERY VOCAL and quite beautiful. They were such compelling birds and very striking to watch through binoculars. Their large heads supported beaks resembling black daggers that were used to capture high-speed fish. Their white and black-striped neck plumage gave them an appearance of always being dressed in formal attire. The rest of the upper body was a spectacular array of white on black. The chest and underside were snow white and could be seen whenever the bird stretched up and flapped its wings forward.

It seemed that they did this "flashing" of the white areas of their bodies as a display because I saw it often. It appeared methodical and I wondered if it was a beacon defining their territory. They floated low on the water, just rolling with the reservoir. Rising with the swells in bad weather, they took advantage in calm waters for feather preening. They were made for the water as evidenced by their fluid movements. Their heads scanned from side to side and then abruptly dipped below the surface, peering into the underwater world.

These nine to fifteen-pound diving birds needed a combination of flapping and running to break the surface of the water and

LOONS ON QUABBIN

become airborne. Their watery runway needed to be at least a quarter-mile long. Since they have one of the smallest wing surface area-to-body weight ratios of any bird, getting off the water is difficult. I could see where a loud and convincing voice and unmistakable vocabulary could save the bird much time and energy. Such a defense would decrease the effort of flying around to protect their territory and still get their point across to intruding rivals.

Bird Calls

They woke me up in the middle of the first night with what was called a "yodel." It was quite loud and angry sounding. I recorded in my notes that two loons yodeled thirty-eight times at midnight and ended with two high "kee wees." I thought they came from the resident pair but read later that only the larger males could make that call. It was an aggressive and frightening challenge issued by the resident male in a border confrontation with another male. It must have been the eerie, haunting quality of the goose bump-producing call that instantly drew me to it. I became addicted to the sound. Thereafter, any time I heard the yodel, I would hold my breath so that I could listen to every note produced.

Another call I recorded in my notes was the "o-louuuu" call, which was made throughout the day. It was technically called the "wail." The wail was lengthy and drawn out and carried great distances over the watery landscape. It was used to locate an absent mate when the pair strayed apart. The call seemed to say, "Where are you?" It served as communication from one loon in the bay to the other who was nowhere in sight. At night the sound took on a mournful quality because the air was so still.

My loons sounded a rather nervous laughter or "tremolo" when a boat or an eagle came within view. I defined it in my notes as "oo la lo." They became very serious as the intruder encroached on their territory. Their vocalizations would put me on alert because I began to recognize the differences between warnings.

My "watch dogs" could see the object of concern long before I could because of their open water vantage point.

Only the MDC police boat was allowed on the water where I camped. The open fishing area ended far to the north of the eagle hack site and was marked with large yellow barrels strung across the water. When the watchful loons broadcast their angry warning, I would move to where I could view the reservoir and search for the disturbance. Then I would observe the loons and memorize the call, matching it to the different intrusions. Even small private planes would bring a tremolo or a special yodel if it flew too low.

The heavy but agile loons spent virtually all their lives on or under the water pursuing fish. Their massive streamlined bodies were built for an aquatic life. Their hips were positioned far back with flattened lower legs that helped them maneuver more efficiently underwater. They even had patellae (kneecaps) shaped like forward-facing rudders. Because of their superior adaptations to water, they were unable to walk upright on land like ducks or geese.

Water rolled off their backs in beads when they surfaced and I watched from shore as they methodically used their oil glands when preening. I sat and smiled as I watched them float on their sides and flap a large foot as if they were waving. They were definitely at home on the water.

Nesting

I was fascinated as I watched the loons build their nests at the water's edge. They practically had to push themselves on their bellies by digging their webbed feet and toenails into the sand as they drove forward. It was an effort for them to lift and push their large bodies up a dirt slope to where it was level enough to hollow out a depression. They then lined the crude nest with grasses pulled up from under the water.

I sat for hours and watched through my spotting scope as they tirelessly built their shallow nests. It was a rare and exciting treat to watch them work. Loons usually nest farther north than

Massachusetts, so I treasured the opportunity to observe their nesting behavior and private lives from my summer campsite. This was one of only a handful of nesting pairs in the state that year. I remember watching one loon crawl halfway up the slope and turn to face the water. It began pulling up grasses that were in the shallow water. It threw them over its shoulder to the other attentive loon, who stretched and collected the grass and lined the hollowed-out depression. Then the loon in the nest excavated a little more by pressing forward on its dirty chest and scratching backwards with its toenails to widen the depression in the dirt. That energetic loon kept turning every fifteen seconds in order to place all the grasses around the perimeter of the nest. At this time the loon nearest the water slipped down the slope and swam away from shore and disappeared under the water. It surfaced, reared up, and stretched its wings with a flash of white and vanished under the water again. It surfaced far south of Loon Island and slowly continued south past what I called Gibbs Point. The nesting loon slipped off the nest and crept closer to the water line and then continued to reach for the wet grasses that the other loon had passed to that point. Eventually the loon eased into the water, but continued to dutifully pull grasses from underwater and flip them over its shoulder. The grass was landing in the water, not on shore. Silly bird. Its companion was nowhere in sight.

The female laid two, large olive-green eggs within days of each other. There was a twenty-eight-day incubation period in which they shared nesting responsibilities. When the incubating bird exchanged duties with its mate, the approaching loon crawled up the slope and sat facing inland while the nesting loon always faced the reservoir. This allowed a quick escape to the safety of the protective water in an emergency. After the sitting loon vacated the nest, its mate would clamber into the shallow depression and rock its body back and forth over the warm eggs. It pulled any displaced grasses from the rim of the nest and tucked them under its breast.

I noticed that one loon appeared quite comfortable sitting on the nest with head held high. It appeared very relaxed and looked like it was wearing a German helmet. The mate, by comparison, was very nervous held its head feathers tight and hunched down on the nest, looking like an anhinga or snakebird. The nervous bird was smaller and therefore probably the female; she appeared far more uncomfortable on shore. It was easy to tell them apart because of their distinctly different postures.

During one observation period, again using the scope, I observed the relaxed male sit up and roll the eggs toward himself. Sometimes an egg stood on end and came back to rest, at which time he gently sat back down on them. Next he took his back feet and hollowed out the nest, got up, rolled the eggs again, hollowed out the new section and then pulled more grasses around himself. Now his belly was quite dirty. Thirteen minutes had elapsed and I started noticing the same pattern at each nest change. The loons

LOON TURNING EGGS

initially faced inland and then started in a methodical ritual of egg turning and hollowing out the nest and gathering grasses around themselves. That process would keep them moving in a clockwise direction and eventually facing the water again.

Whoever was sitting on the eggs during any time of danger would scurry off the nest with surprising speed, almost like an otter, to reach the safety of the water. The threat might be a boat, an eagle, or an intruding loon from another territory.

Visiting Crows

A family of crows lived in the immediate area and flew to the island several times a day to inspect the loon who was tending the nest. The slender shiny-black crow parents and their three obedient youngsters were a constant nuisance to the loons. The youngsters whined a nasal "caw" which kept their parents busy searching for food. The loons would call "oooo" if the nagging pests came too close.

One time only two crows flew to the island, which brought little response or vocalization from the male loon on the nest. The female was nowhere in sight. As one crow walked past the sitting bird the loon's mate appeared instantly at the shore. Her head was down with neck outstretched parallel to the water in attack posture. She shadowed the crow as it walked along the shoreline and lunged at the intruder like a crocodile. It was enough to send the trespasser flying off while the victor dove and disappeared as fast as she had come. The male was in an upright posture on the nest the whole time, seemingly unconcerned.

I worried a lot about those "murder" of crows as they are sometimes called because both loons would sometimes take off for an evening swim, leaving the precious eggs unattended. How could they be so careless? I didn't believe that behavior was normal. I would think the cooling down of the eggs would be counter-productive to the embryo's development. I was always relieved to see that the crows seemed to be off doing their own thing on the mainland when the loons went on their twilight fishing excursions.

On June 26, a couple of days after the eggs were laid, I heard a loud commotion. I looked out and to my surprise saw three loons flying into the little bay from the south. Their wing beats were extraordinarily loud and were accompanied by a haunting tremolo. They came skidding along the surface like a plane without landing gear. I quickly glanced over to the nest and the sitting bird had disappeared.

Moments later I saw four birds swimming together in a tight circle. It had just started to rain and all the birds dove simultaneously. They surfaced and began milling around each other counter-clockwise. Two would dive and the other two would put their heads underwater to check them out. They would all disappear under the surface again. All surfaced, all dove, and then two would surface and then all would be gone again. What a strange game they played. What bothered me was no one was paying any attention to the nest and those exposed eggs. Luckily it was raining, which probably meant the crows were taking shelter under the mainland forest canopy.

When the loons dove, they stayed under the water for fifteen to eighteen seconds at a time. They stayed in a group with either two or four birds on the surface at a time. Three minutes later only two surfaced. I never knew where the other two went. They just seemed to vanish. A crow called from the mainland and as I searched the shoreline for them, one loon made a beeline for the nest. It clambered up the ramp and started the ritual of egg turning, position changing and grass lining. It looked like the calm male. The sun came out, the waves died down and I went to check on the baby eagles to quiet my nerves from all the excitement.

Later that evening, I noted that the loon turned the eggs at 7:30 p.m. Five minutes later the bird dove off the eggs and slid down the slope into the water. It skimmed the shore fast with its neck stretched forward and then disappeared underwater. I climbed the eagle tower for a better vantage point but I didn't see any loons for seven minutes. Then I noticed two loons behind Loon Island, diving and surfacing again and again really fast. Now there were three birds. One sat floating and watching its mate chase the third loon. It was raining and of course the eggs were unattended again. The intruding bird was way out in front as the resident chased it in "motorboat" fashion, loudly splashing across the surface using its wings like heavy paddles. Even when the pursuing bird stopped, the third bird kept pressing onward. Eventually the outcast changed his retreat tactics and moved northward out of the territory. After turning his head to look behind him and peering underwater for any sneak attacks, he dove and swam underwater and then surfaced considerably further away in the direction of Mount Pomeroy Island.

An hour later, the two territorial birds were bobbing in the waves south of Loon Island. One bird came north along the shore, nonchalantly looked around for half a minute and then clambered up the slope towards the nest. It turned the eggs, looked around and then rearranged the drying grasses. The other loon disappeared.

10

Wild Neighbors

 LIVING EIGHT MILES AWAY FROM THE nearest civilization, I felt as if I were in my own little world. Yes, people would show up during daylight hours to visit the site and see the growing eagles, but for the most part, I was happily alone. The assorted songbirds and insects made for a pleasant and harmonious symphony and there was beauty to behold everywhere I looked.

I started to feel as if I was part of the earth. I lived in rhythm with the water and could understand the body language of the animals that I observed. I didn't feel alone at all for there was fellowship in the trees, sky, water, and the earth itself.

I basked in the sun's rays and felt as if I were weathering like the landscape, unspoiled by civilized impurities. My skin was getting quite dark and my once-soft hands were well calloused. Lately I had been pulling my nets and not getting covered by fish scales. Wearing gloves when I chopped up the fish had helped, so everything I ate didn't smell and taste like raw fish. Peanut butter and jelly should taste like peanut butter and jelly, not white perch!

Occasionally I looked up and saw an enormous C-5 military aircraft cruising overhead. I really couldn't hear it until it passed and then I heard the roar of the engines, straining in a high-pitched whine. They were gigantic. Those planes would snap me back to reality.

Every now and then the loons would call out with a tremolo announcing an eagle was near. On the high tower, I could look out the front window. If the adult eagle flew too close to the nesting loon she would quickly scoot off her nest and slide down the banking to the water for protection. I peered into the babies' cages and see if anyone noticed the eagle. Those who were not preening or sleeping had their brown eyes riveted on the graceful movements of the free-flying eagle as it sailed by. If the wild eagle saw the babies it showed no obvious reaction. When the danger passed, the unnerved loon scampered back up the well worn path to settle in on its warm eggs.

One day I watched a wild adult bald eagle bathe along the shore of Loon Island. It waded into the water up to its "pantaloon" leg feathers, gulped a drink, and then started splashing water up over its shoulders by dipping its head down. I could hear the regal eagle flapping its wings on the surface of the water. Because I was looking through the scope, the sound was delayed compared to the image I saw. The adult even rolled right over to get its back wet. I took great pleasure in being able to watch the private lives of these creatures without disturbing them.

Horsefly

There was a very territorial creature that let me know every time I entered its limited airspace between the fish pen and the tower. It was a very aggressive horsefly that flew out from near a pine tree and circled my head incessantly, buzzing loudly. At first the encounter was quite startling as the fly's wing beat was loud and I thought it was a bee. Then it began its annoying circling of my head while escorting me through its territory. When it accomplished this task it buzzed away in the direction of the pine tree. I got used to the fly and found myself greeting it as I approached and wishing it a nice day as I left. I missed it on rainy days and looked toward the pine tree for any sign of tiny activity. At some point it stopped worrying about my daily invasions. Either it became used to me or was eaten by the crafty kingbird that patrolled the area.

Beaver

At dusk the resident beaver occasionally swam out to Loon Island from its shoreline lodge in Prescott Cove. Because the water level was down so far that year, he used a low underwater entrance to his home. I didn't see him too often so it was always a treat to watch him slowly and silently make his way across the little bay. He pushed the calm water aside with subtle ripples that made an ever-widening "V." Once I was mindlessly scanning the landscape in the direction of Gibbs Cove and noticed a dark object a quarter-mile away along the shore. There were no boulders or tufts of vegetation that large that I could remember. I retrieved my binoculars from the dock and peered down the shore. Sure enough, it was not a regular feature of the landscape, but it was the unobtrusive beaver turning to his side grooming his soft wet fur. I was so pleased that I knew the immediate landscape well enough to notice the beaver was out of place. Early man must have been attentive to his surroundings, as any change might have meant either a threat or opportunity. Their powers of observation kept them in harmony with the land while acquiring food or watching for danger.

Reservoir

I began to measure the depth of my own self during that summer, thanks in part to the reservoir itself. On many occasions, I had revealing experiences when I stepped into my boat and ventured out onto the water. The reservoir was my friend, providing me with fish for the growing babies and tranquility on warm, calm days. I rolled with the smooth movement of the waves and my ears became accustomed to the lapping of water against the boat.

In the evenings after my chores, I sometimes went fishing. I gazed over the side of the boat into the glass-like water and wondered at the old stone walls as they disappeared into the depths of the reservoir. The loons used the submerged roads and underwater highways to chase schools of fish. I peered down and witnessed various underwater activities. Once I saw a large bullhead excavating its burrow by carrying silt in its mouth and depositing it in a mound at the entrance. Then the smooth-skinned, whiskered, brown fish curled its body to turn around and disappeared back down into the hole with a wave of his tail. A gigantic smallmouth bass hugged a large, submerged boulder and used the shadows as a hiding spot to ambush unsuspecting bluegills.

Once I saw a white object far to the north on the surface of the reservoir. By the glistening light I assumed it was a Styrofoam

LAKE TROUT BIT OFF MORE THAN IT COULD CHEW

cup. As I approached it by boat I realized it was a large dead lake trout with a fish wedged in its mouth. Now I know why fish have fins on the top, side and bottom. They raise their spines to get predators to think twice about eating them. This large fish had no chance to think twice. He felt the smaller fish's revenge and it was an "end of life" experience for both of them.

Nighttime Visitor

I found out I had nighttime visitors when I put frozen deer meat outside of the tent to thaw. (I had a freezer at the astronomy site for supplementary food for the eagles.) Half the meat was gone the next morning and for a split second my imagination ran wild. What could have possibly devoured it right next to my tent door? Bobcat? Coyote? BEAR? Either I slept soundly or this silent creature had made off with the meat without my hearing him. Oh to have solid walls for protection from those wild creatures.

I set out a plastic bag full of meat the next night and attached a string to it. The line went from the bag to my bed through a small hole in the screen. I wasn't sure if I even had the nerve to peer out through the plastic window into the darkness. I had to find out what was so silent that it didn't go "bump" in the night. I'm one of those people who, as a kid, couldn't go down in the basement after dark or look out a window if I heard a noise. I didn't want to believe in the boogie man but you never could be sure.

The string moved at 2:00 a.m. and I heard the plastic bag crinkle ever so softly. I took a deep breath and hit the switch on my flashlight. Two very startled raccoons were mesmerized by the light and paused a few seconds with their delicate fingers fondling the meat. Then they disappeared up the path. One bandit was dark and the other had a lighter buff coat. The mystery was solved and thank goodness I had remembered to pull the ladder back from the tower each night. The baby eagles would have been easy prey at their young age with no parents to defend them and, of course, I would have been sound asleep.

Alone In A Rainstorm

A tremendous rainstorm hit hard late one night making me feel extremely alone. My tent was under a towering pine tree that protected me from most of the storms, but this one pounded my metal roof with incredible force. It sounded like popcorn sizzling in hot oil. My thin canvas walls shook continuously and my tired ears received no break from the constant rattling noise. Continuous waves of driving rain persisted for hours. I couldn't sleep, let alone hear myself think. I wrote my daily notes to try and keep my sanity and almost called the MDC police on my two-way radio. It was about 2:00 a.m. and I just wanted to know if civilization still existed. I thought about calling the station and imagined hearing a voice responding on the other end. After this mental exercise I was fine. I woke up the next day to the sounds of the loons. I was glad I did not give in to my insecurity about the frightening storm and being alone out here in the wilderness.

Coyotes

I was a little unnerved another night when I was awakened by the startled cries of several coyotes. The darkness didn't help as I reassured myself that the timid canines would not bother me. I felt the tent canvas against my side and moved a little closer to the middle of my mattress and a little deeper into my sleeping bag. I opened my eyes long enough to press the light button on my watch to see that it was around 4:00 a.m. The secretive coyotes only carried on for a few minutes, but they were loud enough to make me pull the covers over my head. I felt really vulnerable and isolated for a few seconds and was glad morning was but a few hours away. Good gosh, this is Massachusetts and I'm all alone out here!

I talked to God every day under many different circumstances. Sometimes it was to help me with my temperamental boat when the motor quit at an inopportune moment or to support me when

I didn't think I had the emotional strength to carry on. So-called "civilized" man is still primitive and only a stone's throw away from our ancestors when it comes to trusting in gods we cannot see but rather feel in our hearts and souls. No, I was not alone nor afraid to be out here. I became one with the land as I learned to coexist with nature on her terms and live by her rules.

11

More Letters From Quabbin

Day 6

June 26, 1985 - 12:00 noon

Dear Paul and Becky,

Everything is going smoothly here. I'm taking a break for lunch. So far it's been anywhere from just me here to as many as five people in a day. Yesterday Jack Swedberg brought down a group of people and I fed the eagles their breakfast while curious eyes peered quietly but excitedly through the mirrored glass.

I watched two Fish and Wildlife workers pull in a fyke net yesterday. Billy D., who will be my weekend replacement, and I accompanied them in the boat so I could learn how to tend the cumbersome apparatus. The net is underwater and serves to catch live fish that I then hold in my floating pen. This way I'm guaranteed a continual supply of fresh fish.

Lee McLaughlin, also from Fish and Wildlife, filleted two or three fish for me and taught me the technique. It was enough to feed two

or three people, but after everyone left I
fed the birds and then cooked the fresh fillets
and ate them all. I had planned to cook noodles
with them, but I was too stuffed. By 8:30 p.m.
I was so tired it was hard to stay awake for
my 9:00 p.m. radio check with the MDC police.

I eat well and don't skip any meals. Sometimes Jack or one of the two Billys brings
me down a thick sandwich from the restaurant
up in New Salem. I eat healthy balanced meals
of bread, fruits, cereals, and now fish. I
sleep until 7:30 a.m. most of the time and
try to turn in between 9:00 and 10:00 p.m.
I don't want to be tired or rundown like I
was during the time we took care of the polar
bear cub. I try to write letters every few
days to serve as a diary, because I'm not
good at keeping a journal and spelling was
never my strong subject.

Becky, I'm glad you and Daddy are coming
to visit me. You'll love the baby eagles.
They eat for ten minutes straight, fill up
and then go back to sleep. Then they wake
up at 3:00 p.m. and eat leftovers until they
have a full crop and then sleep or rest again.
I feed them at 8:00 p.m., which gives them a
full crop again before nightfall. They must
wake up bright and early because when I check
them in the morning, all the food is cleaned
up and their crops are full again. What a
great cycle. It cuts down on the fly population.
I guess they had maggot problems in previous
years because uneaten fish baked in the sun
and attracted flies.

Well, the rain stopped. No visitors today.
Take care.

Love, Dianne

Day 7

June 27, 1985 - 4:00 p.m.

Dear Mom, Dad, Scotty and Louise,

I am able to write because it is raining
and I've done all my chores. I just spent the
last three hours on the hack tower with the
eagles. They're enjoyable to look at. Next I
have to get fish out of my holding pen, but
I'll see if the weather clears up for that.
I keep hand-pumping out that darn little boat
because it keeps raining. I had laryngitis
again yesterday; I am still stuffy and I'm
fighting off a cold so far today.

Last Sunday, I was alone and my boat broke
loose in a very windy storm. It was blowing
from east to west so my little protected cove
was getting pounded. The boat and dock ended up
against the shore and they're quite heavy in one
big mass. Thank goodness Billy Byrne came Sunday
afternoon. He helped me refasten sections of my
dock with some bolts he had in his truck. To
reciprocate, I helped him disassemble his
photography blind that was set down the shore
near an eagle tree. We tried earlier but there
was a terrible storm.

Got to go now,

Love, Dianne

Day 8

Thursday, June 28, 1985 - 4:00 p.m.

Dear Mom, Dad, Scotty and Louise,

I've had a great day today! I just returned
from capturing my first up-close picture of a
wild immature bald eagle. I had used the boat to

put fish heads on the shore south of the tower
appropriately named Fish Head Point. At 1:00
p.m. the loon began calling and issued an alarm
across the bay. The male loon slid off the nest
to the water so I ran to the tower and scampered
up the ladder. I had left the spotting scope up
there and had it trained on the loon nest.

The crows called next and I looked out over
the water and saw an eagle fly by with slow,
deliberate wing beats. Its tail fanned out and
tipped side to side as it was riding the strong
north wind like a kite. Its legs were dropped
like a plane's landing gear. It wouldn't come
down all the way to the fish remains, but just
hung there in the wind investigating the free
lunch. Then all of a sudden it tilted its wings
and soared out over the reservoir and dropped
straight down toward the water. It snatched a
live fish from the surface and flapped back up
into the sky above the treetop level. There it
sailed like a hang glider, back and forth, while
it positioned the fish in its talons so it was
facing head first. The eagle actually looked
down at its feet while making the adjustments.
Finally it disappeared over the distant trees. I
could hear the crow family again announcing the
eagle's retreat. The loon returned to shore,
shimmied back up the slope and settled down on
the exposed nest and eggs.

I took notes on my eagle babies for the
next few minutes and then as I was leaving the
tower, the loon called again. I looked up over
the tower roof. Sure enough, the lone eagle
came soaring back over the choppy water, this
time very high. I immediately crouched down and
froze to remain undetected. He came down a bit
and glided over the loon and his nest. Boy did
the cautious loon scurry into the water to join
its mate offshore. They both had a few choice
words. Bald eagles are one of the few natural
enemies of the loons. The eagle wandered back

over to the fish heads and dropped straight down
in the strong wind with opened wings and feet
extended. The white-capped waves were parading
due south in tight rows and the sky was slate
gray. What a sight.

I shifted from peeking over the top of the
tower, where I could observe the loons'
reactions, to the side where I could watch
the renegade eagle. With my trusty binoculars
I saw that he had bands on both legs but I
couldn't read them because he was too far
away. I quietly slid down the ladder on pure
adrenaline, carrying the scope and tripod. Then
I snuck up the path to the tent and grabbed my
camera. I raced out of sight of the eagle to the
inlet where my boat was docked. I worked my way
up the running brook a ways so that I could use
boulders and a fallen log to jump to the other
side without getting too wet. I bounced through
the ferns and followed a deer trail up over a
forested knob and then I crept slowly down
through the trees to within sight of the water.
I set my tripod down on the soft pine needles
and tried to be inconspicuous, although my
breathing was heavy and my heart pounding. I
first positioned the scope, trying to find the
area where the eagle had landed and then tried
to zoom in on my subject. I could make out #103
on the left leg and a silver federal band on
the right leg.

All of a sudden the eagle looked up from
eating the fish heads and spotted me way up in
the thick woods. He kept bobbing his head trying
to determine what I was, since I was hunkered
down by a large tree. I was peering through the
scope and didn't move a muscle. Finally one of
the nosey crows cawed, which attracted his
attention. When the eagle turned his head, I
jumped aside, grabbed my camera and snuck around
toward his backside. I crawled like a G.I. Joe
to get close enough to use my telephoto lens. I

took one picture, moved closer and took another.
Jack Swedberg had taught me that strategy, just
in case your subject moves off before you get
any photo opportunity.

The pounding waves and the wind stayed strong
from the north. The wind parted the feathers on
the eagle's brown head as he bent down to eat.
He finally finished and flew off. As I walked
back up through the friendly woods I felt on top
of the world. I had my camera bag over one
shoulder and Jack's scope and tripod over the
other. I felt like a real wildlife photographer,
even though the mighty eagle would look
microscopic in my picture.

I returned to the tent, made a hot tea and
decided it was a good time to squeeze in dinner.
I'm eating spaghetti while I write. I heard a
deer this morning whistling like a train again.
I went over the crest of the hill and she was
jumping and snorting, jumping and snorting. She
must be mad at me for the inconvenience I've
caused by making her reroute her way around my
busy campsite.

I still cut up the eagle's meals into bite-
sized pieces. My hands, arms and shoulders get
so tired. I finally got smart and now bring a
radio down by the shore to keep me company.

I haven't had any guests for two days. I make
a point to sing out loud with some of the songs
on the radio when I am cutting up the fish, just
to check my voice, of course.

Today I took the boat out in strong northerly
winds and headed south. I got caught against the
shallow shore after I moved in to dump my fish
remains. I struggled to paddle back out to get
my engine in deeper water. Wouldn't you know it,
the engine wouldn't start. Now I was getting
blown across Gibbs Bay at a good clip, trying to
start the beast. I pulled and pulled on the
starter rope with my foot braced firmly against

the back of the boat. I finally asked God if he could help me get the motor started before my shoulder gave out. It started up on the next mighty pull. (He seems to always be there when I'm in a pinch; so far at least!)

The eagles are at a transitional age. The older ones are in the nest and can keep their feet underneath them now. They used to "clump" around on their ankles, which kept the rest of their bodies low and compact. I'll bet that lessened their chances of falling out of a natural nest. "Nature" is smart! Marjorie, my favorite eagle, can now wander out of the nest onto the floor and sometimes walk, sometimes clump over to the bars and peer out. It's been cold this whole week, considering it is the end of June. No sun, just wind, drizzle, or rain.

Well, it's 4:46 p.m. I have to cut up another ten pounds of fish. I spend about four hours a day cutting up food and cleaning the food preparation area. I then spend two to four hours observing the babies eating and interacting. I keep my third eye on the loons, noting their nesting and territorial behaviors. It takes me almost two hours to pull my fishnets from the reservoir, and then I repair them in my spare time--all good stuff.

When someone from Fish and Wildlife comes to visit, I get to relax and enjoy the few hours they are here. We talk about how the growing birds and I are faring and they help me pull the nets, which is always welcome. I wonder if they think I just sit around most of the day. Yesterday and today have been twelve- to fifteen-hour days of non-stop work except to write a letter at lunch or dinnertime.

Take care. I am.

I love you,

Dianne

Sometimes I just walk along the shore after feeding and cleaning up after the babies. I tend to walk with my head down and enjoy picking up washed pebbles. Some years the reservoir is full to capacity while other years it could be down as much as eleven feet. With water levels fluctuating, the soil keeps eroding along the shore and exposing new treasures. I found a wooden-handled jackknife without the blade and a child's metal ice skate.

There are many kinds of beautiful stones of all different sizes, shapes and colors. My favorites are the smooth, round orange gems and the pepper-colored ones. I bent down and picked them up and twirled them in my fingers and marveled at their creation. As a child in school, I was shown some of the more common varieties of rocks like quartz and granite. I don't remember which are which anymore, so I just take simple unscientific pleasure in their natural beauty.

Day 11

Monday, July 1, 1985 - 8:57 p.m.

Dear Paul and Becky,

I miss you and wish you were here, even though I was with you both just yesterday. I'm having a late dinner and have three minutes until I call in to the MDC police for my nightly check. I hope you two ate well today. How are those dinners holding out? I'm eating noodles and fish.

Something is going on here at Quabbin. I just went to do my radio check but the police were transmitting so I waited. Then they radioed "Eagle One," which is me! I was surprised since they've never done that before. Besides, I only have the radio on when I'm about to make my two daily calls. Otherwise I try not to waste my batteries.

They wanted to know if there was an MDC police
boat in my area. I went outside to investigate
because the loons were yodeling, which means
something was out of place on their part of the
reservoir. I looked myself, but couldn't see any
boats from shore, so I ran back in to report
that I saw no activity on the water. They said
to radio them if I did because there was a
boating emergency in one of the distant fishing
areas. I kept an eye out and I am monitoring the
emergency frequency. Besides, it's getting dark
outside so there's not much to see. I never
found out what the emergency was.

Billy D. helped me cut fish and set a gill net
yesterday. He built a table from scrap wood over
the weekend when he relieved me. Jack gave me a
heavy, sharper knife with some real authority.
Gosh, it is like using a thick machete! It used
to take me two hours to cut up the food and now
it only takes me forty-five minutes. I used to
sit on a plank like a see-saw and cut the fish
up on that same piece of wood. Now I can stand
at the table and chop away with room to work. It
gives me three extra hours each day to watch the
eagles, check the loons, or do my chores.

Eaglet Snoopy, who is in the same cage as
eaglet Woodstock, is under close watch. When he
breathes he sounds like a child's birthday horn.
I taped it so I would not have to describe it to
the Tufts veterinarians if they came out.
Sometimes he even croaks like a frog. He's
eating fine though and is alert.

Marjorie jumps on and off the scale constantly
now. She weighs 9.1 pounds before eating and
10.2 after gorging herself. She is probably a
female because of her higher weight. The
"probable" males on the tower weigh closer to
seven or eight pounds.

I got a little too much sun today. I really
enjoyed the warmth since all the days of dismal

rain last week. I had a bathing suit and shorts on. I keep my shirt tucked in my belt so when guests come I can put it on.

I just had something crawl down my arm and it was a wolf spider!!! Ahhh! I don't mind them outside or in my Port-a-Jon, but I nearly had a coronary brushing it off me here in my small tent. Of course every little movement after that or anything that rubs near me causes another coronary. Right next to my bed too! I leaped up and hit my thighs on the underside of the table. Did that hurt! What's worse, he's in here somewhere.

I saw a couple of deer in their beautiful summer coats this evening. I also saw an adult bald eagle fly south out of Gibbs Cove at 8:00 p.m. He must have been sitting in a tree and I didn't even know it. The alert loons sounded an alarm call about an hour earlier and the nesting loon even got off her nest to join the mate. They both swam to the east of the island, one in front of the other. I couldn't understand why they were so careless to leave their nest unattended. At the time I had written in my loon notes that the waters were calm and there was no sign of any threat in the area. That shows how observant I was that evening. The seasoned loons knew the eagle was there. I need to pay more attention and trust their primitive instincts and keen senses.

I caught my first three mice early this morning with my old beat-up mousetraps from home. They're still peeing all over my canned goods, the bums. The traps went off at 11:00 p.m., 3:00 a.m. and the last one at 5:30 a.m. With all this nighttime activity I need a nap during the day. I'm glad I keep all my chewable boxed goods in the sealed refrigerator. Without any electricity it serves as a vault and the crafty mice can't get into it. Don't worry; I'm not eating the mice like Farley Mowat did in *Never Cry Wolf*. I'm giving them to the eagle babies in the morning. I open my door at night and place the deceased up on the roof until morning. The raccoons can get their own meals.

The other morning I went up to feed the growing babies and noticed some little droppings coming from under the stiff tarp that covers one of the back windows looking in on the eagles. After inspecting the canvas, I noticed a small bump in front of me. I cautiously touched the mound and it squeaked! I touched it a few more times and it squeaked each time. I slowly and carefully lifted the material up and there appeared a small brown bat. How awesome. I lowered the tarp and left it alone.

The fish nets work well. It took me two hours to haul them up and take the fish out this morning. I bring my radio out in the boat now and sit on an overturned bucket. As I pull up the lines, the fish come to the surface and I have to untangle them from the nets. Some big fish are just caught by the lips so I usually let them go. Sunday, before I returned, Billy D. caught an enormous smallmouth bass, just under five pounds. He put it in the live pen and, after showing me, he let it go. I didn't set the net tonight because the men from Central District of Fish and Wildlife are coming to use my boat to check the fyke nets tomorrow. The forty fish I catch feed the eagles for a day and a half. I also add vitamins and thiamine supplements. I don't want to catch any more than I need. The fyke nets should give me a fish supply that I can put in the live pen in my little bay.

Kiss Becky for me.

Love, Dianne

Day 13

Wednesday, July 3, 1985 - Noon

Dear Mom, Dad, Scotty, and Louise,

I'm boiling eggs for lunch and am having tea because it's chilly out. It is the first hot tea I've had since last Friday, which was one of those cold, wet, long-underwear days. Yesterday was a beautiful day.

A Fish and Wildlife crew came down to check a fyke net yesterday. Here's how it works: The fish follow the underwater nets and funnel into smaller and smaller compartments. We pull up the line, untie the knot and take the live fish out. It's hard to pull up and try to get the hoops up over the bow and steady the boat at the same time. You must then try to net the fish out while trying to maintain your balance. A third person anchors the boat from the stern and acts as a counterweight so we are not tipped too far forward. When Billy D. comes again on Friday for weekend coverage, we will attempt to empty the fyke net again and will commandeer any other person who happens to visit.

I usually fish a gill net daily. Two orange buoys help me find the ends of the net the next day. Heaven help me if I don't let the net out straight, as it sinks to the bottom of the deep reservoir. I have to set it while standing up in the unsteady boat, which is puttering in reverse. My foot is on the steering bar to guide the boat backwards while I attempt to feed the net out straight. It's not too difficult to do, although I have gotten the length cord and the netting wrapped around the prop two or three times since I first tried doing it solo.

On one occasion I backed up and had the whole net down under the rolling waves without a

twist, in fifty feet of water. I then threw
out the end line and attached marker buoy and
proceeded to turn the boat the wrong way. Not
only did I wrap the line around the prop, but
I cut the gosh-darned line and watched the
bobbing buoy float off. Good thing there was
no one around to witness my error, or so I
thought. While hanging upside down over the
motor and struggling to unwrap the line from
around the prop, I saw the police boat way off
in the distance, heading north on its patrol.
Of course the loons were the ones to bring the
intruders to my attention.

All of a sudden the police boat stopped, so
I stopped what I was doing and picked up my
binoculars. Wouldn't you know it? A police
officer was staring back at me through *his*
binoculars. I'm sure he had been watching me
hanging off the back of the motor. I thought,
"Oh great! He'll have a good laugh back at the
station about the girl alone in the wilderness!"
I once read a book about a woman, Erma J. Fisk,
who did some bird research in the wild. She
wrote how I felt, "Damn, damn, damn, they sent
a woman to do a man's job!" I could use a little
confidence in myself here.

I saw two immature bald eagles yesterday
and one wandering osprey. The loons are still
housekeeping and doing okay. My babies are
looking good except for one who sounds like a
horn. Jack Swedberg said he has heard it before
in previous years from other growing babies and
they've been fine. That information let me relax
a little.

No visitors today. The weather is warm and
the day is peaceful. I painted the tower's white
tar-papered roof yesterday. What a view of the
beautiful reservoir from on top of the second
floor. I was up on a short ladder behind the
babies so they couldn't see me. At one point I

reached up on top and one of the babies saw me
and grunted. I'm sure it was Bert because the
vocalization came from the top left cage and he
doesn't like anything that's different. Jack
told me to be very careful because he knew I
was going to start painting after he left. He
worries sometimes. I do my best work alone
though. There are no distractions except for
the wonderful scenery, and I'm starting to
familiarize myself with the landscape more and
more. I've already filleted my dinner and it's
in my cooler. I'm having white perch with
noodles, green beans and milk tonight.

   Well, it's 12:30 p.m. I'm eating eggs
because I need a break from peanut butter and
jelly. I eat plenty of food out here. Last night
I ate four pieces of fish that filled my frying
pan. I eat well but burn it off during the very
long hours.

   I want to set my nets far to the north of
the tower and see if I can get fifteen pounds
of fish for the babies' dinner. Ten pounds of
it will go to the youngsters and five pounds
of heads and tails will go to my compadres,
the turkey vultures.

   I took my shorts off and fixed the dock in my
bathing suit today. Some bolts came undone and
I had to find them in the mud, underwater. It's
a gorgeous day so far, but the radio predicts
thunderstorms. I hope the storm doesn't arrive
when I'm out pulling my nets. Once I start I
just can't quit until the whole net is in. I'm
a sitting duck out there when I'm tied to the
bottom of the reservoir.

   I was just going to end this when the loons
started a loud panicked yodel. I dropped my pen
and ran outside the tent and down to the bank
overlooking the shores and saw three adult loons
in the bay. No one was on the nest and a crow
was on a boulder right next to the eggs! I

tensed up and threw my hands up on my head in anticipation of the loons losing their eggs. The male turned away from the other two and raced back over to shore, loudly chasing the crow away. After the crow flew back to the mainland the male loon went back out to chase the intruding loon away. What excitement, what noise! I wish they would be more careful when they're both off those large conspicuous eggs. It's just a matter of time before the opportunistic crows are going to get lucky and have their way with those eggs.

Take care. I love you and think of you all the time.

Scotty, how's your bird doing with her molt? When I am home, Habiba's mews look like snow with all the feathers she's losing. Her new feathers that are coming in look great.

Again,

                    Love, Dianne

Day 13.

Wednesday
7-3-85
12 pm Noon.

Dear Mom + Dad, Scotty + Louise,

Hi, hope everyone is fine. Say hi + Jr + Dot for me mom, I think about them too. Their special people to me!

I'm boiling eggs for lunch and am having a tea. First tea since last friday during those cold wet, long underwear days. Yesterday was a beautiful day, had bathing suit + shorts on. got burnt over my tan. The boys came down to see if there was any fish in the fyke net. There were some. Friday Bill Davis will be coming down and we'll be doing them alone. It usually takes at least 3 people to pull them. I bet we'll struggle but come through it alright. Heres a diagram of how it works. The fish follow the underwater nets and funnel into smaller + smaller compartments.

we pull this part up, untie first + take fish out. Its hard to pull up and then try to get the hoops up over the bow and stern enough to go in the net to net out the fish.

Now I'm using a gill net alone. Its not to difficult to use although I got the cord wrapped around the prop 3 or four times plus the netting! Its then fishing line

LETTER ILLUSTRATING FYKE NETS AND GILL NETS

12

Scotty

Quinton Scott

 SCOTTY (QUINTON SCOTT) WAS ONE OF my closest friends. Tall and lean, the 66-year-old resembled an old Scottish sea hand with snow-white hair complemented by a fisherman's beard trimmed neatly against his face. He visited twice while I was at Quabbin.

We met seven years earlier, as falconers who shared a common interest in birds of prey. We both flew seasoned red-tailed hawks. I often traveled to the Cape in the off-tourist season to hunt the sandy dunes of Chapin Beach with Scotty, his female hawk, Fred, and his loyal beagle, Annie. Both of our hawks were eight-year-old females but Fred was a giant at three pounds compared to my hawk, Habiba, who flew at two-and-a-quarter pounds.

I remember one time Scotty and I met on a winter weekend with our birds standing tall on our gloved hands while looking out over the wind-swept dunes. The elusive rabbits were just as experienced, for our birds chased them a lot but had difficulty coming "talon to tail." Annie snuck in and out of the tall grass and nonchalantly tunneled through the thick brush, sniffing the ground obsessively. Occasionally she let out a soft drawn-out "roowww" as her tail swayed back and forth. Scotty knew she had picked up a cold trail (bunny scent). Fred, who was Annie's hunting partner, rotated her head toward the sound with slight interest and then looked back over the dunes.

When the bunny trail was "hot" (fresh), Annie picked up the vocal pace and it held Fred's interest. Scotty stood there interpreting the barking language and taught me the relationship between his dog and bird. Habiba showed no interest because she normally did not hunt with a dog and quite frankly found the canine's barking extremely annoying.

Fred, on the other hand, was focused on Annie's every move, her furrowed avian eyebrows now prominent. Her head feathers stood on end when she turned and looked downwind. Her long wings and distinctive red tail were outstretched as she balanced in the salty breeze. Scotty let Fred fly freely to wait for Annie's next howl.

SCOTTY WITH FRED

With a high-pitched yowl, both rabbit and dog were running through the underbrush. Fred sailed through the air, allowing just enough wind to pass through her feathers to stay suspended over the action. Seconds later the bunny was in Fred's sights and she transformed her body into a high-speed missile, slicing through the air and crashing into the high bushes. Habiba was too distracted by the yelping dog to join in the chase and stayed put on my thick glove. Scotty moved in to assist Fred and stopped to listen if contact was made.

That day we heard the hasty retreat of one very fast bunny while Annie tattled of its escape. Fred walked out from under the bushes, flew up to Scotty's glove, and we called it quits for the day. Darkness was approaching and Louise, Scotty's wife, waited with supper.

"Another good day," Scotty said as he put Fred in the van with a generous morsel of food secure between her talons. "Doesn't matter if we get anything as long as Fred can soar over the dunes and we return home together."

Scotty loved life and taught me many of its secrets. If anyone brought him a sick hawk or owl, he had the bird standing on the glove and eating out of his hand within half an hour. He had a special gift. He felt that you always had to give back to nature in both word and deed.

When I started the eagle project Scotty came to visit. He showed me how to make the most of my day at Quabbin by knocking on my tent door at 5:00 in the morning! (He slept in his van at night.) He also taught me how to eat sensibly and his wife, Louise, sent granola cereal, fresh fruits, rice cakes, and the like for me to eat. I never ate better. Scotty also told me to take one hour each day for myself and relax or catch a nap. Getting up at 5:00 a.m. helped me remember why I needed it.

He instructed me on how to properly repair my nets. He had lots of experience since he was a fisherman who grew up on Cape Cod and also was a twenty-year Navy veteran. We enjoyed watching wild eagles sail by and loved hearing the haunting loon calls in the early morning hours.

Every day we made a game of pulling mystery fish out of the nets as they emerged from the clear waters. As we pulled, white shadows came out of the depths, becoming larger and easier to identify. Until that time we had caught large, small, and rock bass, landlocked salmon, lake and rainbow trout, white perch, blue gills, pumpkinseeds, bullheads, and white suckers.

Later Scotty and I sat under the eagle tower at midday to savor the solitude that the wilderness provided for us. We enjoyed listening to the baby eagles clumping around in their nest boxes above us. Occasionally a stream of "white wash" would shoot through the front of the bars and spray white rain noisily on the bushes below. I was delighted because it meant the bird ate heartily hours earlier. Scotty and I commented on how wonderful natural behavior was in these birds, to aim away from their nest and not soil it.

SCOTTY AND DIANNE WITH FRED AND HABIBA

The day Scotty left he was sad because he truly enjoyed the break from civilization and the hustle and bustle of cars and noisy traffic. On returning to the Cape he wrote me a long letter and commented on the silence he enjoyed while visiting. He had watched Cape Cod change over the last fifty years from vast areas of undisturbed scrub oaks and pitch pine to an area overrun with people, commercialism, and crime. (He was a retired police officer, having served the town of Yarmouth for twenty years.)

I remembered one day back in 1981, when we took an afternoon excursion during the summer months behind Chapin Beach in the tidal marsh. I was visiting my parents who also live on the Cape. The weather was beautiful, but extremely windy and I had trouble keeping up with Scotty as we paddled our kayaks in the estuary. At one point I had to hold onto some tall marsh reeds that were rooted along the side of the inlet. Every time we paddled forward I swear I was going backwards.

Scotty got way ahead of me and I had to shout for him to slow down. He turned his sleek kayak around and drifted down to me. He laughed and said the reason he retired from the police force was that he had suffered two heart attacks. I was shocked and began to worry about his health for the first time. I remembered being embarrassed because I was thirty years his junior and was out of breath and out of energy. We turned to head back and I paused from paddling. I said, "Scotty, how do you want to die?"

He smiled and pointed directly over the estuary to Chapin's Beach where he and I flew our red-tails on rabbits in late fall and winter. "I'd like to go while flying Fred over the dunes and have Annie hot on a bunny's trail at Chapin's Beach." He paddled a few strokes and added, "But before I die I would like to get a pole up so Fred can perch on its height and reign over the dunes in the winter. Ospreys could raise their young there in the summer months." Scotty always wanted to give back.

Scotty Gets His Wish

That was one of the last times I saw Scotty. Late one night, a few years later, I received a call from Scotty's wife, Louise. Scotty had died a few hours earlier and she had been trying to reach me to let me know. Through suppressed tears I asked if she was all right and how he died.

Scotty had gone hawking as usual with his bird, Fred and his beagle, Annie, at Chapin's Beach. When darkness approached and Scotty didn't come home for dinner, Louise said she felt that Scotty had died. She sent Kenny, one of their sons, to the familiar beach. Kenny found Scotty's van in the parking lot next to the dunes. He called for his father in the dark and eventually followed his tracks in the snow until he came across Scotty's body in the dunes. He must have had a massive heart attack because Kenny said he fell straight forward with his walking stick still in hand. Annie was curled up on his back and gave a soft growl as Kenny's darkened figure approached. Fred was nowhere in sight.

I raced down to the Cape the next day at first light to be with Louise and help other falconer friends find Fred. We needn't have worried. Kenny said Fred was next to the van the next morning, possibly waiting for that extra morsel of food and a trip home with Scotty.

Months later the small falconry community helped raise an osprey pole with Bill Davis in the Dennis estuary across from Chapin's Beach. Billy was the osprey coordinator for Fish and Wildlife and worked with many local towns around the state to bring back the ospreys as a nesting bird now that DDT was banned. It was yards away from the water where Scotty had confided in me about his final wishes.

A plaque under the cross arms of the osprey nest reads:
In Memory of Quinton Scott,
a Dedicated Falconer
and a Friend to All.
1919-1987

Within a year Scotty's second wish came true. Ospreys raised three young, and Billy banded the babies in the company of Scotty's two sons. Fred still hunted the dunes with another falconer who took over guardianship for a while. Eventually Fred retired from hunting and was given to a friend of mine who gave programs on birds of prey.

I miss Scotty dearly and feel fortunate to have known an "elder" who was willing to share the knowledge and wisdom that comes from many years of life, rich with experiences.

IN MEMORY OF
QUINTON SCOTT
A DEDICATED FALCONER
AND A FRIEND TO ALL
1919-1987
MASS FALCONRY HAWK TRUST

13

All Grown Up

 THE BABIES SEEM TO BE IN A NEW PHASE of their young lives. Their undeveloped bodies no longer restrict them. They used to clump around on their ankles and hold their board-like wings folded up against their bodies. To get in the nest they had to struggle with their wings and try to brace themselves up into the nest box.

All that was changing as most of them entered their eighth week of life. They were making progress in their ability to stand on their sturdy yellow feet, hop, and even jump around. Attila and Marjorie were flying into the nest on increasingly powerful wings. They exercised when the strong wind came up and showed great interest in nest sticks as play toys.

Day 21

Thursday, July 11, 1985 - 3:04 p.m.

Dear Mom, Dad, Scotty, and Louise,

What a day! The supplemental deer meat is not quite thawed so I'll feed around 6:00 this evening. I took a very rare, quick dip up to the north, beyond the eagle tower point, to wash off the fish scales that were accumulating on my

arms and legs. I usually take showers at the
astronomy site after the babies are tucked in
for the night. Today however, I have almost as
many scales on me as a large fish does. The cold
water was quite refreshing. I'm now in a loaned
canoe and the warm breeze is drying my hair. I
hid my wet towel up in the woods past the tower
so no one would know I took an invigorating but
illegal dip.

Jack had come with three other men to discuss
a new system for the eagle perch scales. I had
been using D cell batteries for the four
disguised scales but they had run out of juice
too frequently. One man was an expert with
radios and tried to upgrade my CB. It didn't
work though. I gave them all peanut butter and
jelly sandwiches and soda and then went fishing
while they worked into the afternoon. I didn't
even get a nibble. They left around 2:30 p.m.

I'm finally getting this job down to a science
and have more time to myself, both physically
and mentally. I'm alone with no thoughts at all
this afternoon because the scenery is pleasingly
distracting. It's hard to even concentrate on
this letter. Every time I write a sentence or
two and then look up, I am in a lazy dream
world. (I need a nap!) I look at the passing
clouds or a painted turtle sunning itself on a
beaver cutting. A fin breaks the surface of the
water; probably a pumpkinseed sunfish. When the
sun goes behind the billowing clouds the water
turns from olive to black. Now with the wind
from the west and the sun gone, the water
ripples like black oil. It's so serene and
peaceful here.

Dr. Sedgwick is coming tomorrow from Tufts
Veterinary School. He hasn't seen this year's
birds yet. I hope I've done all right with the
babies. I'm relatively confident things are
going well.

I lay down in the canoe for an hour and fell fast asleep in my little cove; I slept so soundly. I finally figured I'd better get up to eat and then fix the babies' supper. I'm having ravioli and they are having fish and some deer meat that finally thawed.

Scotty, I'm so glad you got to spend some time out here. I appreciated your help with the daily chores and thanks for teaching me how to repair my torn nets more efficiently. I also enjoyed your wonderful company and talks about the wild ocean locations you experienced by submarine during World War II. Knowing your special appreciation for nature, hearing whales serenade while you were on night shifts must have touched your soul deeply. It doesn't surprise me at all that you took the time to listen to the whale's song in the middle of wartime.

This project is so great because it doesn't end after my three months or even after the next three years. It is, I hope, forever. Five years from now maybe one of my babies will come back as a mature adult to set up a nesting territory and raise young. Boy, that sounds like a long way away. Then their offspring will grow up and repeat the cycle and so on. I hope my grandparents are happy "upstairs" knowing one of their own offspring is helping a species that almost died out in their lifetimes.

Love, Dianne

Day 28

Friday, July 18, 1985 - 9:10 p.m.

Dear Paul and Becky,

While I am writing this letter to you, I heard something outside. I went out and sat in

my chair and heard a bang far off, then another
bang that echoed across the calm water. I
decided to radio the MDC police and boy did that
open a can of worms. The dispatcher radioed all
units separately and asked them if they heard a
shot. No one did. They asked me if I saw a
plane. I said they fly over all the time and
just as I said that, the loon began hollering
and a plane flew right over the tower. They
wanted to know if it was heading north or south.
They then had their units try to get numbers on
the plane. It's never a dull moment here.

Brad Blodget came today. He helped me take
in my second gill net and saw how I was doing.
He's a pistol! He stayed for lunch and into
the afternoon.

I went fishing for a few hours in the canoe
after he left. The air was so still and the
reservoir was like glass. I looked down through
the sunny water at the rocks and then gazed all
around at the peaceful landscape. I saw a
cormorant snaking his way along in the water.
Cormorants hold their black bodies low and slink
along with their long "S" shaped necks. Their
heads and sharp beaks are turned up in a
snobbish position. They are voracious fish
eaters and quite good at catching their meals.
The loons made it clear that they were not happy
with his presence. He moved on through.

My mother and father arrived safely this
morning to be with me for a few days and met
Jack. My father and I set the gill nets as a
thunderstorm was fast approaching; we didn't
make it back to shore in time. We put empty
buckets over our heads and it took forever to
get back to shore because of the heavy downpour
and an underpowered motorboat. We were soaked
to the bone. It rained all afternoon, which made
the tent steamy and cozy because we had to keep
the plastic windows zipped up. We all slept
soundly that night.

Our clothes were laid out all over the warm
rocks the next morning, drying in the sun, when
the loon biologist and her friend arrived
unannounced by boat. I asked Mom to quickly hide
the underwear and bathing suit at least. Thank
goodness for the early warning by the loons.

After greetings and introductions, I started
to go over my loon notes with Jennifer Weaver,
the loon warden. My father, who was sitting on
the point watching the loons through the scope,
mentioned that one of the loons was halfway down
the well-worn nest ramp. It was dipping its beak
from the dirt to the water. It repeated the
delicate action over and over. I peered through
the scope and still could not figure out this
new behavior. Whatever the loon was placing in
the water was shiny and the dirt seemed to
glisten in the sun. I did notice that one egg
was missing. I had seen it that morning during
the loons' changing of the guard at the nest.

As I watched, the busy loon slid into the
water and joined its mate, who was mingling with
two other loons offshore. Where had they come
from all of a sudden? There were no
altercations, vocalizations and no hysteria.
They all were circling each other and taking
turns putting their heads underwater in a
seemingly social greeting. I was baffled. I had
no explanation to give my guests who were here
to observe this pair of loons.

We began asking questions, seeking logical
answers to these unacceptable interactions
during the loons' egg incubation. Just then
black objects moving toward Gibbs Cove caught my
peripheral vision. It was the crow family, about
to make their daily reconnaissance flight to the
island. I watched in horror as the first crow
made the short trip and found the nest
unattended. "Oh noooo!" We ran down to the dock
and jumped in the boat. We yelled and screamed

to scare the crow away. I wanted to save the
egg but my boat was too slow and the scavenging
crow was too quick. It took advantage of the
inattentive loons. He continued to peck at the
remaining egg until it broke.

As we approached the island the crows finally
flew and we solved the mystery of the other egg.
We found a blob of gel on the sloping nest ramp
with little egg fragments scattered along the
edge and in the water. That's what the
meticulous loon had been depositing in the water
when my father was watching through the powerful
scope. The inside of the egg that the crow tried
to have for breakfast, looked like nothing more
than yellow yogurt. I didn't get it. Where were
the developing chicks? This was day twenty-two
of incubation. They should have been almost
ready to hatch. Instead, one looked like a clear
jellyfish with a hint of red bloodstains and the
other was just smelly mush. Both eggs had been
infertile all the time.

While all this was happening the negligent
loons were still socializing offshore with the
two intruders. I went back to the mainland to
tell my parents of the tragedy and grabbed my
camera to get photos of the crime scene. I took
pictures of the carnage, the nest area and what
remained of both eggs. I was relieved that it
was all witnessed by the loon biologist because
it was all too hard to believe.

It appeared to me that it wasn't human
disturbance, enemy eagles, or low-flying planes
that caused the careless loons to ultimately
fail at their nesting attempt. It seemed the
interaction with other loons in their territory
would have been the cause of failed parenthood
for this pair. I'm sure the nightly absence from
egg-sitting duties didn't help the development
of any embryos if there had been any.

Yesterday, after my parents left, Herm Covey
from Fish and Wildlife and his friend, Hank,
came by to bring my radio. It works great. The
police come in loud and clear. Herm has been
with Fish and Wildlife for thirty years and has
been pulling fyke nets for almost all that time.
What a pro. We pulled a six-pound largemouth
bass out of it. I thought it was a porpoise when
we were netting it because its head was so
massive. Herm took many pictures of me with it.
No way could I feed this magnificent fish to the
hungry eagles.

Hank, the radioman, had been out fishing in
the little cove while we were working on the
fyke net so we put the fish in the holding pen.
Hank had caught a couple of two- and three-pound
smallmouth bass and let them all go. When he
came in we all let the biggest bass go together.
Hank, who is in his seventies, held the fish by
its lower lip and worked it back and forth to
oxygenate the gills until the fish kicked freely
from his fingers. For a minute there I thought

it wasn't going to make it, but it swiftly swam
back out the channel. What a sight.

Hank gave me some rubber worms and then some
quick fishing lessons. Up to that point I had
been a lousy fisherman. I couldn't wait to apply
my new knowledge. As Herm and Hank made their
way up the road I was off in the boat, back to
Gibbs Cove. I caught a three-pound bass right
off the bat, but as I reeled it to the boat, he
saw me and snapped the line. I looked over the
side and there he was near the bottom, shadowing
a gigantic boulder. I caught a two-pound bass
after that, and he gave me one heck of a fight.
I let him go too. I don't go fishing that much.
Jack is going to relieve me tomorrow. He said he
won't be here until 4:00 p.m. though.

I've been getting behind on my paperwork. I
just don't feel like doing it and it is piling
up. I'll try to get my weights, food intake,
daily log and weather report done tonight. I'll
make myself some tea. See you soon!

                                    Love, Dianne

An Unexpected Visitor

One day I was going to take a quick trip up the road to meet
my twin sister, Linda, at Gate 17. She lives in Arizona and was
going to stay with me for a few days. I pulled back the ladder to
safeguard the eagles while I was gone, walked back past my tent
then headed down the crooked path toward my car. I was watching
my step when all of a sudden I looked up and saw a man on the
path, coming my way. I had never seen him before. I wondered
how he got through two locked gates and as I looked closer, I
noticed he had a large gun holstered to his right side. He was in a
short-sleeved shirt and worn dungarees. I started a quick mental
checklist of who this man could possibly be. I also could feel my
brain working out an escape route, bolting up a deer trail to my
right. I would run until I couldn't run anymore.

As he approached I thought of the self-defense class I had taken that spring in anticipation of just this occasion. The instructor had said, "Show the attacker you're not intimidated and stare him right down." I decided to try that tactic first instead of bee-lining it up in the woods like a scared madwoman. He might just be an environmental police officer in plain clothes. The MDC police always came in uniform and by boat, so he couldn't be one of them. I looked at him with a long serious stare, glanced down at his gun and then back up to his eyes to let him know I was aware of the weapon. I said, "Can I help you?" with a voice of steel and legs of trembling rubber. He said, "Hi, I'm Kenny Stolgitis." All the adrenaline drained right out of me and I approached him with a big smile and an outstretched handshake. He was indeed a MDC police officer in plain clothes who came out to view the eagles. Jack had mentioned Kenny's name in the past as one of the officers at Quabbin.

Kenny said he liked to look in on the eagles and look for arrowheads along the shore since the water level was way down. I had a few minutes to spare before meeting Linda so asked him if he could show me some arrowheads. I looked all the time and couldn't find any. Within two minutes he surprised me with many "chips." They were the discarded chips from an arrow or a tool that was made eons ago. I left to meet my sister; I never found a chipped stone on my own, but I found a new friend.

Linda wrote a letter to our brother, Ronnie, about her adventure at Quabbin. Ronnie later sent this copy back to me to keep with my journal.

Dear Ronnie,

    I got here on a Friday afternoon for what I thought was going to be a lazy, fun, easygoing weekend in the woods. Get some sun, eat, drink, and be merry. Well, we got settled in Dianne's popup tent. Not bad, I thought, and she said we needed to go in the boat and catch fish for the

eagles. Cool, I said to myself. It was a neat
little boat and we jetted out to an area where
we gathered the net to get the fish. What an
eye-opening experience. It was pretty neat.
There were fish of all kinds and she was
gathering them out of the net like she'd done
it a million times before. The first one I
touched jabbed me with its fin. Ouch!!! Dianne
realized that there were many holes in the net
to repair and was going to take it in this
weekend to fix them.

That night we had some fish for dinner,
fresh from our afternoon catch. Most of it was
for the eagles, but she took some prime perch,
I think it was, and cooked it for us. It was
so much fun watching her feed the eagles and
take on what was such a huge responsibility
with this eagle project.

I was in awe of the pride she took in her
job. She made sure I knew it had to be quiet
and they couldn't see you. It was important that
we not be in a shadow so that they wouldn't see
our image in the one-way glass. They needed to
imprint on the land, not Dianne or me. She sat
forever it seemed, waiting for eagle #4 for
instance, to get on the perch and get weighed.
Her book with the entrants was pages long. It
was a daily task. She made observations and
wrote them down diligently and I was so taken
by the things she wrote. That stuff is that
important for this project? Wow!

Now I am really a city girl but I can
definitely handle a popup trailer. No big deal.
What really spooked me was that we were about
eight miles from anyone. At 9:00 p.m. the call
came in from the police, checking on her as they
did every morning and night. Darkness was
quickly coming upon us and when we got home from
a walk in the woods, we turned on the lights to
get ready for bed. I was tired and ready for

lights out. Within minutes Dianne was sound
asleep and I lay there on my back, listening
intently for the mass murderer to come into our
tent and kill us. I would hear little noises
outside, twigs cracking, leaves moving and it
was all I could do to remain sane. There was no
car to go to and definitely no home within
miles. It was rather unnerving.

All of a sudden there was a noise in the tent;
a pop and some flopping around for about five
seconds. I yelled to Dianne to wake up. She did,
suddenly, and then I said, "What is that?" She
jumped out of bed, grabbed the mousetrap with
the dead mouse in it, took it out of the trap I
think, and tossed the now dead animal up on the
roof of the tent trailer. She made some comment
about it being a great treat for an eagle
tomorrow. Then she got back into bed and fell
asleep without missing a beat. My heart was
about out of my chest! I don't remember ever
sleeping that night, and when the sun came up
early the next morning and the loons started
singing, I finally managed a catnap.

This was not the life for me, but I was so
impressed at being able to witness what she did
for a living. First thing to do in the morning
was to go fishing and get breakfast for the
eagles. They watched us in the boat as we rode
past the huge house built for the eight birds.
They were beautiful and watching us intently.
The days were spent entirely of taking care of
chores, documenting eagle movements and weights
and fishing.

This was no vacation: it was work. Her cut-up
hands were evidence of a job that took a lot of
strength and dedication to those eagle babies.

I remember watching Dianne wave goodbye and
then go right to the boat, as there were fish to
catch and cut up for dinner for the eagles, her
children for the summer, and it was a weekend I

will remember for the rest of my life. It was so
much fun watching her in action and I was so
proud of her and knew that what she was doing
was a great thing for the state of Massachusetts
and the eagle project. I wish you could have
come here, Ronnie. You would love it here.

Love, Linda

Day 29

Friday, July 9, 1985 - 1:00 p.m.

Dear Mom, Dad, Scotty and Louise,

I'm sitting out on the point and waiting for
the water to boil for my hot dogs. I'm out of
fresh drinking water from my jug so I'm
borrowing Boston's drinking water. Linda had a
fun time out here and was great company.

I'm watching a family of four turkey vultures
on Fish Head Point having a field day on the
abundant fish remains I put there earlier today.
One wants the other's fish so he sneaks in and
takes it. The one that had his fish stolen
scurried over to the third bird and took his
fish. It sure makes life easier with a pecking
order. No fights, no altercations, just an empty
belly for the "peck-ee." It's interesting how
everything fits in until the "kids" get into the
act. They were easy to pick out with their gray
heads, not red like the adults. Their baby
squeals commanded immediate attention. With all
the scrambling going on, the adults still stop
to feed the young. I noticed it was the same
with the crow family.

I pulled my two gill nets yesterday and caught
fifty fish. They were mostly white perch, the
finger-slicing kind. My fingers are all cut up
again, but fortunately I'm getting tougher

hands. They don't hurt. I needed fifty more fish
today. Two men from the Fish and Wildlife Valley
District came today to check the fyke nets. I
asked them if they would put today's catch in
the astronomy site's freezer when they left in
case I should need them in the future.

The birds are not eating as much these days.
Their feather growth is complete and they are
full-sized so their food requirements have
slowed down.

I missed monitoring the crazy loons for about
an hour and that was it. I now enjoy my extra
free mental time to myself without looking at
Loon Island every waking minute, especially
since the eggs were infertile anyway. Life is
not easy, even if you're the "Voice of the
Wilderness," as the loons are. Now I can just
watch the handsome loons for pleasure without
keeping a scientific eye on them. I do treasure
their company and early-warning calls though.

I celebrated my new-found freedom. I can now
travel where I want, instead of always hugging
the shore when I motor in and out of the cove. I
decided to make a canoe trip straight across the
little bay since the water was calm. As I
approached the island a huge loon popped up
right at the side of my canoe and both of us
almost had a coronary. I just about leaped out
of my skin and tipped the canoe. The loon was
much larger than I imagined, having only seen
them through my binoculars and scope. The
surprised loon noisily dove underwater, like a
beaver would slap his tail when in danger. He
scared the daylights out of me but I suppose I
did the same to him. He slapped the surface of
the water with his wings and uttered a guttural
yodel. He then "motor boated" around like a
maniac. I stayed motionless for a second so the
loon could make its retreat and then I quickly
paddled in the opposite direction. I hadn't seen

the pair all day and thought they had left the
area for good after having failed with their
eggs. It was getting too late for them to start
over with more eggs. Well, at least I briefly
saw the island up close.

                    Love, Dianne

14

That's What It's All About!

Day 41

Wednesday, July 31, 1985 - 10:30 a.m.

Dear Mom, Dad, Scotty, and Louise,

   How is everyone doing? I'm fine. I'm listening to the radio and eating my lunch at 10:30 a.m. I want to get it out of the way I guess. I'm eating green beans, white perch, milk and orange juice. I use Ritz crackers and melted butter now for the fish and it is mouth watering.

   I pulled a net at 5:30 a.m. to get some fish for the baby eagles' breakfast. I didn't have any leftovers from yesterday. At 8:00 a.m. I went to pull the other two nets that I'm using. I was far to the north of the eagle tower, sitting on my overturned bucket and carefully pulling the fish out of the net when I heard a "kerplunk" beside my net. I couldn't imagine what kind of fish or sea monster could make that hard a splash on the surface. I checked the net and around the boat and then checked the shore. There was Bill Davis. He works for Fish and Wildlife. He said he didn't want to scare me by shouting because I looked deep in

thought, so he tossed a rock. I told him he
just terrified me instead.

   After I pulled the first gill net I picked
him up and he helped me with the other. He
pulled his side of the net up and a six-pound
lake trout came up over the side of the boat.
I was so excited because it was the first lake
trout I had seen in the net. The fish was
caught by his lower jaw and still alive so we
let him go.

   I fed the eagles at 9:00 a.m. today after
pulling in the gill nets. I set the nets out
again at 10:00 a.m. I need fish for tonight
and don't like using my live supply until I'm
desperate. I have twenty-four hours of rain
showers coming around noon so I hope I can get
back out on the water and have some fish in the
nets before then.

   I saw a mature bald eagle on Monday, flying
straight downwind. Was he ever moving with the
wind behind him. Later Billy and I went fishing
and a wandering adult eagle was on Loon Island
getting a drink at the water's edge. We were
about a hundred yards offshore. He just watched
us, aware but unconcerned. "How exciting to be
that close to a wild eagle," I said. Billy
added, "That's what it's all about!" I smiled.

   I traveled back to Quabbin on Sunday with Paul
and Becky. Our neighbors from Methuen followed
us in their car. They wanted to peek in on the
eagles and see where I was spending my summer.
The enthusiastic kids and I fed the birds. I
told them I had to keep accurate records on how
much food the individual birds were eating to
make sure they were all getting their fair share
of the fish. I mentioned that it was sometimes
frustrating because on certain birds I had to
read the blue tag number on their leg bands to
identify them. They were too similar in
appearance and size.

One of my guests, little eight-year-old Stacy, figured out a way to tell the top right and bottom left birds apart from each other. It was so simple but I had never figured it out. One had the blue numbered tag attached to the band on the left leg and the other bird had the blue tag on the right leg. Nothing like "out of the mouths of babes!"

Now I don't have to wait for the birds to move around to read their numbers. I just have to see what leg the silver band is on. Attila and Marjorie, who are paired together, are both around eleven pounds now and look too similar, so it was hard to tell them by size alone. However, I could tell them apart by their behaviors. Attila is still top dog. In the bottom cage, eaglet Woodstock is a big female now compared to eaglet Snoopy, who is quite small.

Do you realize that next Friday we're letting the growing babies go? It doesn't seem possible.

Jack Swedberg came yesterday with the telemetry. It consists of a small transmitter that the birds will wear on a central tail feather and includes a tiny battery and a trailing antenna that runs along the feather shaft. It will be attached using an electrical tie and surgical thread. We will put them on the babies when they get their final physical from the Tufts veterinarians a couple of days before the release. Jack said the birds hardly notice the transmitters and they tend to preen right over the colored antennae.

Jack also brought the receiver, which is the size of a lunch box and picks up the signal from the transmitter. Each bird has a different frequency corresponding to a numbered channel and the blue numbered tag on their legs. I will be able to switch to a different frequency by turning a black knob and be able to receive that bird's signal. When I want to find Attila I will switch to channel one on the receiver. Bert is channel two and so on. Simple! I could handle that. I will have the receiver box in my right hand and have a hand-held pole with a directional antenna in my left.

Jack pointed out the yellow knob at the top of the antennae and said I will point that forward and the signal will be received there. It will then travel down a cord along the pole, which is hooked to my receiver. I will pick up a beeping sound by headphones. A meter also registers the strength of the signal. Supposedly I will be able to pick up the eaglets' signals over two miles by land or boat and sixty miles air-to-air or eagle-to-plane.

I was told that in 1982, the year Massachusetts started releasing young eagles, "Ross" the male eagle hung around but "Betsy" flew all the way to Ottawa, Canada, within three days. Her signal was tracked using a plane. The next day her signal was gone and she was never seen or heard from again.

Jack said they'll bring gas to use for my car when I drive around to find the babies once they're on their own. That will help, because my funds have run out.

Jack watched the birds Friday after I left and on Saturday, Ernie was lying down sleeping when he checked him in the morning. Jack went out, pulled the gill nets and came back and Ernie was still down with eyes glazed over. He even stuck his head down the top where we put the fish in and there still was no reaction. Bert, his nest mate, went nuts, grunting and flaring his head feathers.

Jack radioed MDC police and had them call Bill Byrne to get Tufts to stand by in case they brought the bird in. Billy B. arrived that noon. By then Ernie was on a perch. Jack was relieved. Billy B. drove back out to the restaurant phone

to cancel Tufts. The bird is fine now. I guess
Ernie was just very tired. Last year Jack was
the one who found one of the babies dead in the
cage, so I could see why he would be overly
worried.

Take care. I love you,

Dianne

Day 42

Thursday, August 1, 1985 - 9:07 p.m.

Dear Mom, Dad, Scotty, and Louise,

Well, I'm writing to you outside in the
darkness with the aid of a flashlight. A while
ago I could only see the planet Venus because
it was so bright. Every time I look up from
writing, the sky gets darker and darker.

Rippling waves from the north all morning
built to rolling seas with whitecaps by
afternoon. I pulled my nets in the high winds
and waves. I was getting thrown around in my
small boat while sitting on the overturned
bucket and trying to hold onto the lead line.
It felt like I was riding a bucking horse. It
was fun. I tried to guess what fish was coming
up from deep below the surface. Sometimes it was
a perch, a sucker, or a rock bass. I got a huge
lake trout that was around twenty-eight inches
long and weighed about sixteen pounds. I let him
go. The waves were making a lot of noise.

Tonight it finally calmed down and it sounds
like low tide at Cape Cod. The small waves are
just breaking repeatedly on the pebbly shore.
Every now and then I see a red or white blinking
light in the sky and know that it is a low-
flying plane. I just looked up a while ago and

saw a dim red light moving east across the sky.
There were three white lights following in
perfect formation behind it. I'm glad I'm
near an air force base because I hope those
are planes on maneuvers and not UFOs! It would
not take much for me to get up and walk back in
the tent trailer, never to wander outside at
night again.

There's not a cloud in sight and although the
crickets aren't loud, they are constant. They're
great background music. I can see how animals
must depend on the consistency of cricket
chirping to know everything is copacetic. I just
heard a flying squirrel squeak. I saw some of
them the other night playing in the trees;
they're very cute. Their fur is rippled when not
used for gliding from tree to tree. Their deep
brown eyes are huge for nighttime vision.

I have a young owl friend who is calling. He
sounds like a baby barred owl and makes a sound
like "Eeeee." He starts every night at the same
time. I call back to him but can't get him to
respond or come across the brook. I'm sitting on
the point and he's across from me. I just heard
a kerplunk in the water to my right. The beaver
must be coming out.

At dusk I ran up the road to the second bridge
where there is another beaver lodge. It is my
escape exercise. It doesn't seem far until I run
it. I just want to be prepared to sprint through
the forest if I am confronted with danger,
whether animal or human. It's dark in the woods,
even if it is light out. I'm still not afraid of
living alone out here.

I can hear a loon calling far to the north of
my campsite. The lonely sound is traveling
slowly over the reservoir and the loon repeats
itself many times. I can barely make out the
long drawn-out wail. The water is finally calm
and looks like silk in the approaching darkness.

Looking up as I write, I wonder where the moon is. Two days ago it was full as I looked out my tent window from the comfort of my warm bed. I can see a yellowish slit rising above the dark silhouette of the far shore beyond Loon Island. There are low clouds hovering over the distant horizon now. Venus is more visible in the darkening sky. I notice a change in its position when I glance up after writing a sentence or two of this letter by flashlight.

It's quite cool tonight. I have on warm sweatpants and a sweatshirt plus bug spray because the wind has died down. The clouds are building. The moon is now behind low wispy clouds that are slowly moving in.

I hear the barred owls calling, "Who cooks for youuuuu?" I've always loved that call; it's nicer than the great horned owl's call. It's more civilized. My other little talkative owl hasn't made another call since I called back to it earlier.

Jack Swedberg came down with his wife and two friends today. They said they saw a coyote in the road on the way in. We had a nice chat and they enjoyed seeing the babies. After they left I repaired one of my gill nets. The holes in those nets will be the death of me.

I finally hear my secretive owl buddy far away. The moon is glowing behind the clouds so I think I'll stop writing and watch. It's coming up so nonchalantly. The beauty in life seems to happen whether you're there to watch it or not. It doesn't care. As I write this, some clouds cover up the moon. Here it comes again... second chance. I'm so interested in this simple pleasure because I've spent all my past nights safe and secure in my cozy tent.

I'm going to check my mousetrap because I heard a snap. The eagles might get an appetizer for breakfast tomorrow morning.

I'm back, complete with long johns and a down vest. The moon is almost full and glowing with a beautiful shimmer across the still water. By the way, I got another mouse. That makes nine! I would get a lot more but my mousetrap is as old as the hills. It doesn't work most of the time and I find the peanut butter licked clean most mornings. It's 10:00 p.m. so they're starting early. Usually it's 2:00 or 3:00 a.m. when they try to invade my limited food supply.

The cool reservoir is lightly rippled now. I can hear Prescott Brook because it is flowing fast after all the torrential rain last night. It's a good thing I took a four-hour nap yesterday when the heavy downpour began at noon. I was able to stay up through most of the persistent rainstorm at night, catching up on my paperwork. I finished my notes, graphs, and charts at 1:30 in the morning. I had the radio blasting because the rain was coming down so hard and it was scary to hear it on my canvas walls and aluminum roof. I don't like the sound. I finally read a magazine until I was tired enough to fall asleep.

I have only a short week before the birds are released so I'm getting photos of feeding, preening, and playing with sticks and close-up shots. I can't believe they'll all be gone next Friday. I'm going to miss them terribly.

If all goes according to plan, we will be moving my tent trailer out of sight of the tower so that the eaglets will be able to come back to feed. Then I will be getting ready for the telemetry work, so I'll be working right until dark. I hope to get a good night's sleep Thursday night. I can't wait to get next week over with and I'm glad Paul is going to stay with me for a few days. When we received the birds back in June it was hard to turn around and be alone after everyone took off. I was left

with a flood of emotion inside with no one to
talk to. It was traumatic.

Well, it's 10:39 p.m. and I'm doing fine out
here under the stars beyond the confines of my
tent. Every so often I see a shooting star
streak brilliantly across the sky. This
wilderness is quite dark and there is no
civilization close by although I can see a
distant glow in the southern skies to remind me
that it does exist.

This act of bravery to finally venture outside
after dark began when I was walking down the
path to the eagle tower this afternoon. I had
pulled my nets an hour ago. I looked out over
the reservoir, amazed at how the water had
taken on the appearance of the ocean. The
rolling waves were heading due south,
perpendicular to the shore instead of crashing
up against it. The winds were really driving to
build large whitecaps with wisps of water
spraying out in front of them. I stopped on the
now-worn path. Way off in the distance I could
see something big heading south, riding the
waves. I ran back to the tent and grabbed my
binoculars. I couldn't for the life of me think
of what it might be.

The object turned out to be a big yellow
barrel. It is one of a handful that marks the
watery boundary beyond which fishermen are not
permitted to go with their boats. South of the
barrels is the "no fishing" area where I am. The
runaway barrel was a mile east of Loon Island
nearer the far shore than my side of the
reservoir. It was drifting near Shaft 12, the
outlet where the water from Quabbin starts its
journey underground toward Wachusett Reservoir
and then on to Boston.

I figured the barrel broke loose in the heavy
waves. The barrel and line were probably
anchored in eighty feet of the water over what

was once the valley town of Greenwich. It
seemed perfectly logical at the time to run
down to the dock, hop in my small Whaler and
putt out to retrieve the barrel for the MDC.
I put on my life jacket and headed out. Before
this interruption I was just going to check on
the birds while my hot dogs cooled a bit before
I had a late lunch. Now my hot dogs would have
to wait.

It didn't dawn on me until I got out of my
protected cove and motored into the breaking
waves that maybe this wasn't such a good idea.
With each slam of the boat I felt more uneasy,
but by then I was on a mission! The waves were
hitting me head-on and I was getting soaked by
the spray. The whole bow shot up and came
crashing down until the next wave. It was like
the surf at Nauset Beach on Cape Cod. I first
shot north into the wind. I realized at some
point that I had to swing east toward the barrel
and parallel to the mountainous walls of
turbulent water. It seemed that about every
third wave was a giant swell. I had to steer the
cowering boat back into it so that the water
wouldn't fill my small craft and flip me over.

The barrel was still far away and drifting
fast to the south. I started to feel very
insignificant out there on the churning
reservoir and I was moving farther and farther
away from the safety of my protected cove and
tent. It seemed to take forever to cover the
distance that on a calm day would have taken
about fifteen minutes. The waves were pushing
south as fast as I was traveling east with the
help of my ancient motor. As I finally
approached the barrel I started wondering how
the heck I was going to get this fifty-five-
gallon steel drum in my Whaler. The combination
of waves and the unsteadiness of the small boat
were frightening. When I looked closer at the
barrel I noticed a long cable that trailed deep

into the water's depth. My first attempt at getting the barrel into the boat on the north side was out of the question because it just kept slamming into the boat and spraying water all over me. I valued my healed hands and was not about to have them crushed between the barrel and the fiberglass boat. I worked it around the boat while kneeling because the seas were too rough to stand.

It suddenly occurred to me that once I figured out how to haul this barrel in, how was I going to make it back? I turned and looked to the west, only to see the hack site was over a mile away. I still hadn't gotten the barrel in but held onto it for dear life. I must be crazy! I finally heaved the heavy drum in and began to haul the steel cable and endless length of heavy rope that followed as I drifted south with the rolling waves.

While idling, my motor conked out and I rode the waves up and down, totally at their mercy. I held onto the sides of the rocking boat and tried to plot my next move. All I kept visualizing was being thrown overboard and bobbing up and down in my life jacket, trying to keep my head above water. I would drift and eventually get stranded somewhere along a distant shore or island, miles of water separating me from my campsite and the eagles. There would be no boat, no one around to even know I was missing. If anyone came tomorrow they would find my hot dogs sitting in the pan, untouched from the night before. Even worse, no one would show up for a day and I hadn't fed the babies their dinner. How would I ever swim back across the reservoir? Just maybe the MDC would realize that I hadn't called in for my 9:00 p.m. nighttime check.

I pulled on that darn engine cord one more time and it finally started. Now I had to figure a way back across the waves that were still enormous. I turned the boat around and headed back, watching every threatening wave coming from the north. My strategy was to motor two waves westward and then turn north to meet the next big wave. After the bigger one that followed, I would then head west again for two more waves. It seemed to take forever to get back and I couldn't wait to head due south and have the waves at my back for the last leg of the trip. I looked ahead at the hack tower on its gigantic stilts and eventually could see the babies on their perches. I realized I was almost home.

When I turned the boat southward I discovered a new problem. The boat was being lifted up like a surfboard by the following seas. As the third and fourth big wave expectedly came, my overworked engine came out of the water while the mid-section of the hull straddled the crest. The roar of the motor behind me almost scared me out of the boat but as I got used to it, the high-rise roller coaster ride became rather exciting. I watched behind me for the ultimate wave and found one that lifted me up like a big hand. I rode the crest of the wave back for quite a distance, surfing at an incredible speed. I rounded the corner to my cove just as another large wave was coming for me. I couldn't wait to get off the spirited water. As I entered my protected cove I breathed a sigh of relief.

Once on solid ground I turned to look beyond my quiet inlet to the fury of the angry water and I felt like a friend had betrayed me. The reservoir had been a part of me, giving me pleasure, serenity, and food to feed the baby eagles and me. To have it turn on me was a shocking experience. I wondered what I did to incur its wrath. How could I make peace with the reservoir? Now I could understand how Thoreau gave life to Walden Pond. Quabbin showed me its dark side today.

I had to set my gill nets at dusk and thank goodness the seas had died down some, but they were still rolling. I felt so different out there. It was like thinking you know someone until you see them upset and then you see them a little differently. After that you're more cautious of the relationship.

I feel a little hardened after coming back from that boat ride today. I guess that's why I can sit out here under the brilliant stars for the first time after forty days of camping out here alone. I figured that if I could survive that frightening boat ride, I could survive anything, I hope.

The loon is calling from the far north again and my owl friend is back calling, "Eeeee!" I just heard a big crack behind me in the woods. I think a deer might be coming down to feed by the water's edge but it is too dark to see. The loons sounded again and my owl friend is getting closer. There are two barred owls that just called from the direction of the beaver lodge in the cove. What a racket. It sounded like a lady screaming, then a couple of cackles and then the familiar, "Who cooks for you?" Within seconds I could hear my young owl friend calling way behind me in the woods. I've never heard him on my side of the brook before.

Well, it's 11:15 p.m. I still have to do my daily paperwork to stay ahead.

I hope that I won't hear any "snaps" in the middle of the night. I have to get up, take the mouse out of the trap, bait it again and reset it. Lately I'm wide awake and don't get back to sleep. It's still better than hearing the mice gnawing on my food packages.

Good night. I love you.

                 Eagle One

15

Super Babies

 IT HAS BEEN EXCITING WATCHING THE babies grow over the last two weeks. They are no longer helpless little chicks. They ran, jumped, flew against the bars and played, played, played. Sticks were either delicately rearranged in the unkempt nest or attacked in mock battle. The nest mates could be "beaking" with tender nibbles one minute and then ferociously assaulting one another the next.

Some days they skipped meals and it took me a few panicked minutes of thought and observation to figure out why. They started off eating about two pounds of food each day while their bodies and feathers were growing. When the babies were full-sized, their feathers were all grown in and they no longer required as much food to sustain themselves. Subsequently, they started to move around the cages with their newly feathered "super" bodies. They also increased their wing exercises and scaled the bars trying to get out. This last behavior occurs within days of their release so I knew they were ready.

Woodstock And Snoopy

Let's start with Woodstock and Snoopy during their last two weeks of captivity and free food. When they both lie down in their nest, which they occasionally still did, they filled up the nest. Snoopy liked to play with sticks. He would flip them in the air and then be done with them. He often followed this play with vigorous wing flapping and grunting. He still worried me more than the others because he continued to sound like a child's birthday horn when he breathed. Sometimes this occurred while he sat staring out at the reservoir or even while sound asleep on the perch scale.

Woodstock became much larger than her nest mate and didn't mind demonstrating that fact, although it didn't get her anywhere. She sometimes tried to push Snoopy off the long perch but usually ended up walking him down the branch and then nibbling on his toes.

Snoopy, on the other hand, could easily get his point across. Toward the end of their stay Snoopy was obviously getting quite "antsy." Once, Woodstock was minding her own business, had just pulled straw up around her body and lay down in the nest. Little Snoopy, who was standing nearby, practically took her face off with a swipe of his talons. Woodstock, who had maintained her "baby qualities," went immediately into a submissive posture with back hunched, squealing voice and head down, staring blankly ahead.

By the final week Snoopy was exercising regularly and flying from perch to perch. Towards the end I was dropping in small live fish. Both Woodstock and Snoopy were intrigued with the flopping morsels.

There were still five days of captivity left and Woodstock was going wild. She ran and jumped onto the scale perch. As I tried to read the scale she would be tearing at it and bouncing up and down. Before I could get the weight, she jumped back off, grabbed a clump of straw, jumped back up on the scale, jumped off, ran over and attacked a dried-up piece of fish, clutched it in her talons and carried the prize back over to the scale. Finally she jumped off, discarded the dried fish, and sat contentedly back up on the perch (11.3 pounds, finally)!

One day the light must have been just right in the dark room between the cages. As I peered into Woodstock's window she glanced up at the mirror and bobbed her head back and forth and from side to side to focus better. It was as if she was slowly realizing that there was something more than a reflection of the ceiling. She extended her neck, slowly fluffed up her feathers in a defensive mode, and her stance became more erect. Her dark piercing eyes glared through the one-way glass and her mouth opened slightly. I must have had just enough light behind me to reveal my ghost-like appearance to her. I leaned back away from the glass and she relaxed.

At dinner on August 1, I wrote in my notes that Snoopy was going absolutely wild eating a fish. He was completely crazy, tearing it apart on the perch scale. The next day he tried to squeeze out between the bars. His voice changed to a whistling noise. By August 5, Snoopy was just about ready to leave home. At 9:00 a.m. he jumped on the scale (bear with me) to the bars, scale, perch, deck, scale, perch, deck, and scale and finally stayed on the deck. I wrote, "Very fidgety." No kidding. After all that perch hopping, I never got a weight. He sounded like a horn again for the rest of the morning. The next three days consisted of the same activity but I managed to steal a weight (8.3 pounds).

Dick And Jane

At T-minus one week, Dick and Jane, who resided in the lower left cage, were enjoying a morning rain shower. They were playing "beaks" by gently tapping their large beaks together in a non-threatening manner. Suddenly Jane jumped down to the deck. After seeing her reflection in a little puddle, Jane tried to take a bath on the wet plywood floor thinking it was a wading pool. She even went through the motion of dipping down and flapping her wings as if letting the imaginary water run down over her back. Five days later, during a noon to midnight rainstorm, Jane stood at the edge of the nest where water was pouring down through a small hole from the top cage. She took a bath with her wings open, flapping as if showering.

By August 1, both birds wanted out. Dick tried to walk out between the bars by pressing against them and pushing his head and neck out toward freedom. When his attempt to escape failed, he just walked back and forth until he grew tired of pacing and climbed on the scale perch (8.9 pounds). One day he bounced back and forth between the scale and pole perch ten times in one session. He finally got the hang of "bar" jumping and literally did

SIX WEEK CHICK WEIGHING ITSELF ON PERCH SCALE

just that; jumped up to the top of the bars and hung there with wings folded down. I took a picture through the one-way glass.

Jane flew aggressively right at the bars from the perch scale (10.7 pounds). Dick ducked when Jane sailed over his head. As the days went on, Jane's jumping imitated the carnival game of hitting the ball with the strike of the mallet. She jumped higher and higher until she finally hit the top. She was ready to go. In her spare time she liked to carry sticks and was quite ambidextrous.

On August 6, I served a meal of raw deer meat. Jane jumped down and wanted to spar with Dick who was eating some meat on the scale. Dick smacked Jane with his wing. Jane jumped into the nest and attacked Dick from behind. Dick got off the scale and Jane took over the prized deer hide. Dick, who retreated to the pole perch, watched in silence as Jane ate his meal.

Bert And Ernie

Ernie, Attila, and Marjorie enjoyed a bath on the same day as Jane. Ernie went so far as to believe the wet floor of the cage was deep water. He got down, curled his legs underneath him, crouched forward, rolled on one side to the wet deck and flapped sideways with the opposite folded wing. He almost tipped over trying to simulate getting his wings wet. This behavior is identical to a house sparrow taking a bath in a birdbath, only on a much larger scale. I was observing the same instinct to bathe that must have been shared by these species dating back to a common ancestor.

Three days later, Ernie was carrying around the backbone and legs of a road-killed rabbit that Bert had greedily eaten days earlier. Ernie was going absolutely crazy transferring the prey item from his beak to his talons. He brought it to the perch scale (9.0 pounds). There wasn't a trace of meat left on it.

Bert, enemy of all who walk the earth on two feet, loved to flap his wings in the wind. He would pump the air or just hold his mighty six-foot plus wingspan outstretched and hover over the perch in the slightest breeze. He loved to carry sticks around and became quite fidgety toward the end. His little games included running, jumping, and tearing the perch scale rug to shreds. His antics included dominating Ernie with scare tactics. Bert would fly into the nest unexpectedly and terrorize Ernie. He would jump out and then right back in and try to look Ernie in the face. Of course Ernie already had his head down in the submissive position and turned away from Bert. Bert needs to be free with lots of personal space.

You could tell who the boss was in each nest enclosure by who claimed the best food first. Snoopy might have been smaller than Woodstock but he had the mental advantage. Snoopy and Woodstock seemed the most compatible because they both tried to hold their own. However, Woodstock seemed to get her point across more effectively by having that extra pound over her nest mate. Bert dominated by quick action and pure tenacity. In general, the six birds in these first three enclosures could work out their differences quickly without any real hassle or lasting hostility toward one another.

BERT FLAPPING IN THE WIND ON THE EAGLE TOWER

Attila And Marjorie

Attila and Marjorie were a different story. They were the birds we had to break apart that first day when we paired them together. There were occasions when I had to tap on the tinted window because of Attila's overbearing personality. She was an outright bully. Attila constantly was a "bee" in Marjorie's emotionally-torn "bonnet."

Attila knew all the buttons to push. I had to sit and watch her torment Marjorie day after day. Her tactics were described by the following in my notes: bickering, pecking, pushing, lunging, stealing food, and adjectives like nasty! It got to the point where I would just write "altercation." Sometimes the birds would play "beaks," feed off the same chunk of deer meat and lie down in the shade side by side. Marjorie once dropped a stick on Attila's back while playing and Attila just moved out of the way. Marjorie even sat and watched Attila eat some fresh fish I threw in, then hopped over and stole it from Attila and there was no fight. However, sometimes Attila could be downright cruel.

ATTILA ON THE ATTACK

On August 2, I observed both birds lying down together. It was 8:34 a.m. At 11:00 a.m. I was down at the dock when I heard an eagle screaming. I could see the tower as I ran toward it and knew the ruckus was coming from Attila and Marjorie's enclosure. I scaled the ladder in record time and peered in the window. I saw Attila repeatedly grabbing Marjorie with her

ATTILA SHOWING MARJORIE WHO'S BOSS

talons. Marjorie screamed and Attila attacked again. Then she jumped on Marjorie's back and footed her a few more times. Poor Marjorie scrambled to the far corner and squeezed her large body between the nest box and the wall and put her head down. Attila jumped to the perch scale, arching her head and neck feathers in an aggressive manner. Boy was she upset. Marjorie, in the meantime, stayed in her submissive pose for a few minutes and Attila resumed her place on the perch pole. Marjorie then jumped into the nest, keeping a watchful eye over her shoulder. She scrambled across the nest to the other side and jumped out. She was breathing hard and never stopped watching Attila. Attila relaxed her posture so I left to finish up my chores.

At noon I heard Marjorie screaming again, so back up the path and ladder I went. My legs were in great shape with all this ladder climbing. Attila was at it again. She was attacking Marjorie who was pinned in the corner. Finally Attila relented and jumped into the nest. This gave Marjorie the opportunity to back out and scramble toward the front of the cage, again in a submissive manner. Attila seized the chance to jump on the perch scale and assault Marjorie again. Marjorie screamed and ducked under the perch pole and pressed her lowered head into the front corner bars for ten minutes, staying in a crouched position. Attila then jumped on the perch pole, right over her nest mate. She had her mouth open and body erect. Marjorie didn't move a muscle. At 2:00 p.m. round three began. I missed the temper tantrum but witnessed the cowering shown by Marjorie. Attila was nonchalantly preening her own feathers.

I don't know what Attila's problem was, for that day was the worst day of their stay together. After that they resumed their friendly "beaking," perching, or lying side by side, bouncing, hopping, and exercising together. On August 6, they both had voracious appetites and ate like wolves. Attila momentarily stopped eating and preened Marjorie's back while she ate. Marjorie didn't even flinch. The next day Attila had a fish in her talons. She ran over, grabbed Marjorie's fish, and continued her playful antics by flapping around from area to area with a fish in both feet. Attila made a point of denying Marjorie either fish. She finished both and filled her crop. Then she sat back and watched Marjorie eat what was left over.

16

Leaving The Nest

Day 60

August 19, 1985 - 6:15 p.m.

Dear Mom, Dad, Scotty, and Louise,

On "Transmitter Day" the eagles' sequestered world was turned upside down. We had to capture the "teenagers" two at a time to have the doctors and vet students take follow-up blood samples. Then Fish and Wildlife personnel attached the radio transmitters to the central tail feathers.

The week of the babies' departure was a hard one. The *Worcester Telegram* newspaper interviewed me. Jack Swedberg said the reporter was going to make a special article from our talk.

That day was understandably stressful. It brought me back to the tension of the polar bear days when there was all the media attention. I went out at dawn and pulled my northern net. As I motored back I eased back on the throttle and peered over my right shoulder and looked up at the eagle tower. Whoever was perched and could see me looked at me with indifference. I said goodbye so only I could hear. I will miss them.

I fed the birds early so they could have a
couple of hours to digest their breakfast.

At 9:00 a.m. I could hear all the cars
coming down the road and went to greet everyone.
Tufts personnel set up under the shaded tower.
Meanwhile Jack, Billy D., and I, sat at the
campsite and went over the telemetry one last
time before we affixed the transmitters to the
birds' tails. These devices will be very
important in the first few days and weeks of
the birds' freedom. They will allow us to find
a bird that is in trouble or hurt. If they have
demonstrated that they can make it that far,
then the transmitters will have served their
purpose and then fall off when the bird molts
next summer.

It was after nine and the loons sounded their
warning. "What's up with them?" I wondered.
Minutes later I looked out over the reservoir
and saw the MDC police boat cruising toward my
area. "Oh my gosh! I forgot to radio in at 9:00
this morning." I leaped up and ran down to the
shore and waved my arms, signaling that I was
alive. I could see they had slowed down and had
their binoculars up. They turned around and
left. I was so upset with myself for neglecting
my radio check that I ran into the tent and
radioed the police my apology. Damn, damn, damn!

We joined up with the Tufts doctors, students,
media, environmental police, and assorted guests
of the project. Jack and I coordinated our
efforts and climbed the ladder to retrieve a
bird apiece. We opened the door to the top right
cage and cautiously walked in. The birds were
quite surprised and flew to the bars. It was not
easy to walk in empty-handed and grab a bouncing
bird with a six-foot wingspan. I had worked with
hawks and owls, but this was something new.
School started when we walked in that door
and realized there would be no second chances.

DIANNE AND MARJORIE

Jack captured Attila and I grabbed Marjorie.
We came out the back entrance door on the top
level so Tufts' veterinary students could wrap
the birds' feet in protective bandages. That way
the eagles wouldn't hurt themselves or us with
their needle-sharp talons. They're not little
helpless babies anymore. They're full-sized
regal eagles with large powerful talons and
biting beaks. The feeling of having a massive
eagle in my hand was exhilarating.

Marjorie's head was next to mine and her dark
eyes sparkled. Her body was strong and forceful
and I held onto her for dear life. One of my
hands held her large legs and the other hand was
cupped around her neck. She couldn't understand
the restraint and tried to tune me out by
staring away with her mighty head down. I held
her firmly under my arm like a football and
began my journey down the ladder. We had to turn
around and back down the ladder, keeping control
of our robust birds. We caught each rung with
our other hand and slowly lowered ourselves to
the ground.

The veterinarians worked on Jack's bird first.
Billy D. weighed the bird in a basket hanging
under a scale. Billy B. unobtrusively documented
the event with his Nikon. The vet students took
a blood sample from the underside of one wing. I
was standing off to the side, totally awed by
this new experience. It must be hard to live in
a sequestered world and then be exposed to the
outside all at once.

It took a while to get blood from Attila and
then the sample clotted so that the vet student
had to do it again. The two doctors were so
patient with the students because this was their
first wildlife experience. They were used to
handling dogs, cats, and horses.

Then they affixed the tail transmitter to the
bird's tail. That took a while and I could see

that Jack was getting a little antsy. I knew he
wanted to get the birds back up in their living
quarters. At this time I was sitting down with
one vet student, holding out the left wing while
another student was pouring alcohol on the vein.
They did a good job and it was time to kneel
down so the transmitter could be put on. My arm
strained from holding the 11.5-pound bird in the
same position while still holding her feet in
the other hand. I needed help getting up because
my knees were so cramped.

Jack, by this time, was starting to sweat
as the vet students were patiently teaching
him better surgical knots to fasten the
transmitters to the tail feathers. Finally
we were finished and headed back up the ladder.
We gratefully released our birds back into their
living quarters.

Tom French, assistant director of nongame and
endangered species for the Fish and Wildlife

FOREGROUND LEFT TO RIGHT: JACK SWEDBERG AND DR. CHARLES SEDGWICK
ATTACHING RADIO TRANSMITTER TO TAIL FEATHERS.
BACKGROUND LEFT TO RIGHT: DR. MARK POKRAS, DR. TOM FRENCH

Dept., came today to observe the project. He was
up on the tower when we went to grab the first
birds. I had met him when I applied for a bald
eagle educational permit last year. It was nice
to see him again.

Jack and I looked into Bert and Ernie's cage.
We stood in the observation room, took deep
breaths with arms at the ready and mentally
prepared ourselves to storm the cage. Our
intention was to catch the startled birds
quickly without anyone getting hurt. Jack
said, "Are you ready? Go!"

We pushed open the door, ran toward a bird
with arms out and tried to grab the backs of
their wings. They were desperately trying to get
out through the bars. Attila and Marjorie in the
adjoining enclosure could see us and they flew
toward their bars again. It was very noisy for
those few seconds until we got hold of our
respective birds. I seized my good buddy Bert,
and he instantly turned his head and lunged
toward me and tried to bite my face. Billy D.
quickly stepped toward me and tried to keep his
hand and a roll of gauze between Bert's open
beak and my cheek while I was stretching my neck
in the opposite direction. All the other birds
were inclined to put their heads down and
distance themselves from us but not Bert!
Regardless, we wrapped their feet for our
protection and brought them down.

I put Bert on his back to get weighed, and we
wrapped him up in a sheet so that he could calm
down. Then I held the bird's feet in one arm and
pulled the exposed wing out with my other hand
for blood to be drawn. Well, I'm in shape, but
not in good enough shape to hold my body in that
position for long. I started shaking and all of
a sudden a vet student jammed her legs under my
back and told me to lean against her side and
legs. I couldn't thank her enough. Bert was

starting to get hot. Jack's bird was too. Things
were starting to go like clockwork though. It
was up the ladder after everything was done. I
told someone to take the sheet off Bert to give
him some air and cool his body.

Going up the ladder was a challenge because
Bert was lunging at me again and had his head
feathers flared out. He had piercing wild eyes
and strength in his body so I held him tight to
my side. I wished we had a falconry hood to cover
Bert's eyes and calm him without getting his
whole body hot. I had to hold my head in the
opposite direction going up the ladder. Then I
pulled the bird in close to get us both up the
ladder between decks. He took that opportunity
to grab my neck with his hooked beak and twist.
Thank goodness my neck was stretched in the
opposite direction. My neck felt warm and wet.
I hurried into the enclosure and waited for Jack
to bring his bird in. We unwrapped the gauze on
the birds' talons and let them go together as we
backed out and quickly closed the door. We just
stood there trembling. What a rush! He said he
was going to have Bill D. and Tom French take the
next two birds down because we needed a break.

I went down off the tower and tried to stay
to the left of the people so they wouldn't see
that I had been bitten. I was so embarrassed. I
touched the spot to make sure I wasn't bleeding
that much.

We heard commotion from above us and saw an
eagle's wing flapping outside the bars. A vet
student saw my neck and told Dr. Sedgwick to
take a look. They swabbed my neck with betadine
solution. While I was receiving first aid, Billy
D. was above getting talons taken out of his
hand. He went to grab his bird, either Dick or
Jane, and the frightened bird flipped on its
back, sharp talons up and spread his long wing
out through the bars. Billy didn't want the bird

to break flight feathers or a wing so he reached down and got a thumb and wrist full of talons. The vet students nervously tried to pry the talons out and just as they wrestled the last dagger out, the bird "taloned" Billy again. We finally got all the birds completed and back up in their respective enclosures. I brought out the soda and we all mingled afterwards.

Wendell Dodge from the University of Massachusetts came and taught me how to work the telemetry that I was to use to track the babies after they were freed. He mentioned I should go out in the boat and head north and try to find the birds' signals coming from their tail transmitters. The birds were still confined to the tower and would remain there for two more days, so I figured this was going to be easy. Wendell said that I should switch to each frequency and see if I could get all my signals. He said to move around and learn about detecting false signals from the pulse bouncing off island ridges and trees. I thanked him very much for his practical advice. I appreciated the guidance and respect he offered through his quiet demeanor.

After everyone left I was exhausted. What a feeling to have eighteen people there one minute and none the next. After Jack, Bill B., and Bill D. left, I put food in with the juveniles, took notes on their lack of appetite, and came out on the back platform. I sat down on the edge and hung my legs out over the ladder. All I could do was stare out at the trees in front of me. I just wanted someone to come back to talk to me.

I heard footsteps pounding up the trail and looked down the pine needle path thirty feet below. Billy B. came to the bottom of the ladder and looked up in puzzlement. He came up the ladder and we talked about how the day had gone well and he gave me the telemetry frequencies that they forgot to leave. He said Billy D. had gone to the hospital for a tetanus shot and antibiotics for his talon wounds. His hand and arm had swelled noticeably by the time he left here. We said goodbye and I thanked him for the company. I was fine then and went out in the boat to set my three gill nets.

I had fed the birds at 5:30 a.m. so they had eaten before all this happened. It was a good thing, because they didn't eat after their ordeal. All the fresh food I dropped the next day was left untouched. They remained quiet. I even gave them their favorite foods: salmon and deer meat. I started noticing their feces were less in volume and green in color, which meant there was nothing in their stomachs. Fortunately, they were heavy enough and had good fat reserves so that I didn't worry too much.

I had a day to practice with the telemetry so I took advantage of it. As I listened, I could pinpoint the birds' signals at the hack tower. This was easy, I thought. However, if I moved out of sight of the tower I found the signal coming from the opposite direction, from Pomeroy Island to the east. What the heck? Wendell had told me that if I got beyond line-of-sight, the signal would then start bouncing off the islands, ridges and surrounding forest. He said the best thing to do was to get a signal and then point the antenna in the opposite direction. If that didn't work, he suggested moving a little bit to see if the signal held true or got weak quickly. It took me a while to get comfortable with the equipment but I was gaining confidence in my ability the more I practiced.

Take care all,

Love Dianne

DIANNE LEARNING TO USE
TELEMETRY ON THE WATER

Release Day

I never wrote anyone about "release day" on August 9, because Paul stayed with me for a short vacation at the hack site after the eagles were liberated. The details of that momentous occasion, however, were seared into my memory and years later it was easy to recreate it.

I was nervous that day but that was no surprise.

People filed down in cars as they did two days earlier on "transmitter day."

This time the media, VIPs, and invited guests also came. Paul Nickerson from the U.S. Fish and Wildlife Service came and it was nice to see him again.

The people at the Tuft's Wildlife Clinic had rehabilitated an eagle knows as "91" who was found shot that spring at Quabbin. He was from the eagle "Class of 1984" and had been released as a baby last year as part of the project. Since the last two digits

TOM RICARDI RELEASING EAGLE 91

on his original alpha-numeric band read "91," that was used as his nickname. My falconry friend, Tom Ricardi, who also was an environmental police officer, had housed the bird during his final stage of rehabilitation. That morning, Tom brought the eagle to the hack site and Jack put a transmitter on the bird's tail. We released the two-year-old in my cove for all to see an hour before my babies were freed. Instead of heading out of the cove and over the open reservoir, 91 ventured up the narrow Prescott Brook valley and into the tangled woods. Silly bird.

People who came to witness the release were shuttled to "Media Point" located across the mouth of the cove from the hack tower. This vantage had been used in previous years.

When everyone was in place, Jack and I simultaneously opened the doors remotely with ropes. He was on the top floor opening Attila and Marjorie's door and then he released Ernie and Bert's. I opened Snoopy and Woodstock's cage and then Dick and Jane's. Within seconds the tower became a flurry of noise and wings.

Attila bolted right away, which I expected. She quickly flew north out of sight around the bend.

Snoopy burst through his door as it was still being pulled open. He pumped his wings and sailed down past some excited people who were behind a camouflage screen. With a few more wing beats, he started to rise up to meet a tree branch. The problem was that his feet did their part by grasping the limb but the body and wings did not work as a team to break his momentum. He pitched forward and then back as he tried to compensate for the error. He eventually found himself upside down and hung there for a few seconds before he pushed with his mighty wings and righted himself.

Woodstock came out and immediately banked right and headed due south. She flew beautifully, but lost altitude and crash-landed beak first on Fish Head Point. She walked into the water and took a long-awaited bath.

DICK'S FIRST FLIGHT

Marjorie left and flew to the Gibbs Brook area and landed smoothly on the ground. She opened her wings slightly and ran up further from the shore to settle in. I'm glad her hell mate, I mean roommate, Attila, flew north.

Dick and Jane were in no rush to leave. Dick finally walked to the edge of his door and sprang in the air and flew south on light wing beats to Gibbs Shore. His plumage was so beautiful. The white on the under tail was bordered with a dark stripe. What a gorgeous bird.

Eventually Jane walked out and over to Woodstock's and Snoopy's empty apartment. Then she hopped out on the outside perch pole in front of the cages. This time there was no floor under her feet, but rather rocks and bushes thirty feet below. Her movements were confident and direct. Her brain must not register a fear of heights. I took a picture of her through the one-way glass. She looked around a while and finally tested her wings by flying south to Gibbs Cove. She alighted perfectly in an oak tree.

Bert and Ernie stayed a long time in the security of their condo. They initially jumped at the bars when all the commotion started but never grasped the idea that complete freedom was now just a few feet away. Bert kept jumping nonchalantly from the perch pole to the scale and back again. Finally he figured it out and sprang into the air and flew north out of sight. Ernie stayed so long that we decided to leave the tower and let him take his own sweet time. There was no rush.

Jack asked me to go down and talk to a newspaper reporter from Providence, Rhode Island. He was polite and we had a pleasant conversation. I left the TV reporters to Jack and stayed away from the majority of the media people. I was still going to live alone for another month and we didn't want to advertise that fact.

Everyone was quite satisfied with the release and a core group of Fish and Wildlife people stayed to help move my tent. Wendell Dodge came back out from UMass and gave me a few more pointers on ways to combat false signals with the telemetry

MARJORIE LEAVING THE HACK TOWER

receiver. I had been practicing for the last two days and still had some trouble finding the stationary birds while they were secure on the tower. Wendell suggested we try and locate 91, who had flown up Prescott Brook, which paralleled the road. That way we would not bother the newly-released inexperienced birds who had left an hour earlier.

We tracked 91's signal up the road and after a few turns and adjustments of the antenna, I surprisingly found him sitting in a tall tree. I was awestruck by this ability to find the yearling with just headphones and a receiver. I looked up at Wendell's weathered face and we shared a simple smile. I thanked him for the lessons. I was becoming a field biologist, eager to learn from my on-the-job training.

The next day it was clear that something was bothering Paul, although he wouldn't tell me what. He got upset when I had to caution him about putting the gill net back out straight. He said, "F- - - it!" It shocked me because he never swore in front of me. He

JACK SWEDBERG FILMING EAGLES

went home a day later and I turned my full attention back to the released birds. I put a road-killed deer carcass on an island for them. I also had to get a fix on Woodstock. Her signal was very weak but I finally got it by going up on the tower. Jack installed a big antenna, which worked much better than my hand-held one. The signal put her out near Mount Lizzie Island to the southeast. I decided to check it out.

Later, Natural Resource Officer Bruce Bennett picked me up in his cruiser. We drove south to the MDC police administration building and launched his boat for me to use. My six-horsepower was just too small to go over great distances looking for the babies with telemetry.

Bruce's boat is a forty-horsepower outboard mounted on a thirteen-foot Boston Whaler with a steering wheel. He cautioned that it was very fast. He sometimes had trouble with the engine quitting on him and he had just had the motor checked out. I decided to wear my life jacket and bring an emergency pack with me in the boat at all times. In it is a warm jogging suit, a flashlight, first aid kit, snacks, waterproof matches, and space blanket, just in case I get marooned somewhere.

I informed the MDC police when I was going on the water, for how long (three or four hours), and when I'm "off the water" as they like to call it. They told me if my boat quit and I got stuck on an island, to start a small smoke fire. They were all polite and the radio contact felt like a giant wing protecting me from a distance since I didn't know any of the officers personally.

I picked up all the telemetry signals from the birds this morning. I went up on the tower to use the larger antenna and as I was coming down I spooked an eagle off Loon Island. It was Ross, an eagle released during the first year of the eagle project back in 1982. His head has white on it but his tail is still brown. He has a blue tag on his wing and that's how I could identify him. He flew to the north past Mount Pomeroy Island.

It is so different out here now. I'm not camped out on the point near the water anymore. My tent is at the end of the road near my car. This makes my view of the reservoir limited because I'm tucked back in the cove and can't see to the north and south. I guess I'm there so the birds don't see me coming and going as much. It makes sense but I miss the visual contact with the watery landscape and the open sky. I'm under pine trees again next to Prescott Brook. My nights are not that noisy, though, because the brook is just a trickle now that it is late summer.

The reservoir has dropped to eleven feet below capacity. Last year, when I saw the eagle release, the Quabbin was full.

I don't have to cut up the fish anymore or observe the birds through one-way glass. That took so much of my day. I do still have three nets out that I have to pull daily. I put the fish out after dark so the eagles can find them in the morning and not associate them with me.

EAGLE TOWER, THE EAGLES HAVE FLOWN

Day 61

Tuesday, August 20, 1985 -10:15 a.m.

Dear Paul and Becky,

   I was glad to talk with you last night, even
if it was for only a minute. I have signals on
all my birds today. My new boat sure feels like
having a G-force effect when you give it gas.
The only problem is that it stalls out when I
idle the motor down to check out an eagle
signal. It took me forever to get it started
again. It has a pull-cord starter inside the
housing. I finally yanked so hard that the rope
half came out and the backlash almost pulled me
out of the boat. On the next try the cord came
all the way out and I fell backwards on the
telemetry antennae and bent it. Damn it! I
finally got it started and headed in after that
incident. I'll only use that boat if I have to
travel a fair distance to locate wandering
birds.

   I have nets to pull and then it's waiting time
again until I check signals on my birds at 6:00
or 7:00 p.m. this evening. I just had two eggs
and an English muffin. I had a two-and-a-half-
pound small mouth bass last night for dinner.
It was okay but nothing like the sweet taste
of white perch.

   Commissioner Hoyt of the Department of
Fisheries, Wildlife and Environmental Law
Enforcement, and Brad Blodget are supposed to
be coming today. I have three nets to pull so
I'll have to keep an eye out for anyone walking
along the shore while I'm out on the water.

   I got a road-killed fawn yesterday from
Environmental Police Officer Chuck Connors and
put half on Loon Island and the remainder on
Gibbs Shore. Billy B. put up his blind at Gibbs

Shore again. I baited the rocks all around the blind with fish. I haven't seen any of the birds too close to the blind though.

Well, I suppose I should do my dishes, make tea, go up to the point, watch for eagles, and then go out and pull in those nets.

Love, Dianne

Tuesday, August 20, 1985 - 6:00 p.m.

Dear Mom, Dad, Scotty, and Louise,

Surprisingly last week I didn't eat fish at all. I wasn't in the mood. I had to get the telemetry mastered, which was no problem. I also had to find things to keep myself busy. I have so much time on my hands now that I might start going home nights. I'm missing family life more because my mind is not occupied all the time. I find my birds by 8:00 in the morning; pull my nets and its only 9:30 a.m. I have the whole day until I set my nets and check the signals at night. I try to put the food out after dark.

You're not going to believe what happened last week. The very first time I took some time off, Wendell Dodge was calling all over the place looking for me. He's the UMass "telemetry" man who tracks bear, bobcat, and other animals by airplane with an antenna and receiver. He wanted to take me up in an airplane to track my wandering birds by air. He has my frequencies so he can home in on the eagles' signals. He took NRO Dennis Brennan up instead. They saw a bear in a cornfield having lunch! Wendell left for Washington, D. C. the next day. He'll be back next week so I hope I get another chance.

It is so beautiful out near the water. I'm under the trees in my tent listening to the radio. Some politicians arrived at 5:00 p.m.

in the police boat. Brad Blodget was with them.
Some climbed the tower where the eagles had been
to get a better view of the Quabbin. The VIPs
all had ear-to-ear smiles. Brad could spot only
one eagle chick along the shore. They stayed a
little while and I shared my supply of soda.
One person made a "startling" discovery that
the soda cans didn't have a five-cent deposit
return. I told him that I live on the
Massachusetts/New Hampshire border and buy my
groceries in New Hampshire. That seemed to calm
him down. Brother, what some people get worried
about! Just after the people went out of sight,
with binoculars I located five birds sitting in
the trees in their favorite perches. They were
all deeper in against the trees when the people
were visiting.

   I got a six-pound lake trout up north today.
It was the only fish in the net. I let it go
because there wasn't a mark on him and he was
very much alive. I caught a three-and-a-half-
pound smallmouth bass (dead) in the next net
plus many smaller bass and white perch. The
third net came up empty. Sometimes I try new
areas and I guess I'm missing the flow.

   Take care. I love you,

                    Dianne

Day 64

August 24, 1985 - 2:00 p.m.

Dear Billy D.,

   Billy and I just got back from paddling all
the way from just north of Little Quabbin
Island. The engine died and we sailed with two
sweatshirts, life jackets, and one paddle. You

should have been there. What fun!

Billy's still working on the sorry engine
while I write. He cleaned the spark plugs but
still can't get the engine started.

The nets are set: two south at Gibbs Point
where we set them before and one south at the
red rock ledges before you round the corner near
Little Quabbin. Billy said he has had good luck
there since we didn't catch many fish today. You
were right; the fish must be in deeper water
because of the warm temperatures. We got into
trouble coming back from setting that one. I
guess you'll have to use Bruce's boat. Good
luck. The last net has one buoy up on the
deepest end.

Well, have a good time Sunday.

Dianne

Don't forget to call in to the MDC. They want
you guys to call too. The radio is in the locked
shed. You might want to put the nets right back
out because there's not much room in Bruce's
boat.

Day 67

Tuesday, August 27, 1985 - 6:30 p.m.

Dear Paul and Becky,

I'm sitting outside on the point. The eagles
have now been on their own for eleven days. They
are still out in the trees and on the rocks near
the water. They come back every day because they
are still dependent on me for their food.

Now I have lots of time on my hands but it's
too far to commute. That's why I call you every
so many days and last week I just got in my car
and drove home for the night to be with you

both. I'm glad you were very surprised.

Day 64

2 pm
8-24-85

Dear Billy,

Billy B. and I just got back from paddling all the way back from just North of Little Quabbin. The engine died and we sailed with 2 sweatshirts, life jacket, and 1 paddle. You should have been there!!!

notice sweatshirts

What FUN! Billy's still working on the engine while I make some lunch! He cleaned off spark plugs but still couldn't start it.

I hate to tell you but the NETS are set... 2 South at Gibbs point where we set them before and one all the way south at ROCK Ledges before you round the corner near Little Quabbin. Bill said he has had good luck there since we didn't catch much fish today. We got into trouble coming back from setting that one. I guess you'll have to use Bruce's boat. LAST NET HAS ONE MARKER UP. FAR OUT.

Well, have a good time Sunday.

P.S. Check the "tin" stump! We saw some birds in that area. (SAY hi to RICK please!)

Dianne

Don't forget to call in to MDC. They want you guys to call too. Radio in shed.

I'd put the nets right back out because there's not much room in Bruce's boat.

THE SMALL MOTOR DOESN'T WORK!

LETTER TO BILL DAVIS: "SAILING ON QUABBIN"

I miss you so much, Becky, but you seem to be adjusting very well. Daddy tells me that you tell everyone that your mom is at Quabbin taking care of the baby bald eagles. I like it when you ask me how they are doing. It's hard to believe you're only three years old.

Daddy enjoys getting out of work at 5:30 p.m. and going to pick you up at the baby sitter. You two have become so close. If anything else, out of this whole eagle project, the bond that was created between you and Daddy was worth it all. A mother's love for her child is special. Daddy has experienced that love by feeding you, changing you, taking care of your needs, and being your friend and companion.

You have two parents that love you, hug and kiss you a lot and spend quality time with you, even if it is separately for this summer. We'll get together after all this is over and we'll all be happier because of it.

I'm sitting among the pines with crickets providing the background music. They are joined by many different songbirds. There's a catbird in the brush crying like a kitty. There's a song sparrow singing his tea kettle song, and a kingfisher racing back and forth on stiff wings, trying to find a vantage point from which to hunt the small fish in my cove. He likes to sit on the dock post. There is a red squirrel behind me in the pines. A loon out in the bay is calling, "O-looouuu." The water is dead calm, which is very relaxing. Occasionally I hear one of my baby eagles crying to another on a far-off shore. I'm sitting on the point behind green screening so the babies can't see me. I have a scope focused on one of the babies. She's watching two other babies up in a pine tree. I'm not even going to figure out who they are right now with the telemetry because I've had "visuals" on all my birds today and I just want to enjoy them as wild eagles.

It is so peaceful out here. The sun has set behind the trees but it is still light out. You know, I don't think animals perceive this beauty. They just live! They hunt to eat and watch out so they don't get eaten. The goal of life out here is to see if you can go to sleep with something in your stomach.

The woods are a place to make a home or hide. The loons live their lives on the water because of their anatomy. They float on the water in the rain like a cork, manage cold windy days, and journey onward in choppy waters. Eagles flying overhead can leave them hysterical and an intruding loon can lead them in a frenzied chase over the surface of the water. Territory—just like people with fences around their property—there is a primeval drive to defend it. It didn't take me long to tap into the loon's private conversation and early-warning system. I saw some deer along the shore when I was out in the boat earlier today. They "flagged" their tails as they ran into the deeper woods. Even they silently signaled my presence.

The loon is calling a long drawn-out wail again. Sounds like he's saying, "All's right with the world," because it is his "I'm here" call. I have to put a deer carcass on the island in front of me. I took it out of the freezer at the astronomy site. It should be almost thawed so I'll put it out tonight after dark. That way the birds can feed on it first thing in the morning without any disturbance from me. Besides, they usually fly to the island, eat, and go back to perch by the time I get up.

Take care.

Love, Mommy, Dianne

Deciphering Individual Signals

I wrote notes on the eagles' first take-out breakfast of deer. The hide was still on so I made a cut through it so the babies could get at some of the red meat. However, they would have to work at getting to the rest of it. I put out fish I had caught in my nets the evening before so there was a generous surf-and-turf for the birds to choose from.

I was still developing my own techniques for telling who was who while looking through the spotting scope. Trying to decipher the individual signals and match them up with the different birds was sometimes difficult, especially when they were all standing side-by-side, squabbling over a meal. I had nine visuals and 91 still hung out with my inexperienced birds. That morning I had the receiver turned off and just took notes on the interactions between the birds. I could guess at the identity of some birds because of their size and color-coded transmitters. My notes read: "Two birds together here and three birds there on Loon Island." A few were on Gibbs Shore where I also put some fish. Some were vocal. They still made baby peeps when they called, echoing across the still water to my appreciative ears. One on Loon Island walked down to the calm water, took a drink, and then grabbed at green tufts of grass with its beak. Then the bird walked over and grabbed a stick with its talons and transferred it to his beak so he could walk around with it. Now he is biting pieces off, even though there is food all around him.

One large bird was at the southern tip of the island. She hopped up on a rock where I had placed a fish the night before. She cautiously inched closer to within reach while looking around at the other birds. She pounced with one foot and her hackles (head feathers) raised up in a defensive posture. Other birds called out. She took flight and flew to the east side of the island with her prize.

On Gibbs Shore, two birds seemed to be enjoying each other's company. They were running around each other and searching the

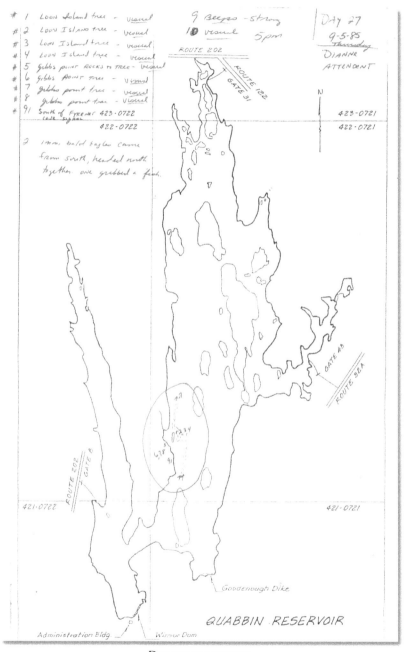

DAILY TELEMETRY MAP

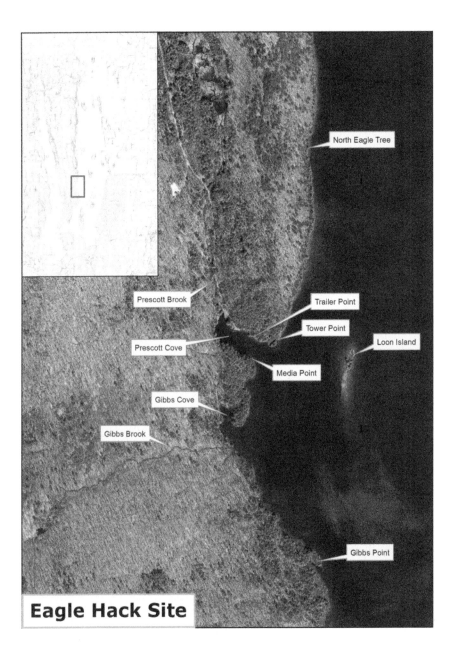

North Eagle Tree

Prescott Brook

Trailer Point

Tower Point

Loon Island

Prescott Cove

Media Point

Gibbs Cove

Gibbs Brook

Gibbs Point

Eagle Hack Site

ground for something: food I guess. One was Attila, who grabbed a stick and both birds puffed up and cried out. She became quite frisky and ran around dragging her stick and biting off pieces. Woodstock was the other bird and she grabbed her own stick. Attila flew over to steal Woodstock's stick and they both ran behind a large stump. All I could see were wings flapping and I could hear Woodstock peeping. Two birds were at Gibbs Point when all of a sudden 91 came from nowhere. He circled the other two birds as they screamed in unison and 91 landed.

Back on Loon Island an eagle was on a rock, mantling (wings covering food) and screaming. With crows cawing, the bird jumped down in the grass with his prized fish and began eating. One of the birds from Gibbs Point took flight and flew just above the water all the way to Loon Island. That was an awesome sight to see him slice through the air, touching the water with his wingtips. He pumped for most of the way and then glided as he made his final approach to the island. His flight was premeditated and as he made his way over land, his intentions became perfectly clear. His mission was to steal the fish from the bird in the grass.

Just as contact was made, a third baby flew over and attacked the intruder, who turned out to be Ernie. Ernie flipped over on his back. Feathers were flying and after a talon to his body, Ernie high-tailed it back to Gibbs Shore in no time flat. I guess it didn't matter if the eagles were confined to the hack tower as caged youngsters or out on their own and a quarter-mile apart; they still fought over food. Their "battling" instinct for food remained strong.

Finally one of the babies showed some interest in the deer carcass I had boated over last night. Two birds were watching a third youngster tear at the fur. While this was going on, a lot of screaming came from Gibbs Point. Three birds were on the ground below 91, who was watching from above in a tree. One bird chased another with outstretched wings until the second bird took refuge in another tree. The first bird then turned his attention to the third bird who just kept his distance. It wasn't any friendlier on Loon

Island with the deer. A fight erupted among the three birds around the carcass. They appeared to be mock battles but feathers were flying. A fourth bird joined in. The birds stood in a circle with mini-battles ensuing. I could hear a baby eagle in the Loon Island tree, so that made nine birds accounted for this morning. Yea!

It was better when I didn't have to go out searching for the birds by boat for their morning check. This sitting and watching was less disruptive to their daily activities. Good, one bird was finally eating off the deer carcass. Two managed to work some of the hide off and were standing together on a rock, tearing it apart. The fourth bird walked over and watched the first bird gulp down large pieces of meat.

For the next twenty minutes others joined the party until six birds were together at the south end of Loon Island. One eagle tried to fly off with a heavy fish but dropped it. Four birds were locked in battle over nothing; one was eating a fish on a rock and another walked down to the water to get a drink. Four birds suddenly spread their massive wings and flew off in different directions. There seemed to be a lot of activity but very little eating. By 8:30 a.m. only three birds were visible through my scope; 91 had been complacent all this time in the Gibbs Point tree and the remaining two were still lunging at each other on Loon Island with hackles up and wings extended.

All the babies came back to Loon Island for breakfast and dinner from the day of their release back on August 9. The birds spent most of their time in the Gibbs Shore area. My daily maps helped me keep track of their last locations for the day. The telemetry was an integral tool to insure the identity and the whereabouts of the eagles.

Marjorie and Woodstock wandered south along the shore during the day but returned in the late afternoon to feed at Loon Island with their buddies. Attila's favorite spot was still in a dead tree north of the abandoned hack tower. Dick and Jane were the first birds I saw actually soaring. Dick was down over Fyke Net

Cove past Gibbs Point and Jane was further south, soaring high over Little Quabbin Island.

Fourteen days after their release, Ernie was so high over Loon Island that he was just a speck in the sky. He flew out of Fyke Net Cove and proceeded to circle higher and higher as I watched from my boat. I lay in the bottom of the boat with my hands behind my head, staying out of the wind and marveling at the incredible skill with which he soared. What a spectacular view he must have of Massachusetts and beyond.

Twenty days out, a sub-adult (four-year-old eagle) joined the gang for breakfast. His head and tail were ninety percent white with a dark stripe behind his eye, yellow iris and two brown bands on his tail. I couldn't see any leg bands. The ranking senior gorged on fish for forty-five minutes until his crop was full. Three of my babies were screaming at him and watched him attentively but from a respectful distance. The seasoned adult ambled down to the shore for a drink and lingered there for another fifteen minutes. Then he flew to the southern tip of Loon Island and stayed fifteen minutes there. He nonchalantly looked around in between preening his semi-adult plumage. His posture was different from my young birds. He stood upright with his tail out straight behind him. I saw the same stance earlier this summer in other wild adult eagles. My youngsters tended to have their tails touching the ground.

Day 71

August 31, 1985 - 9:00 a.m.

Dear Williams and Jack,

   I'm cold, wet, and my hands are trembling. I am sitting here by the Coleman lantern for light because it is so dark and gloomy outside. It has been raining buckets. The tea water is boiling so I'll be back. To top this whole morning madness, my cream is sour! I made new tea and put half a cup of Coffee-Mate in.

My left arm is immobile. I had such a time
hauling (and I do mean hauling) my nets in. The
long one almost hauled me in on the other side
of Loon Island.

I was trying to get out of here early this
morning to help Mardi Snow, my falconry friend.
Her husband is having a big auction and wanted
me to help. They're way up in West Newbury so
it's going to be a long ride. I'll head home
after that. First, they're going to have to wait
until I change out of my drenched clothes and
regain my composure. The tea tastes great. Ahhh!

I had all my birds accounted for by 6:00 a.m.
I had five eaglets on Loon Island, one on Gibbs
Shore, and the rest had strong signals from the
Gibbs Cove area. I figured this was going to be
easy; I'd pull my nets and then be out of here.
It was ominous out with very dark clouds to the
north but I figured I could get the nets in
before the rains fell.

The first net took me over an hour and by that
time the heavens opened up. I was netting north
of the tower in a new area to see what kind of
fish I could get. I used Bruce Bennett's boat
and that was my first mistake. It was a
challenge to say the least. I got stuck on the
bottom four times, caught on old tree trunks and
wait until you see the tears in the net from
those! Twice I had to tie off to the cleat and
use the boat to pull me off the bottom.

On the second net, I almost had a heart
attack. As I was pulling up the net I peered over
the boat's edge. It seemed like an octopus or
giant Alaskan king crab was caught in the net
with all its legs stretched out. It turned out to
be the imposing waterlogged stump I was caught
on. I deep-sixed it and carried on. But my net
was getting tangled as I put it in the bucket.

I then tried to get my engine started so I
could put the net back out. I pulled on the cord

repeatedly. I pushed the choke in and then pulled it out. The water was getting deeper in the bottom of the boat from the "monsoon" that had carried over from the weekend. Finally I got the motor started after drifting all the way south along the backside of Loon Island. I went back north and tried to put the difficult net out. The buoy rope drifted toward the back of the boat while I was in reverse, trying to keep the net from pulling a "one-eighty" on me. Sure enough, the motor cut the rope, which started the buoy drifting south in the waves. The rope attached to the net was wrapped around the prop, which stopped the engine. I had to lean over in the pouring rain and unwrap the line from the prop. It was like déjà-vu from the beginning of the summer. However, this time it was cold and I was soaked. Finally, the engine started. I dropped the net out straight without any tangles. You guys just remember that the net has only one buoy up near shore. Ask Billy B. about his tangled net on Monday.

By this time, the rain was coming down in sheets with two more nets to pull. I started to head in because I couldn't see in front of me, but figured I had to get those troubling nets in. Ultimately, I turned back and went to the Gibbs Point area. It took me a while but I finally found the buoy in the choppy waters. The rain was loudly dancing on the surface. I started to pull the net up in the drifting rain. This net was also tangled, but only one twist around. Halfway through, a lightning bolt hit due east of me on my side of Mount Lizzie Island. Man, I prayed to God to not let me die on that one! The crack of thunder almost knocked me out of the boat with the shock waves alone. I looked around me and noticed I was standing in two inches of water. I momentarily jumped up on the front seat and crouched down in case another lightning bolt struck. I pulled that net in as

fast as I could while peeling one salmon after
another out of the mesh. Then I tried to get the
net back out and had the same trouble starting
the engine. I worked at getting the net back in
the water without any twist, which was fun in
the turbulent water.

The third net was the same. The one twist in
it was just enough to hinder the whole process
of getting the net back out smoothly. There were
only three white perch in the whole net. I only
got those three, twelve salmon, three suckers,
and one lake trout out of the three nets. I
decided to bring the last net in. It was raining
so hard I couldn't see.

Finally the motor started, but by then I had
drifted way down past Fyke Net Cove. The thunder
and lightning part of the storm was slowly
moving east but remained just as frightening. I
sped over to Loon Island, dumped my small load,
and headed in by instinct. It was impossible to
see because the rain was hitting my face like
machine gun bullets. I kept thinking it was hail
because it hurt! I scooped all the water out of
the boat so that it wouldn't sink and ran to the
tent.

I called MDC to let them know I was off the
water. Don't forget to call them. I asked them
for a portable radio on Thursday but it doesn't
reach them, because they are on a standby radio.

I missed a plane ride with Wendell Dodge
again. He will call MDC at 8:00 a.m. and tell
them he will meet me at Gate 17 if he is flying.
You guys or I can call every day to find out if
he called. Maybe someday one of us will get up
there. Well, this has taken forty-five minutes
and I should have been helping Mardi. I have a
two-hour ride ahead of me.

Dianne

17

I Can't Make You Love Me

 MY WORLD SUDDENLY TURNED UPSIDE down with a surprise trip home to visit Paul and Becky on September 4. It was a Thursday and I usually came home on Friday afternoon. Paul told me that he wanted a divorce, just like that! No arguments, just me pleading for him to reconsider our love for each other and especially Becky. He finally said that if I didn't leave, he would just walk out on Becky and me and never return. I would have to move because we lived in a house where he worked as a shelter manager for the Massachusetts Society for the Prevention of Cruelty to Animals. I could see the pain in Paul's eyes that came from the longing in his heart for someone else.

Looking back, the song, "I Can't Make You Love Me If You Don't" by Bonnie Raitt summarized my feelings perfectly. I couldn't make Paul love me. I couldn't make his heart feel something it didn't. Eventually I would have to lay down my heart and give up the fight.

When he visited me at Quabbin after Release Day he seemed distant and now I knew why. I was devastated just the same. I learned years later that divorce was the number one stress in life, with death of a loved one number two. At least with death you can mourn a loved one and not see them in love with someone else.

I returned to Quabbin. I had to put food out for the wandering baby eagles and needed time to think of my bleak future. I walked up north through the woods, past the hack tower to my rock ledges where I had known peace, happiness, and solitude. My life was shattered. The air was cold and still. The water lay motionless and quiet. My ears heard nothing and my body was numb. What were Becky and I going to do? Where were we going to go? I hadn't furthered my education beyond high school because I stayed on at the Worcester Science Center and married Paul. What job opportunities would allow me to raise a three-year-old and be home with her at least on the weekends? Should I first find a job or a place to live? Who would take care of Becky while I worked?

How was I going to tell my parents? They were going to be shocked. Paul and I were about the most compatible couple in the whole world. We loved each other and didn't fight, argue, or insult each other like people we knew. Our jobs both dealt with animals. We both worked with endangered species. Paul had worked a whole summer on the red-bellied turtle project in Plymouth, Massachusetts, back in 1980 and I didn't leave him. I thought it was the chance of a lifetime for him to do something he really felt was important.

I began to build an impenetrable wall from that moment on as I looked out over the vast reservoir from the rock ledges. I had to block out my shattered emotions first. Sore eyes from crying and a tired body would just make things worse. I would tell everyone I was just fine and I didn't need any help. I had to learn how to breathe through the lump in my throat and relax enough so that my head wouldn't burst with so many held-back tears. I sat on those smooth colored ledges for quite a while with my arms folded over my knees to keep warm. "I am going to be fine. I can do this," I vowed.

I went back down to the cove and thought briefly of pulling my nasty nets. I stood at the dock for hours looking out over the inlet. I stared through the water and the landscape, not at it. As the chilly breeze picked up, I felt the cold wind whistling in my ears. I glanced up at the swaying trees and rustling leaves. The air was dry and I felt truly alone for the first time. Tears ran down my cold cheeks and my heart was filled with sorrow. My chest hurt and my knotted stomach ached.

At dusk I finally persuaded myself to get out in that darn boat and haul in my nets. I brought a flashlight and held it in my mouth as a source of light after darkness surrounded me. My fingers were frozen and a chill crept through my exhausted body. I had my usual set of problems with the worn nets. Why was God doing this to me? Why wasn't He helping me like He had done in the past? At one point I let go of the lead line. My red hands were too numb. I had been trying to pull the net that was stuck again on the bottom. I stood up straight and looked north up the reservoir in the darkness. I shouted to God with clenched, half-frozen fists, "You can throw anything you want at me but I'm not going to give in and quit! Do you hear me?" I couldn't feel an answer.

By the time I finished, it was pitch dark. As I looked toward my small inlet, the landscape blended into the darkness. I didn't know where the water ended and the land began. I could find Loon Island all right and threw the fish up on the bank. As I pushed offshore, I looked over to where my inlet was supposed to be. It all appeared as one dark area. How could I dock if I couldn't find the inlet? I noticed as I slowly motored that there was a dip in the forest canopy. That must be where the inlet was and I aimed for that. I crept along and eventually made my way to the dock. I tied the old boat to the cleat and walked slowly in the darkness up to the tent with my flashlight lighting the way

I radioed MDC to let them know I was off the water. A very concerned voice responded with, "Where were you?" I apologized and said I had a late start and my nets were a problem. They radioed back to stay put and that a cruiser was coming down to the hack site. They had never done that before. I apologized again and wondered why they had to come down here. I hoped I wasn't in too much trouble.

I had a hard time staying awake. In fact, the rumbling sound of the car making its way down the dirt road woke me up. A silver-haired MDC policeman came out of the cruiser and introduced himself as Officer O'Brien and handed me a pizza with everything on it and a Pepsi. I was tired, cold, and extremely hungry. I accepted it with open arms and a look of bewilderment. The officer said it was from Sergeant Z who had brought some young kids out to see the eagles a few weeks earlier. This was his way of thanking me for my hospitality. I thanked the officer and retreated to my tent and ate by the light and heat of my Coleman lantern. I felt that God was letting me know that everything was going to be all right. I crawled in my sleeping bag piled high with extra blankets, curled up, and fell fast asleep.

The next morning I got down to business and decided I had to keep busy so that my mind wouldn't keep wandering. The waves were monstrous so I decided to hold off going on the turbulent water. I had learned my lesson not to challenge the reservoir in a situation like this. I sat on the tower to get the babies' radio signals. It was an interesting morning.

All the babies noticed three "strangers." Ross from 1982 sailed through, flashing his blue wing marker. A "second-year" bird called Mr. 01 from 1984 stood on Gibbs Shore for a short visit and a gray-headed "third-year" bird sat in the eagle tree out of the wind. Attila, Snoopy, Bert, and Marjorie were soaring together above him, high in the sky. Ernie, Dick, Jane, and Woodstock formed their own little social circle and soared out over the open water. But 91 stayed put in the eagle tree, unimpressed with the strangers.

Day 82

Wednesday, September 11, 1985 - Noon

Dear Mom and Dad,

   Thanks for all your moral support this past
weekend with my bad news and all. I just
finished lo mein with sliced kielbasa in it. I'm
making the habit of eating again high on my list
of priorities. I'm up on the tower sitting down
on the deck outside of the top floor. The wind
is strong and gusty. The sounds of fall are here
in the rustling leaves. It's cold but very
comforting. The waves are from the north and
rival any you have in Lewis Bay down there on
Cape Cod. I got in at 6:30 last night and pulled
and reset my nets well into the dark so that I
don't need to pull them yet. Today I'm hoping
the wind calms down a little because it is quite
treacherous out there. You could surf on these
incredible breakers. The brilliant sky is bright
blue and the sight and sound of the waves are
very uplifting. It makes me glad I'm alive, no
matter what else is troubling me.

   I'm deeply sad now about what's happening in
my life. You said I would go through this, Mom,
and it's upon me. You are both with me right now
in the trees, the sky and earth. I can cry here
alone at Quabbin but still be comforted by you
both. I am just fine and am stronger when my
thoughts are with you. I'm not one bit afraid of
the future. I am looking forward to it.

   I saw one of my birds grab a dead fish from
the water for the first time. It was Marjorie!
She has two middle tail feathers missing so
she's easy to identify. Way to go Marjorie!

12:29 p.m.

   I'm sitting on a stool on the top floor of the
hack tower again. The front door is open and I'm

watching two of my eagles. One is lying down at
Gibbs Shore while the other is playing with a
stick. He is attacking it first with two sets of
talons, then his beak, and then one foot. Now he
is trying to throw the stick over his back. He
dropped it and is getting a drink. The wind
moves the feathers aside showing the white under
feathers. It is the tip of each feather that is
brown to make the bird appear brown.

I appreciate being out here right now because
you can see that this place keeps me occupied in
an incredible way. I'm not running away but just
admiring the natural world. It's enjoyable to see
an eagle just lying in the grass. A third eagle
is soaring in, approaching Loon Island. I need to
put the scope on him and turn on my receiver to
see who it is. I'll sign off for now.

8:34 p.m.

It's very cold out tonight. I'm writing this
in long johns and a sweatshirt with a hood and
vest on. My feet are cold so I keep moving my
toes to stay warm. I've had an all-around
productive day. After I wrote you earlier, I
came off the tower and broke open the fence we
made this spring to keep the suckers up the
brook. They had all escaped before the eagles
came because of heavy rains and water
overflowing the banks. It seems like a lifetime
ago. I rolled up the mesh and put it behind the
shed along with the poles. Then I went up on the
tower again and observed four eagles soaring
leisurely together in formation. Occasionally
one would glide up and then dip down over
another bird with its legs down. The lower bird
would turn upside down to greet him with its
talons. I'm sure they're just playing.

Jack Swedberg came up around 2:30 p.m. with
his dog, Fritz. I confided in him that Paul
wanted a divorce and he was shocked! He knows us
both and couldn't believe it. I said Paul and I

aren't even mad at each other. I told Jack I was absolutely fine but that I could use a job. He's going to call Dick Cronin, the director of Fish and Wildlife tonight. Jack said they just filled a new position at Fish and Wildlife for a spokesman for the Non-Game and Endangered Species program. He'll make some phone calls anyway.

Jack and I talked a long time like we always do and we're going to meet Saturday morning with Roy, his longtime friend, up at the New Salem Restaurant. He said to order the biggest breakfast I could eat since I haven't been eating much lately. I will take him up on it. Then I'll head home.

Jack left with a reminder for me to be careful out here now. I understood what he meant by the fatherly look in his old Swedish eyes. I told him I have too much to look forward to in the future, so not to worry. (My wall was getting stronger.)

Jack left at 4:00 p.m. I watched my birds from the tower for a while and took more notes on their whereabouts. Later I saw two immature eagles heading north, flying toward my boat. I quickly turned on my telemetry and checked all the frequencies. Surprisingly, they weren't mine. One had a yellow wing marker, which meant he was banded and tagged from New York's hacking program. The other bird was a Massachusetts bird from last year because it had a blue marker. That was rather neat!

MDC got a little concerned over me again. The waves were so high this morning that I waited the whole day for the "seas" to die down enough for me to pull my nets. I radioed them at 5:00 p.m. and told them I would be on the water for two-and-a-half hours, pulling nets. Well, one of my new buoys was missing because it had snapped in the waves. I pulled out the fish and had to bring that net to the dock so I could get another bucket to pull the other two nets. That took time.

Then I tried to locate the second net. I knew
I had both buoys up when I set it last night.
Finally I found one. I pulled over thirty white
perch out as darkness was approaching. The seas
were rolling but no white-capped waves. It was
bitter cold with no sun and my hands were bright
red and numb again. All the perch were tangled
in the net and I had trouble again, just like
last night, trying to get them out. My fingers
felt like they were not working and were
painful, like the first week on the project when
my hands were all cut up and sore.

I floated most of the fish in the water,
hoping they would land on Gibbs Shore, and left
the rest on Loon Island. By the time I got in to
shore and finally up to my tent, it was pitch
dark out again. I called MDC and they said that
because I was overdue, they were just about to
send a cruiser to look for me. I apologized and
said I had a ton of fish and my hands were numb
so it took a lot longer.

I was so cold that I zipped up the tent
windows and turned on my Coleman lantern and
stood over it until my hands and face warmed up.
I filleted two white perch and ate them for
dinner. Now I'm full and toasty warm. The stars
are so bright tonight. Two or three flying
squirrels are squeaking away in the trees next
to my tent trailer. I'm so tired and I can't
wait to get under the warm covers tonight.
Tomorrow I have to sit down and mend at least
one of my nets. They are in such disrepair.
There are enormous holes in them. I lost a buoy
on the second net too because of the waves.
Maybe tomorrow, if it's calm, I'll take the NRO
speedboat out and check the shorelines in an
attempt to find them.

4:13 a.m.

Well, I'm writing you to get this done in
journal form. I've been up since the loons woke
me up at 1:30 a.m. You're not going to believe

where I am. I'm camped out up on the eagle tower. I feel like I'm a kid up in a clubhouse. I never did it as a child, but always wanted to. Another dream fulfilled. The moon is a sliver with Venus to the right. It is so beautiful. I looked at it through the scope but it is more impressive just looking at it with the naked eye. The stars are bright, twinkling and beautiful too. I'm on the lower deck with my lantern for a little heat. The air is cold and I'm wiggling my toes. My vest is on and my hood is over my head. I brought up a thermos of hot tea, two couch mattresses, my sleeping bag, the telemetry, and a book Scotty gave me to read. It took me a few trips in the dark, but I've walked the long path so many times I'm familiar with the twists and turns. I'm very comfortable and wide awake.

Actually, I've been awake since the loon wailed and wailed and wailed! I just couldn't sleep. No problems except for thoughts of how Paul is going to do in the long run. I hope these thoughts don't last forever because I can't concentrate on the future if I can't let go of the past. I hope to be awake at first light. I really want to see how early the eagle babies come to feed. I also want to take good notes on their interactions. I guess they are my children too.

I wish Becky were here because she enjoys coming. I remember on one of her visits, while eating her pop tart, she wandered too close to the point near the tent and within seconds disappeared. I ran to the edge and looked over the four-foot embankment. There she was, holding onto the clumps of grasses. I pulled her up and she was still holding onto her pop tart. She smiled and said, "Look at meee!" We both laughed. Now if she were here I would worry because if I had to go in the rough seas like yesterday, Becky would have frozen to death while I pulled my nets. I do love it when she is here though. Well, I'm going to try to get an hour of sleep.

5:42 a.m.

I'm in my sleeping bag. I opened the two doors on the tower. One is facing out front and the other facing east so that I can see the sunrise. The sky is now powder blue with only the brightest stars showing. The moon has risen steadily in the sky with Venus as its companion. The mist has set in and the placid water is soothing.

One eagle is calling from Gibbs Shore area. I'll bet that's Woodstock who is still such a crybaby. A barred owl is hooting as the morning comes to life. The eastern sky is a little pink now. I just got the scope set up in here so I can stay in my sleeping bag and look at the sunrise while propped up against my pillow. If I look sideways to Loon Island I can see when the hungry birds come in to feed.

This is so exciting! The air is cold but I'm comfortable. I'll write my eagle observation notes to you since I didn't bring my notepad with me. I'm writing by flashlight now. I never got any sleep.

5:52 a.m.

A song sparrow is singing. He is the only animal making any noise other than an eagle baby peeping. I just put my sneakers in my sleeping bag to warm them up before I put them on. Time for more tea. Does that hit the spot. I have to laugh. As Jack Swedberg was leaving yesterday I told him that at least I sleep like a log. I should have knocked on wood.

5:55 a.m.

Four ducks just flew over from north of Mount Pomeroy Island. As they approached their

destination I could hear them skid across the
water. The lower atmosphere is gray-white while
the upper sky is blue. The sunrise area is
turning light pink and yellow with a cloud
moving in. I'll bet it will hinder the splendor
of the sunrise. It would be my first one on the
project.

5:59 a.m.

I can just start to read what I'm writing so
the flashlight can be turned off. I can hear a
bee buzzing so they're now getting active. A
loon is "O-looing" and a group of blue jays are
initiating their noisy chatter.

6:05 a.m.

A loon is now yodeling a lot. Something has
him in a tizzy but I don't see eagles flying.
The mist on the water is growing thick.

6:12 a.m.

An eagle went to Loon Island and is screaming
like a baby all the way over, circled twice and
flew back over to Gibbs Shore. I can tell it is
Woodstock by her tail and voice. In the eagle
tree is 91. He stands out like a lantern because
his chest feathers are so light. The plumage of
second-year birds varies a lot. Their heads have
a golden crest and their bodies sometimes
lighten up. Their eyes and beak start changing
slightly from a chocolate brown.

6:15 a.m.

The first red squirrel is chattering away
behind me in the pine trees. The loons "Ooo'd"
again. The sun is still not up yet and 91 is
calling to someone while I'm watching him
through the scope. The sound reaches my ears
long after I see his beak move. One bird is in
the Gibbs Point tree, silhouetted against the
reservoir.

6:23 a.m.

An eagle is flying to Loon Island from the
north and landed on the north point of the
island. He is the first one to actually land
that I could see. He muted (defecated) and gave
two loud chirps. There still is no sun. Now that
eagle flew to the island shore at the southern
end where I put the food out the previous night.

6:27 a.m.

An eagle just flew north from the Loon Island
area. I can see the other eagle still on the
shore so I'll bet this bird going north was the
eagle that the loons were making such a fuss
over. They don't miss a trick, even when I do. I
finally can crawl out of my sleeping bag. Now
the island eagle is eating the fish.

6:34 a.m.

I just noticed there's an eagle in the Loon
Island tree. I'll bet it is Marjorie. The one on
shore looked up and peeped. I am going to
determine their identity with the telemetry.
Ernie is the one on shore and Marjorie is indeed
the one in the tree at the north end of the
island. Now she is flying to the southern tip to
eat. The fog is thickening. Bert is at the Gibbs
Point tree and 91 is still in the eagle tree.

6:43 a.m.

The sun is fading in and out of the low clouds
like a big round globe. Another eagle is coming
from Mount Pomeroy. It is Jane. I have my
headphones on and the signal is getting louder
and then softer as she circles around the
island. She dipped down behind the island and
disappeared in the fog. She landed, judging by
the steady signal pulsing in my headphones.
Marjorie was just sitting on a rock but is now
moving to the right. I love switching to her

frequency because I feel like I'm a part of her
flight and movements. I am watching Ernie and
he's moving, so I switched on his frequency. The
first signal to my ears was a normal volume, and
then the signal blasted as the eagle turned the
tail antenna in my direction and then became
almost undetectable as he landed. Now he's
flying north and the signal is getting weaker
but steady, so I'll bet he rounded the point and
landed in the northern eagle tree beyond the
tower. I can't see him, though.

6:50 a.m.

The sun turned from a dull yellow globe to a
bright light that is too bright to look at. Here
comes Ernie, back from the north. The signal is
really loud now as he passes over Loon Island
heading south to the eagle tree in Gibbs Cove.
He flew in and landed on the same limb as 91. No
interaction.

7:00 a.m.

Snoopy just flew from Gibbs Shore to Loon
Island. His signal was strong-to-weak as he
landed on the east side out of sight. I could
see him coming in for a landing the way he beat
his wings rapidly as he disappeared. While I was
writing this his signal got stronger and I
looked up as he hopped up on a rock within my
sight. He jumped back down and the signal went
weak again so I turned up the volume on the
receiver. He flew a little and my ears got
blasted through the headphones. It shows that a
bird could have a weak signal by being on the
ground but be right in front of you. The
kingfisher searching for breakfast just caught
my attention at the water's edge. His blue head
crest is quite prominent as he studies the
water. I wish the fog would lift because I can't
see the shores on Loon Island.

7:09 a.m.

I don't believe it! I've been watching all
this time and didn't notice that there are five
eagles together under the cover of mist that has
been forming on Loon Island. One moved closer to
another and I could see through the scope that
wings were flapping and mouths were moving. I
can see four birds in one location because of
their movements. Ernie, Marjorie, Snoopy and
Bert are all eating. I can see their heads when
they pop them above the ground fog to look
around before they dip back into the fog to eat.
Three are eating side-by-side while one is
apart. One bird walked over to where the fourth
bird was drinking water along the shore. He
started drinking too and there was no
interaction. It is wonderful to see them free!

7:20 a.m.

Another bird appeared out of the fog. Now
there are five grouped to the right and one to
the left. Great, the lone one to the left is
Dick. Now all I need to see are Attila and
Woodstock and it is only 7:22 a.m. The crisp sky
is clear except for the low clouds. The fog is
hovering over the water like a thick blanket. One
lone bird just flew over to Fish Head Point. It
is Ernie. I have never seen a bird over there
except for the day we released the birds when
Woodstock crash-landed. The crow family is with
him, foraging. Ernie is now playing with a stick.
He is attacking it and then leaving it alone. Now
he is flying back to Loon Island and his signal
is very strong. No vocals. Twenty mallards just
flew south from Loon Island. None of the eagles
paid them any attention. The ducks don't seem too
concerned about the eagles either.

7:38 a.m.

I heard eagles calling, looked up, and one
bird was heading south from north of the tower.

She went to Gibbs Point. I put my receiver
channel on Attila and the signal is coming in
loud and clear from her direction. She still
likes to sleep north of the tower in the
northern eagle tree. I tend to pick up her
signal late in the day after the eagles go to
roost for the night in that direction. She
kicked another "noisy" bird out of the tree and
of course that bird was Woodstock. Dick is on
Gibbs Shore again. Attila flew down to the shore
to grab a dead fish and Dick fought a little
over the same fish. Attila took off to the right
and around the point with the fish in her
talons. They're learning.

7:53 a.m.

One bird flew from Loon Island to the southern
eagle tree. They flew incredibly! Everyone's
signal now is loud and clear. It figures because
the fog just cleared and the eagles are all done
with their breakfast. As it stands, four birds
are hanging out on the Loon Island shore while
one is in the Loon Island's only pine tree. Two
are in the Gibbs Point tree and one is in the
eagle tree but 91 is missing somewhere. He is
easy to recognize so if I see him and don't have
the telemetry with me I can still tell that it
is him.

8:05 a.m.

Well, I'm going to drive up to a pay phone
and call MDC to see if I can fly with Wendell
today. When I stepped down on the ladder I
spooked two eagles out of the pine tree on Loon
Island. One started to fly toward me and then
turned north. I'm glad they're wary of me. There
is a mother doe and two fawns drinking at Gibbs
Brook so I paused for a little, just to watch
while leaning my body against the ladder.

9:00 a.m.

I called MDC; no plane ride today. I'm sitting
on the shed doorstep. It is going to be my
salvation. I washed my dirty dishes from last
night and my hands are frozen, and my feet too.
Sitting here in the sun warms me right up. I
fixed myself some eggs and fish for breakfast.
"Delisheus!" Boy it's a shame I can't spell. I
know that word is spelled wrong but I can't
figure out how to spell it right. It gets me mad.

The only thing on the agenda today is to fix
my nets. All my birds were visuals, meaning not
only did I get their signals but I also saw
them. I'll pull my nets early today. What a
beautiful day! I feel I should be home with
Becky, though. I miss her terribly.

5:07 p.m.

Jack and a camera crew were here filming Jack
for a television program. The group was out of
Washington, D.C. Jack is going to mail this
letter, so I'll sign off.

I love you. Take care.

Dianne

18

Finding A New Beginning

 I SPENT THAT FALL AT QUABBIN PULLING nets and leaving food along the shore. The loons were getting their winter hues of grays and whites, replacing their summer speckled black and white attire. They congregated in close flocks and were ready for migration with no border disputes.

In my spare time I took a few trips down to the Cape with Becky to find a job and be with my family. A falconer friend had told me of a job training dolphins at the Zoo Aquarium in West Yarmouth. By the time I talked to them the position was already filled.

Budgeting

My conscientious father sat me down and wrote out a detailed budget that he had revised from his own budget when he retired. He had his house paid off, so my budget had to include a larger chunk for rent. Believe it or not, I had never written a check before. My father did a great job of explaining how to budget for car insurance, car maintenance, telephone, electricity, food, clothing, rent, and daycare. There were many more miscellaneous costs that would creep in too. He used his calculator like a pro and worked his magical figures with his #2 pencil. He calculated that

I would have to earn $8.00 an hour to be able to support myself and Becky. I was shocked. Where was I going to find a job like that with a high school education?

I stared straight ahead for I could not show that I was scared. My wonderful parents had offered me the opportunity to go to Colorado State University in the fall of 1972, but I had declined. I assumed I would be married and at the Worcester Science Center forever with polar bears, mountain lions, and Paul.

Job Search

My mother said this was the time to stand up for myself and call some people in the environmental field. I made a call to an environmental police officer I knew through falconry. He said he was stopping by the Tufts Wildlife Clinic in Grafton, Massachusetts, and would ask Dr. Sedgwick if there were any job opportunities at the new veterinary school. He called me back that same day and said they were looking for a part-time wildlife technician. I couldn't believe my ears.

I called Tufts and set up an interview. I thanked my mother for her advice and left with my father's budget. Tufts would hire me part-time mornings starting November 1, at $7.10 an hour, which was great, but it was not enough. I had to find another part-time job that made up the difference. In the employment section of the Worcester Sunday newspaper was an ad for a job that paid $9.00 an hour.

"This is it!" I shouted.

"Where?" My father asked.

"UPS, unloading tractor trailer trucks," I answered.

I was in great shape from pulling those darn fish nets. I could do it! My father was a little skeptical, but I drove to Shrewsbury and filled out an application and was hired on the spot. My UPS supervisor told me a month into the job that I was one of their better "unloaders." (As a woman, I felt I had to prove I could do it.)

Now that I had jobs within five minutes of each other, I found an apartment in the town of Grafton, right in between the two. It had a large yard and plenty of room in a nice quiet neighborhood. Becky had her own bedroom and an immense pine tree in the back that beckoned her to climb. My landlords were wonderful. Their names were Dick and Jane, just like my parents (and my eagles)! Life was working out okay.

Since I was to live in Grafton, I went to visit Mr. and Mrs. Elvidge, whose farm I worked on as a teenager. They still lived on their farm on top of a hill in that town. Wesley had retired from the dairy farm business but still grew lots of vegetables. Eleanor was just as sweet as ever. They were so happy to see me, and we caught up on the past fifteen years. I joined their church so that I could keep in touch with them at least once a week.

A Letter From My Father

September 11, 1985

Dear Dianne,

I'll probably talk to you before you get this letter, but I want to put this in writing so you can refer to it as things develop.

Bob Hoaglund, who is our attorney and lives in Shrewsbury and practices law in Worcester, is a friend of mine since grammar school. He suggested an attorney up in your area who handles divorce cases. Since this is a "friendly" divorce, you might be able to have one lawyer represent you both in a "no fault" divorce. Inform him that there is not much to divide except furniture. If the lawyer you choose can't help you, Bob will handle it.

As I told you last weekend, you are going to need close to $18,000 to $20,000 per year to survive. You are going to need a job, pay daycare fees for Becky, health and car insurance, clothes, food, etc. It's not cheap to live these days and where you and Paul lived in a house at the MSPCA shelter, you didn't have to pay for rent, electricity, or phone bills. You're kind of out of touch on what those cost. It's not going to be easy and I guess you know that. You must have an idea of how much money you can reasonably expect to have so you can plan for the future sensibly and fairly realistically.

You know that we and your brother and sisters are all behind you and we'll do anything necessary to help. Our homes and pocketbooks are open to you any time you need them. Put your pride in your pocket and accept help from us when we offer it. You're going to need help and we're going to offer it, so don't be stubborn.

As we said before, we are all behind you; no one thinks you are a failure or anything like that. We love you and will do all we can to make it easy for you and Becky in the future.

You've got guts; you've proved that on the Eagle Project. We are proud of you and I know you will come out of this strong and a better person for it.

Our love always,

Dad

Day 84

Friday, September 13, 1985 - 7:25 p.m.

Dear William D., William B., and Jack S.,

Just letting you know everything is okay. I'm sitting here in the trailer eating. I came down to the site this morning and was able to get all my birds from the tower identified. It's easy if you're there from 6:30 to 8:00 a.m. They all come in to feed then and if you don't see them flying, they're usually on Loon Island or in the Gibbs Cove vicinity. By 8:00 a.m. sharp the last bird leaves the immediate area.

They all come back in the afternoon at various times. Once one bird shows up on Loon Island at the big rocks, all the others fly over within half an hour. Five birds ate hungrily at 3:00 p.m.

I sat and leaned against the shed door today but not as long as in the past few days. I worked near the dock yesterday for three hours and today for four hours straight, repairing my worst net. Now I know where the phrase "back-breaking work" comes from. I only mended about eight to nine feet in from the small end. I couldn't believe the holes. A great white shark could fit through them and not get caught.

If you don't see the net anywhere, that means I have it. I might take the net and bucket down to the Cape with me this weekend when I go to visit my parents. I have to keep Scotty busy when I visit him. It doesn't have any buoys on it anyway. Both were lost "at sea." I combined two buoys from two nets to one net.

I just want to tell you all that I have had one of the best summers of my life. Your friendship and companionship came at a time in when it means the difference between much sorrow and hope for the future. I found a special bond with my daughter and see her as a neat little person to cherish and grow with. I pray to the good Lord that my friendship with you three lasts forever.

I love you all very much,

                    Eagle One

Hurricane Gloria

My baby eagles were becoming increasingly independent at Quabbin. Eaglet Snoopy had disappeared by September 15. I searched everywhere, including drives around Quabbin with the telemetry, but with no success.

In September, Hurricane Gloria was heading up the east coast. Predictions showed it would continue along the Cape and the islands. I wasn't too worried. I radioed MDC for my morning check and they had a message for me to call home. I drove up to the astronomy site to use the phone and asked what was up. The new storm track for Gloria had it moving through the middle of the state where I was. Paul wanted me to get out of there. He said he still cared about my welfare, even though we were getting a divorce. I told him I'd head home after I pulled my nets and secured the campsite.

I knew I couldn't do much alone, so I thought I'd start with the hack tower. I could at least pull the opened doors closed so they wouldn't tear off in the high winds. I had left them open after the birds flew away just in case they wanted to visit their "surrogate home." I climbed the ladder to the vacant tower and walked in through the bottom door to the observation cubbyhole. I pushed a blanket over to the side so I could climb up the ladder to the top floor. I still enjoyed getting up early and wrapping up to keep warm while I watched for the birds to fly over to Loon Island for their breakfast.

I walked out through the side door to the left cage where Ernie and Bert had lived. I missed seeing them up close, but I enjoyed seeing them fly to Loon Island for a snack twice a day now that they were free. As I walked to the front of the cage I looked thirty feet down to the rocks and bushes below. It was a good thing the eagles flew fine because it was a long drop.

I heard a helicopter off in the distance and looked over toward Mount Pomeroy Island. I had never seen a chopper while on the project so I thought it was strange to see one low over the water. It was painted in army colors. I continued with my mission and carefully inched my way along the front catwalk in front of Marjorie and Attila's cage and grabbed hold of the right front barred door, pulled it closed, and secured the ropes to a cleat. There was a little debris under the door from the nest, but it was easy to close. Then I came back through Ernie's cage and closed the door behind me and fastened the rope. I climbed down the inside ladder again and unlatched the left blind door and walked out into Dick and Jane's old home. All the old fish remains were dried up but the cage still smelled of fish and eagle.

An Attack

I carefully walked out on the catwalk and looked to the left at the helicopter that seemed to be facing my way and hovering. I guess they were wondering what this immense tower was. I didn't know if they could see me or not. My attention turned to the narrow ledge and the door in front of Snoopy and Woodstock's cage. I pulled on the door but it didn't budge. There must have been a lot of debris that collected under the door. I decided to give it a gigantic tug while being careful of my footing. As I yanked the door a loud noise filled the air around me: bees!

They attacked with such fury that I must have been the cause of their rage. My waving hands and arms immediately went up to my head for protection and, for a split second, I almost ran in to Woodstock and Snoopy's cage to reach the observation room. That would have been a terrible mistake because I would have run to a door that was latched from the inside! The bees were swarming and stinging me from all sides; I would have been trapped in the corner and bombarded. Instead, I ran along the catwalk back through the other cage, jumped through the open door to the cubbyhole, and slammed it shut.

The noise was terrifying; the bees were everywhere. I dove under the blanket, screaming the whole time. The bees that were attached to my clothes were now under the blanket with me. The muffled noise drove me to hysteria. I was wiggling back and forth, hitting the blanket, trying to dislodge the bees until the noise finally stopped. My arms and back were sore as I killed the last bee against my body. They lay curled up on the dark floor around me. With the light coming in under the door I saw that they weren't bees but bald-faced hornets! Their black bodies with white stripes on their abdomens looked intimidating.

I peered out the front tinted window and saw hornet patrols zipping back and forth. I had to get out of there. There was no helicopter in sight. They must have thought I was a lunatic as I ran along the front landing waving my arms. Good thing they didn't hear me screaming. I wondered if they would have landed somewhere if they saw me fall off the tower.

I slowly opened the back door and carefully peeked out. Hornets were zooming by in a frenzy. I slammed the door tight and tried not to panic. Hurricane Gloria was on its way and I'm trapped up on the eagle tower, hostage to a horde of angry insects. I didn't know where they came from. I had been living and walking near the tower since the birds left. Where were these guys living? I waited for what seemed like forever and decided to make a break for it. I wished the tent were close so I could run to it for safety. I opened the door again, tiptoed to the ladder, and as the hornets flew by, I slid down it. I ran up the path as fast as my legs could carry me until I collapsed where the tent used to be. I remember breathing hard and feeling sore from the hornet stings. I never wanted to go near that tower again. My nerves were shot and I still had to pull my nets and do something with the boats and my tent.

As I walked down the path to the tent I heard a vehicle rumbling down the road. Bill Davis stepped out of the Fish and Wildlife truck. "What are you doing here?" I asked in a frazzled voice.

"I came to make sure you were leaving," he said. "The storm has changed course and you need to get home. We'll pull the boats out with the truck winch and drop the tent and secure it. What happened to you?"

"I got stung by hornets when I was up on the tower," I said. "I tried to close the doors and I was swarmed by them."

"Didn't you notice the gigantic hornets' nest attached to the underside of the tower?" Billy asked.

"Obviously NOT!" I replied.

We walked up and observed the basketball-sized hornets' nest with binoculars from a distance. It was attached to the tower at the front bars of Snoopy and Woodstock's cage. I had torn the nest totally apart when I ripped the door free with full force. No wonder they were angry. I had welts on my arms and back. I'm glad it was cool and I was wearing heavy dungarees. I protected my hands and face when I flung my arms and legs about like a madwoman. I drove home very sore.

Hurricane Gloria came and went and Jack, the two Billys, and I met and observed the damage the next day. Only a few trees had to be chain-sawed out of the dirt road and not much damage appeared at the hack site. We put the boat back in the water and found all the birds. Hurricane Gloria didn't pack that powerful a punch.

By October all but Snoopy were still showing up to take advantage of the free meals. Ernie's and 91's signals were later lost on October 25.

Leaving Quabbin For Civilization

I left Quabbin shortly after that day. I sadly turned in my key to the wilderness, handing it back to Fish and Wildlife. I started work at the Tufts Wildlife Clinic the following week. This time I was scared to be alone, because now I was back in civilization.

Through the unofficial divorce agreement, Becky and I got to keep the indigo snake, Tabitha the tarantula, and of course Habiba. Paul kept the twelve-foot boa constrictor and the two venomous snakes.

Scotty kept Habiba on the Cape while I got comfortable with my jobs. I eventually asked Tufts if I could keep Habiba there in the back of the clinic away from the other birds. They agreed and I enjoyed having her there. I put her out on her outside perch every day and flew her before I went to work during the winter months. We had been together eight years.

Accepting Help

I became quite ill that autumn, soon after I started at both Tufts and UPS. I made repeated trips to my health care clinic with an upper respiratory condition that I couldn't shake. I was losing weight and looked pale and tired.

After my third visit to the clinic I passed a doctor who had treated me earlier. She stopped me and asked why I was back so soon after she had prescribed antibiotics for my illness. I told her that I was not getting better, but worse. My gums were bleeding and so swollen that I couldn't close my mouth because of the pain. I also had painful sores on my lower lip. My chest ached from all the uncontrollable coughing. I was physically and emotionally desperate for help in healing my body.

She brought me in the back room and noticed all the bruises on my arms when I took off my jacket. I think she thought someone was beating me. My thighs were even worse. I explained that the ugly bruises were from unloading tractor trailer trucks and having the boxes come down on me. She asked if I took aspirin and I said yes; I took them before my UPS shift. That explained the horrible looking bruises. Aspirin was making my platelets brittle and my skin was easily bruised. She told me to switch to Tylenol. Great, one problem solved. I pulled my pant legs up to show her a deep reddish purple rash from my ankles up to my knees. "Why wasn't I getting better with prescription drugs?" I asked.

After looking at my swollen gums she finally asked me if there had been any sudden changes in my life. I blinked hard

HABIBA,
SCOTTY
AND FRED

AFTER HURRICANE GLORIA LEFT TO RIGHT:
BILLY BYRNE, BILLY DAVIS, DIANNE, JACK SWEDBERG

and took a deep breath. I reluctantly listed: my divorce, moving, two jobs, raising my daughter alone and the anxiety of sending her to daycare.

The doctor asked how I was handling my situation. I responded quickly that I was managing fine. She turned to me and said, "No, you are not fine. Your body is trying to tell you that! You need to take some time off and concentrate on healing."

"I can't!" I replied. "I just started both jobs a short time ago."

She told me the only way I was going to get better was to take a week off from both jobs. Did I have anyone who could take care of my daughter and me? I couldn't believe this was happening. I didn't plan for this kind of setback. I promised the doctor I would try and take care of myself and went home.

I swallowed my pride and called my parents. They were there by the end of the day. I did indeed stay home in bed and let my tired body heal. My bruises didn't look so bad with the change in pain reliever; my gums stopped bleeding and I was able to chew again. My horrible cough diminished.

My job at UPS ended soon after the Christmas season and I practically begged a restaurant near my apartment to give me an afternoon job as a dishwasher. I was a hard-working employee and began eating sensible meals on my break time. I still had ironclad muscles from UPS and pulling those gill nets all last summer, which already seemed like a lifetime ago. I was on the mend.

19

Two Billys And A Blind

Billy Davis

 BILLY DAVIS STARTED COURTING ME IN the late fall of 1985 after my stint at the hack tower. It seemed strange after being married for twelve years. My ex-husband was happy that we were dating because it took the pressure off of him for leaving me. And I was even happier for me; Becky and I were both getting to really know and appreciate Billy.

Billy became the hack site attendant for the next three summers, since I had to work at Tufts and the restaurant full-time to support myself and Becky. When Jack Swedberg retired in 1988, Billy became coordinator of the Bald Eagle Project. We dated for six years, and our love for each other grew. Billy was a "knight in shining armor," noble, honest and full of integrity. He always called me his "ravishing creature." He and I and Becky went fishing, hiking and canoeing together.

Visiting Quabbin

I was able to observe my baby eagles a few times through the winter months by sitting in a blind built by the two Billys. They dug it into the shoreline at Gibbs Cove at Quabbin. Attila, Snoopy, Jane, Marjorie, Bert, and crybaby Woodstock frequented the winter feeding station during December. I went with the two Billys one Saturday morning while Becky stayed with her dad.

We had to be on the road by 3:30 in the morning to get in the blind before first light. It was strange to be able to open the gate to Quabbin like old times. The air was nippy, though, and stung my cheeks as I volunteered to man the gate. The lock was cold as I opened it by the high beams of the headlights. The ride down the frozen road was dark and still and the fields that I could see seemed void of life. No splash of blue from a bluebird or the sight of a snapping turtle along the side of the road, just cold air and snow. The brilliant moon cast eerie shadows through the red pines.

A solitary deer ran across the road ahead of us and seemed to be moving in slow motion in the powdery snow. It disappeared like a ghost into the darkness. Footprints zigzagged across the road and through the woods, evidence of the over-abundant deer population. The only sound came from the car's heater as Billy D. blasted it for my very appreciative hands and feet. I hate the cold!

We arrived at the hack site before 5:00 a.m. It was so cold our boots grunted on the hard snow. We walked over to a fenced-in area where road-killed deer were

WINTERING DEER AT QUABBIN   stored so that the

coyotes couldn't snack on them. While the two Billys loaded the deer carcass on a wooden sled, I was already adding layers of warm clothing to my freezing body. I carried a pack that had my camera, binoculars, more clothing, food, and two spotting scopes.

Billy D. hauled the toboggan with a rope strapped around his chest. Billy B. brought up the rear with his backpack of multiple cameras and a powerful telescope that could read the small federal bands on the eagles' legs.

We had to make our way down in the moonlight. The ice formed after the snow so it was like glass. I was a little concerned because the ice in the cove didn't seem that thick. We moved out of the inlet and tackled the frozen reservoir from there. The ice moaned and groaned as we made our way across the smooth, slick surface. Billy D. warned me to stay well behind him in case the ice broke. That was not a comforting thought.

"If it's safe for my bulky weight, it should be safe for you and Bill," he said. He dragged a long line behind him just in case. I guess I saw the logic, but wondered if Billy Byrne and I could pull him to safety. We moved on with Billy B. dragging another deer carcass behind us.

"What are you doing?" I asked.

"I'm covering our trail in case coyotes come through and pick up our scent. The deer carcass will mask our tracks." Those two Billys were full of tricks.

The sky was still dark and clear with bright stars. As sunrise progressed, the light gray-blue of the sky and the snow made beautiful silhouettes of the hills and my companions. My nose and teeth were cold as ice as we neared our final destination. At one point a loud "crack" reverberated across the bay and stopped us all dead in our tracks. We turned to each other and with nervous smiles picked up the pace to get to Gibbs Shore.

We got off the ice using the same caution as we did getting on a quarter of a mile back. By moonlight, Billy B. was checking on a worked-over deer carcass that he had put out a few days ago. The efficient eagles had cleaned most of it up. Billy D. put out fresh meat and also some frozen fish he had on the lengthy toboggan. He threw the fish way out on the ice for birds that would be too timid to come close to shore. Then he sliced open the deer hide so that the birds could more easily break into the red frozen meat.

Once on land, Billy B. spread birdseed around so that the opportunistic blue jays would come in; the movement of wings should attract cagey ravens that would, in turn, attract the hungry eagles. What a system. I just stood there getting colder as I looked for something to do. I leaned on one leg and then the other, trying to wiggle my toes to keep them from freezing.

Billy D. finally opened the blind and started the propane burner so we would be comfortable. I was instructed to draw up the front tarp and take out the tin cans we used as fake camera lenses so that we could replace them with cameras and scopes. We hoped the eagles that frequented the bait station would not notice the switch.

Once we all had our chores done it was time to head off in three different directions in the dark to use the natural facilities. It is not that easy when you're bundled up and have to expose any delicate skin to the cold. I had made sure I didn't have anything to drink beforehand and was thinking twice about having some of my thermos of hot chocolate. We were going to be "roomies" from first light until after dark so that the eagles would not know we were spying on their private lives.

The blind was quite cozy; it was about eight-by-six-feet with very low four-foot ceilings. We had to crouch as we squeezed our way through the miniature door. A shelf spread across the front to support the scopes and cameras. The camouflage curtain had slits for the front of the equipment to slide through; we used safety pins to secure the material tightly around the lenses. We sat on the edge of a foam cushion with our cold feet next to the heater. I, of course, was in the middle away from the cold sides. The biting wind picked up a little and unfortunately came straight through the front peepholes.

Behind us in the blind was a tattered mattress that we would take turns napping on as the long day progressed. For now, since there was no real action outside, Billy B. decided it was time for me to meet "Zippy." A little crunching of a potato chip bag summoned Zippy, the red-backed vole, who zipped back and forth across the edge of the mattress. I couldn't believe that two grown men had a mouse companion that was busy making holes in the foam mattress.

Billy B. told me to peek out the front curtain and look at the deer carcass as dawn approached. I watched in amazement as a great horned owl was tearing at the meat. I finally met my summer neighbor who hooted his low bellowing notes long into the night from Gibbs Cove. He had good hearing and slipped into the darkness as we set our scopes up through the slits in the camouflage curtain. By now it was 6:00 a.m. and the sun would be coming up within the hour. Billy B. taught me how to take a long-exposure photograph of first light at Quabbin. The pictures later came out beautifully with soft shades of pink and blue.

The chatty blue jays started calling and were followed shortly by the neighborhood crows. The ravens appeared out at Loon Island to our right. They quietly flew over to our cove and lightly touched down at 7:00 a.m. The roar of the propane burner silenced their approach. Even with food aplenty, they bickered and fought each other over a tidbit too small for Zippy. One by one, the ravens hopped, skipped and jumped with a nervous flutter over to the deer carcass while making unusual guttural noises. It was hard for them to break into the frozen meat.

The ravens were so much bigger than the crows. Their black beaks were large and their tails were wedge-shaped instead of straight across. They wandered just to the right of us. I watched them with curiosity because I hadn't seen or heard their raspy call at all during the summer while living here. The two Billys had banded some homely chicks on the east side of Mount Lizzie last spring and we were excited to see that a couple of these birds sported a shiny federal band on their legs. They had their pecking order too. I watched as three ravens ganged up on the fourth with a lot of hollering. The "peck-ee" was on his back and one bird had him by the foot with its vice-like beak.

As we peered through the peep holes we heard the reservoir ice groaning and occasionally cracking as dawn approached. An eagle sounded a distinctive cry similar to a child's squeaky toy, followed by its mimicking of a herring gull's call. The bird must have flown up in the leafless oak tree behind the blind because we could hear his strong wing beat. That tree was the "eagle tree" my birds sat in last summer.

The first sighting of a bald eagle was at 7:30 a.m. With a slow deliberate wing beat, the large bird made its way across the ice-covered reservoir on a direct path to the tantalizing food. Four ravens scattered at his approach. A few quick wing beats brought him slowly to the ice where he straightened his posture with a

RASCAL RAVEN AND IMMATURE EAGLE

roust (shake) of his feathers. He positioned his body to gather up the warm rays of sun that fell as a blanket across his feathers. The heat rose in ripples off the cold snow around him. His immature plumage showed a beautiful design; the front was white, save for a brown necklace and distinctive white eyebrows that added to his already intense look.

The eagle walked over to the food and began tearing into the frozen meat. Because it was solid he worked hard at getting small pieces. A cautious raven approached him with its head down. The eagle anticipated the tactical approach by lowering his head and turning to confront him. The raven kept nonchalantly moving to his backside. Another shadowy figure joined in.

The ravens decided to work as a team and each took a side. As they approached the eagle they bounced around on the snow as if they were on a trampoline. The feathers on top of their heads stood up and they seemed light as they floated in the air longer than gravity should have allowed them. One challenged the eagle from the left. While making head movements he ran in and pulled at the eagle's tail feather. The annoyed bird lunged to the left and the crafty raven to the right snuck in sideways and stole a few

ABOVE: BALD EAGLE ATTACKING
BELOW: ADULT AND IMMATURE EAGLE DISPUTE

pieces that the eagle had worked free. The raven didn't swallow the meat but positioned it with his tongue to the back of his beak and held it there. Now it was his turn to distract the eagle from the right so that the raven to the left could hop in and sneak a tidbit of food. The eagle was aware of their game and tried to keep his tail out of their reach. As one drew closer, the eagle finally decided to stop the game by jumping over to a large rock, and relinquishing ownership of the carcass to the ravens. The eagle resumed his sunbathing but stayed on the alert with constant head movements, taking notice of any small changes near him.

With a few victorious bows, cackles and chatter, the ravens turned, jumped down, and left in glory after their fill of tidbits. They juggled the food in their mouths and then took flight. The hungry eagle tried again to snack but the remaining two ravens played their own cat and mouse game. Back and forth, the torture went on, until finally the eagle took to the air and moved out of sight up over the trees.

More eagles showed up as the early morning wore on. They flew to a tree behind us, watched for a while, and then made their entrance dramatically. The next eagle landed on the largest piece of meat. He stepped up on it and worked into the meat while standing very erect and looking around. Next he arched his neck to display his headdress of feathers and then dipped down and tore off a piece of meat, using his sharp beak and strong neck muscles. He finished, stood erect again, and then looked around.

All of a sudden the feeding eagle opened his wings and crouched down a little to prepare his talons for a strike. Another bald eagle was coming in directly at him. Giving a warning cry, the bird on the ground leaped up to meet the aerial bird's attack. Whoever won the challenge got the best spot at breakfast time. The loser moved over to a less appealing meal. This went on all morning. Some would choose a distant piece of fish and watch the fights elsewhere, but others liked the challenge. It got quite noisy with birds screaming from the trees and others waiting on the ground for the anticipated battles. I guess those who brawled would make out well if there were a shortage of food, for they were well skilled in warfare.

At one point, all the birds on the ground took off, including the ravens. I whispered to Billy D, "Why did they do that?" He said to look to the left. Three cautious coyotes moved in slow and easy. They sniffed the ground as they walked. One was a beautiful sleek female with high legs and an orange coat. The second was a wolf-colored male with a dense fur coat of grays and blacks. The third one was extremely disheveled with hardly any fur on its hindquarters and a stick for a tail, a result of his affliction, sarcoptic mange.

"That's Mangy Mike," Bill said. "He's been hanging around with the other two." I was surprised that they didn't also have mange. It's caused by a burrowing mite that gets under the skin resulting in fur loss and was common in coyotes sighted at the Quabbin.

While the orange-furred coyote and Mangy Mike were timidly tearing at the deer meat, the third canine was playing a game of "catch me if you can" with a raven. The coyote would nonchalantly meander toward the bird with what looked like little or no interest. The raven did the same, moving sideways as if there was no danger at all. He hopped, bounced, and made amusing little guttural noises. As they inched their way toward each other the coyote suddenly lunged at the quick-reacting raven. Miss! The coyote resumed his pretended indifference as the raven fluttered just far enough away to escape the canine's jaws, and the match continued.

This harmless game was important to rehearse for both the coyote and the raven. Their practiced tactics helped them survive when food was scarce. Meanwhile Mangy Mike wandered out a ways on the ice. He was walking along at a guarded pace when he abruptly stopped as if he hit a wall. He turned and ran off like a shot back up in the woods with his stick-like tail between his legs.

"Now what happened?" I asked the two biologists.

ORANGE COYOTE
AND MANGY MIKE

COYOTE CHASING
EAGLE WITH
FISHER
CARCASS

"He must have caught our scent from when we crossed the ice early in the morning," was their reply.

The wolf-colored coyote was now chasing an adult eagle with food in his talons over the ice. The canine soon gave up the chase.

While all this was going on we took turns sleeping on the worn mattress. While Billy B. was napping the watchful eagles took off again. Now what? Did the coyotes come back?

"No!" whispered Billy D. "Look straight ahead at that bird coming directly at us." As he landed, any remaining birds scattered. "Do you recognize what kind of a bird that is?" Billy asked.

It looked somewhat like an immature bald eagle to me, but the beak was too small and the feathers on the legs came all the way down to the toes.

"A golden eagle!" I exclaimed, as I swung my scope around to view him better.

"Shhhhhh! He'll hear you and don't move your scope too fast or he'll detect the movement and take off," Billy cautioned.

The "golden" walked over to the main carcass and stepped up on it with authority. He ate his fill, uncontested for a few short minutes, and then was challenged by a first-year bald eagle. He contentedly moved over to a stump and watched the underling eat in his presence. The immature bird turned out to be Jane, as we were able to read her leg band. Dick, Bert, and 91 also showed up for the free meal. It was good to see them all fending for themselves among the older birds. Ross, an original bird from 1982, was there as a sub-adult now with a dark tail, nearly white head, yellow bill, dirty crown and dark eyes. There was a bird from New York's reintroduction project that sported a federal band on his right leg and #X14 on his left leg. The state of Maine also bands young in the nest, and there was a young bird with a federal band on the right leg and a red band on the left leg. These sightings help confirm that Quabbin is an important eagle wintering site on a regional scale.

The birds took flight one by one during the long afternoon, leaving for their nighttime roost. Finally, with all the eagles gone, we slowly and stiffly made our way out of the hidden blind. It was dark now as we crossed the ice again. Time seemed to have no meaning because we had come in the dark and exited in the dark. The stars were shining and on the far shore we could see the shadow of the abandoned hack tower. It sure looked desolate out here in the wintertime. There were no warblers, loons, or insects for background music, just the eerie sound of the ice cracking and groaning.

BALD AND GOLDEN EAGLE

20

Turning Point

 AFTER THE WILDLIFE CLINIC COORDINATOR at Tufts University had left, I was given a lot more responsibility in teaching the fourth-year vet students. I had also been given a token raise. I was thankful, but eventually asked why I received such a small stipend for the added responsibility.

"Unfortunately, you don't have a college degree," replied the uncomfortable assistant dean. Well, there it was. My lack of a college degree finally caught up to me. How could I ever achieve the goal of graduating from college with two jobs, a child that depended on me, and limited finances?

I flew Habiba in the winter months and became more acquainted with other falconers in the state. Because of my past work with reptiles at the Worcester Science Center, I got to know an older hawker named Ed Phillips. He had tagged sea turtles in Florida every summer for the past twenty years during his vacation from teaching industrial arts near Springfield, Massachusetts.

Every year he took some of his high school students along to share the wonderful experience. He had told me in the past that I would be welcome any time. I finally took him up on his invitation, and went to Florida for ten days while Becky visited her father. That turned out to be another turning point in my life. Ed met me at the airport and we joined a small, energetic group of high school students who had arrived the previous week. They called Ed the Turtle Man.

Even though Ed and I had flown our hawks at falconry meets together, I didn't know at the time that we shared similar situations in our personal lives. We both found ourselves working two jobs and raising a family alone. With eighteen years as a single parent he understood the lack of confidence and insecurity I was feeling. He would sense when I was down and say cheerfully, "You can do it kid! You'll see!" He had unknowingly invited me on an adventure that helped me regain my confidence and think about my future with hope. We had long talks about our lives, and what was important to us, as we walked the beach each day. At night we tagged sea turtles and talked with people who were interested in what we were doing.

Our nightly routine consisted of tagging loggerhead sea turtles from the moment the sun set until just before it reappeared over the Atlantic Ocean. Those giant, passive creatures only emerged

LOGGERHEAD COMING ASHORE

ABOVE: DIANNE TAGGING LOGGERHEAD
BELOW: MEASURING LOGGERHEAD

from the sea after dark. We tagged a front flipper with a minimal amount of disturbance to the turtle. The best times to tag and take measurements were when she was actually laying her eggs. She seemed to be in a hypnotic trance and little bothered her.

We worked in teams of two, riding on an ATV, the roar of the engine mixing with the sounds of the waves crashing against the shoreline. One person watched for turtles or their tracks and one would be ready to tag.

Sometimes we were lucky to come across a turtle appearing as a giant shadowy mound at the surf's edge. We would shut off our red lights and motor and watch in silence. Any unusual light or vibration would make her turn around and head back into the ocean. With only the light of the stars we witnessed the miracle of a three hundred-pound sea turtle emerging from the surf. She would pause, appear to sniff the sand, and slowly crawl out of the ocean dragging her great bulk. She was guided by an ancient instinct to bury over a hundred eggs the size of ping pong balls on a land she hadn't seen since her hatching. Many times each night we stopped along our six-mile study area to tag a left front flipper. A number, address, and an offer of a five dollar reward for finding the turtle were inscribed on the aluminum tag to gather information about the turtle's fate.

We also banded the endangered green sea turtle. While the loggerhead's name referred to the size of its head, the gigantic green turtle had a smaller, more proportional head by comparison. They tended to nest further up on land, almost into the shrubbery. They each dug an immense hole, large enough to bury their whole body, and then laid their eggs. We had to shield our eyes from the sand that sprayed far and wide. After the rubbery eggs were laid, the turtle carefully covered them with sand. With the completion of the mission, each turtle turned back and headed for the security of the distant water and its welcome weightlessness for their massive bodies. With one last crash of the waves over their shells they disappeared into the sea.

The ten days I spent tagging sea turtles dramatically changed my attitude toward getting a formal education. During the long days and nights, I spent more and more time talking to passers-by who were interested in the project.

I also found myself talking to, and teaching, the wide-eyed students about the turtles and the project. I felt the joy of sharing all I had learned from Ed, and the turtles themselves, and passing that knowledge on.

At the same time I wanted to know more and be able to teach more, and this desire gnawed at me. Thoughts of Ed and his earlier struggles haunted me. Did I have the same strength? His happiness in his ability to teach kids and raise his own children to adulthood gave me the clue. "You can do it, kid!" This phrase kept echoing in my mind. I found an inner strength that week: strength enough to plan to go to college and learn all I could. I knew I would struggle but hoped my drive to gain and share knowledge would keep me going.

DIANNE AND TURTLE MAN, ED PHILIPS, WITH LOGGERHEAD

In all, we tagged and measured fifty-three turtles. Our last night in Florida was the most successful. By 5:00 a.m. the last of the turtles were heading back to the ocean. My body craved sleep, while my spirit fought to stay awake a little longer to watch the brilliant sun rise out of the sea. With burning eyes and a tired smile, I turned to an equally tired Turtle Man to say thank you.

As the plane lifted off for my journey back to Massachusetts, my heart pounded in my chest as I thought with confidence, "Kid, you can do it!"

21

Buckling Down

 THE NEXT DAY I DROVE TO WORCESTER State College and asked how to start the process of enrolling to earn a degree. The woman told me it would take eight years at night to get a bachelor's degree. If I took any summers off, it would take me longer.

I said, "Where do I sign?" I tightened up my belt and was able to pay for my tuition, one semester at a time without any loans.

I worked during the day, picked up Becky afterwards from the babysitter's, played on the swing set at home for a while, got something to eat, and then went two miles down the road to Tufts to type my papers on the new scary contraption called a computer.

I had to teach myself the commands: *Insert, Home, Page Up, Delete,* and *End*. I had no clue what they all meant! It was frustrating but I struggled through with a thick computer self-help book. Becky drew at the desk beside me and I put her to sleep on a futon after reading her a bedtime storybook. The soft bed lived in a closet at the Clinic. There were times when I stayed up all night, bringing Becky to the babysitter's in the morning and going back to work during the day. It was tiring but we made it work.

My first two classes in the fall of 1986 were botany and English I. I remember crying on my way home from class. "What am I doing taking classes twice a week at night for the next eight years?" When I arrived at home, I sent the nighttime babysitter home and sat down to stare at my English book, and try to remember what a subject and a predicate were.

I started crying again and Becky heard me from her bedroom. This was the first time I had cried since those last desperate days at Quabbin. She asked me what the matter was and I told her I couldn't do something. She was only four years old so I couldn't explain it to her. I led her back to bed and started reading her a story by Hans Christian Andersen, "The Little Match Girl" who froze to death with a smile on her face.

Becky and I sat in silence. "What kind of story is this?" I shouted. I got up and went into the kitchen and threw the paperback book in the trash. Becky came out and held my hand and told me it would be all right, so I gave her a kiss goodnight. I sat at the desk and battled my homework. I woke up the next day and felt refreshed. I had done my homework and woke Becky up to say that I did it!

She put her hand in mine and told me, "Mommy, you are a very good girl!"

I truthfully can say I did not enjoy studying for tests at 2:00 and 3:00 a.m., but I enjoyed the sciences, art classes, and cultural geography. I was able to take a college course that allowed me to get credit for life experiences. I did very well and received enough credits to reduce my course-load by two years. It was a relief to know that it would make it possible for me to graduate in six years.

Eagle 1060

At Tufts, we were working on a bald eagle that couldn't fly, but didn't seem to have anything wrong with her. She was an adult and she had leg bands that told us she was from Maine. Her case number at Tufts was 1060, so that's what we named her. Blood work was normal and her X-rays looked fine except for an old healed fracture in her femur. How did she ever survive long

EAGLE PATIENT 1060 READY FOR RELEASE

enough to hunt and catch food with a broken leg? It was a mystery. We put her in the eagle flight aviary and wanted to see her move around. She could run all right and she was very feisty, but she couldn't fly.

Around that time, state-of-the-art technology was installed in a new building next to the University of Massachusetts Medical Center. It was called Magnetic Resonance Imagery (MRI). We asked if we could bring a bald eagle there to look at her brain for any visible reasons why she couldn't fly. I stayed in the room with 1060 while the machine was making images. We anesthetized the bird with injectable anesthesia so that she wouldn't move during the process. We found out that she had a mass on her brain. Nothing could be done so we took her back and kept her out in the flight aviary with some other recuperating eagles.

One day, some months later, I went into the eagle flight aviary to feed 1060. To my amazement she was up on the upper platform, fifteen feet over my head. She quickly flew across to the other fifteen-foot platform. We let her exercise for a week and then called Maine Fish and Wildlife and I made arrangements to meet them half-way.

When I talked to the biologist who was going to release 1060 near where she was found, he said, "There is a funny story behind this bird." He just happened to look in his records and said that after the baby bird was banded in the nest she had later fallen out over the side and was found on the ground. He remembered the bird because it was one heck of a big eagle's nest that they had to climb to put her back in with its nest mate. I thought, *That's when 1060 broke her leg!* By placing her back in the nest and allowing the parents to feed her, the baby nestling was able to heal on her own. Mystery solved.

22

New Animal Experiences

Full-Time At Tufts University

 TUFTS UNIVERSITY WAS AN EXCEPTIONAL place to work. We received over 1,400 sick, injured or orphaned wild animals every year. Because the clinic was so busy, my job became full-time in 1987. I was sad that I had to quit my job at the restaurant. Becky and I never ate so well. I was able to buy a take-out dinner every night and put anything I wanted in it for her. My weight had returned to normal and I felt healthy.

At the wildlife clinic we handled, cared for, X-rayed and took blood samples from birds ranging from eagles, to tiny humming-birds, and everything in between. We treated bear, deer, bobcats, squirrels, porcupines (including quills)–mostly hit by cars. There was an American kestrel (small falcon) soaked in motor oil, a blue jay caught with a fishing lure, a kidnapped baby bear, loads of bunnies grabbed by household cats, and even a baby moose with a broken leg.

Dr. Sedgwick, the wildlife director, taught me how to catch my first golden eagle out of the flight cage. "First, you walk in with your shoulders slumped and your arms by your side," he said. "That makes you look like less of a threat, as if you were a deer walking through the woods. You are not a predator. Bring a sheet in with you and walk with it in front of your legs and body as you get near."

Doc was kind enough to let me try on my own and stayed motionless in the corner. I proceeded slowly and the watchful eagle took off to the other end of the aviary. Doc let me try a couple of times and then said, "Watch carefully." He took off like a shot and cornered the eagle and swooped him right up in seconds. Wow, no net, no gloves. With his help I became quite proficient with a sheet for larger birds like eagles and great blue herons, and a towel on smaller birds, like hawks and owls.

Once I acquired skills and confidence, my job was to teach the fourth-year vet students how to work with wild animals. Although they had a working knowledge of dogs cats, horses and all other domesticated animals, they didn't know how to take an eagle out of a large carrier, restrain it for X-rays, take blood from a delicate vein bandage a wing injury, and tube-feed the bird until it was able to eat on its own Knowing what diets to feed different animals was a skill that was valuable to the students.

Once we received a porcupine with a broken leg

DIANNE AND MOOSE PATIENT

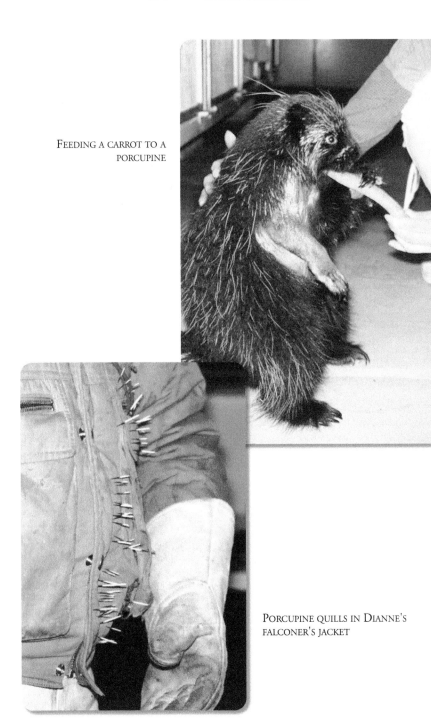

FEEDING A CARROT TO A
PORCUPINE

PORCUPINE QUILLS IN DIANNE'S
FALCONER'S JACKET

All that was required to change the bandage was a carrot. Handling him for an X-ray was a little trickier. I wore my falconer jacket for the sharp quills that covered the front of me. What's a few quills lost when he has thirty thousand more like them!

Loon Mortalities

One thing that saddened me was receiving injured loons, since I had been able to witness so much of their private lives in the wild while at Quabbin. We could place them right on the X-ray plate and anesthetize them with little trouble. They didn't have the ability to walk on land so they didn't jump off the table. We kept most of them in a bathtub with water and live fish. A curtain around it gave them privacy and relieved a little of the stress of captivity. Every once in a while a loon would call its "wail" which could be heard throughout the clinic. Some had trauma like a broken wing or chest trauma because they landed on pavement on a rainy day, thinking it was water. Many, though, died of lead poisoning. They either swallowed a lead sinker from fishing gear, or thinking it was a pebble, picked up the discarded shiny sinker on the bottom of a lake to help it grind and digest food in its gizzard.

Dr. Mark Pokras, our other veterinarian, took the lead sinker problem to heart and obtained grants to study the issue. He asked biologists and anyone else who found a dead loon, to send it to Tufts Wildlife Clinic so that he and some student helpers could X-ray and necropsy (dissect) them. Well, he received hundreds and hundreds of loons in the 1980s and 1990s. I know because I helped X-ray the dead loons in between working with the live patients.

By the summer of 2011 Dr. Pokras had done necropsies on nearly two thousand dead loons! Many loons die as a result of human activities: things like fishing line entanglement and being hit by power boats. Current data show that about half, between 49% and 50%, of the adult loons that die on fresh water in New England are dying from lead poisoning.

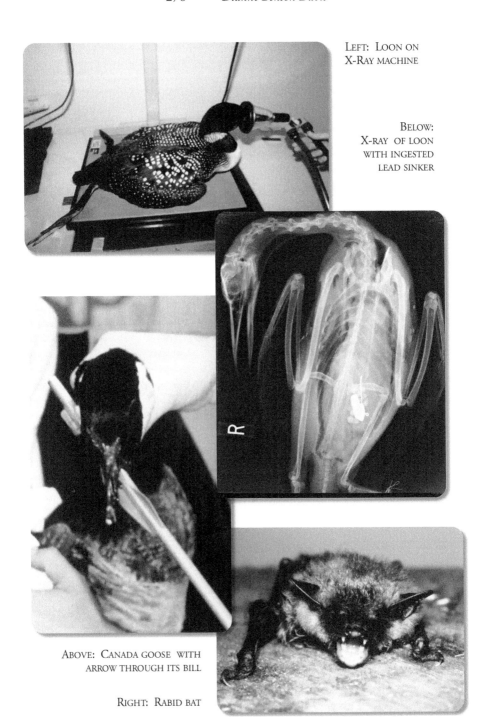

LEFT: LOON ON
X-RAY MACHINE

BELOW:
X-RAY OF LOON
WITH INGESTED
LEAD SINKER

ABOVE: CANADA GOOSE WITH
ARROW THROUGH ITS BILL

RIGHT: RABID BAT

In 2012, after years of research, writing articles to raise awareness of the problem, and meeting with legislators, a bill was passed prohibiting lead fishing sinkers and jigs weighing less than an ounce in all inland waters in Massachusetts. The dedication of one person can make a difference!

In 1985, bats were the only wild animals reported with rabies. In the early 1990s, rabies entered the Bay State and spread throughout the wild mammal population. We handled rabid skunks, raccoons, foxes, and coyotes with great caution.

Many animals came in with injuries caused directly or indirectly by humans. One patient was a Canada goose that was brought in with an arrow through its beak. We had to cut the end of the arrow off and then pull the rest of the shaft through his nostrils. After we flushed the wound daily and gave him antibiotics for fourteen days, he was placed back in the wild.

We received word one day that a bird was hanging from a tree branch by kite strings. The fire department was called and they used an extended ladder to retrieve the exhausted bird. It turned out that it was a long-eared owl and the right wing feathers were torn up pretty badly from its struggle to get free. The patient was fine otherwise, but it would be a year before he grew new feathers after a molt.

To enable the owl to fly before then, I used a falconry technique called "imping" that replaces damaged feathers with feathers from a deceased owl. People who work with animals often save animal carcasses in their freezers for mounted specimens in museums. The Wildlife Clinic had a long-eared owl carcass so we cut off the wing feathers to match our patient's damaged plumage. We used bamboo splinters and super glue to attach the new feathers onto the wild owl's wing. This allowed his wing to function again. We test-flew the bird in a flight aviary to make sure the feathers would hold and then gave him a few days of rest and mice to make him strong again. We placed a silver federal band on his leg like we do with all birds released. That way we can be notified if

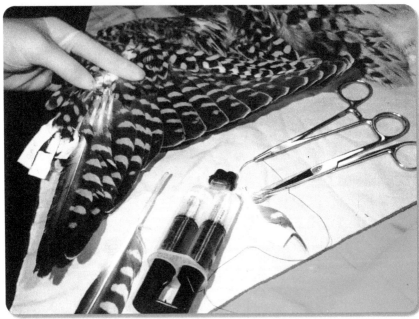

TOP: LONG-EARED OWL WITH DAMAGED WING FEATHERS
BOTTOM: REPAIRING PEREGRINE FALCON FEATHERS

the bird is ever found dead or injured. What a joy it was to release the owl where it was found.

Other animals suffered gunshot wounds, were hit by cars, or poisoned. There were even misguided kidnappings of young animal babies that were fine but were thought to be orphans. We used to say, "If you care, leave them there." The parents are not too far away.

One day a woman brought in a litter of baby squirrels that were just about ready to be on their own. We started our spiel about returning the babies to the wild, when she interrupted and said that when she first saw the babies, she thought it was a hairy octopus moving down the street. We were puzzled. When we lifted the six feisty babies out of the box, they were all attached to each other. It seems they were in a leafy nest that also contained a thorny vine. With their normal, squirming activity, all the babies were eventually tangled together by their tails.

After anesthetizing all six babies, two vet students delicately shaved some of the hair off the tails to find out whose was whose,

and then untangled them and threw away the vine. The babies slept it off for an hour and then the woman who had rescued them took them back to the place she had she found them. Sure enough, the mother squirrel reclaimed her young. She grabbed one at a time and each held on to her by swinging its body around her neck. She eventually retrieved all six babies. This story had a happy ending.

It took a little longer to achieve a happy ending for an injured doe. The vet students and I were working on a red-tailed hawk that had a broken wing caused by a gunshot. As we were finishing with the X-rays and bandaging the wing, two animal control officers arrived and asked us to come to their van. When they opened the sliding door, there in handcuffs was an adult doe. My first words were, "Is she under arrest?" According to the officers she was grazed by a car and knocked unconscious. They handcuffed

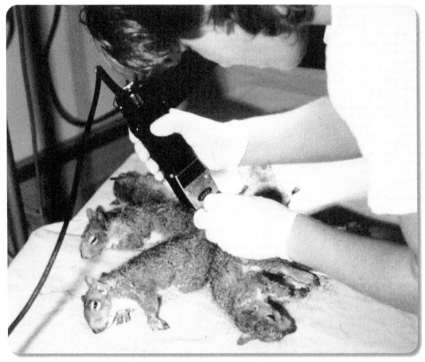

SHAVING THE SIX SQUIRRELS' TAILS

her to hobble her legs so she couldn't stand up in their cluttered van. She didn't seem startled, so before she could really come to her senses, Doc Sedgwick, who had joined us to assess the situation, decided to anesthetize her immediately.

Carrying her was awkward and cumbersome, particularly since we had to get her to the tiny X-ray room on the second floor! After determining her injury was not life-threatening, we called the Fish and Wildlife Department and asked if we could borrow two deer crates. With a manageable fracture, pain meds, and the crates to keep her calm and still, she would have a chance to heal. The crate was dark and cozy so she couldn't move around and hurt herself; food and water were kept close to her head. When we needed to clean her, we put the second crate next to hers and quietly lifted the guillotine doors on both crates. With a little gentle prodding she would move to the other deer crate and lie down.

Many weeks passed and we X-rayed the doe again and felt the leg was finally healed. It was time for her release. It took a little preparation on our part, as we wanted to make sure the doe could be identified if encountered again. We met outdoors and the game plan was for one of the vet students to open up the guillotine door slowly from above. Two other students had a large board they placed across the front to keep the deer in. Doc would reach in and grab her head and I would put a yellow cow tag in her left ear to identify her. It all sounded easy: one, two, three. So the door was eased up, the board was put across the front and Doc grabbed the head. The deer reacted like a bucking bronco. Doc was getting tossed around, up and down, and side to side. You can imagine the racket! Once Doc had her by the head I tried to put the cow tag in the moving ear with a grommet puncher. Doc was straining to keep the head steady and I couldn't believe how fast and strong that deer was. Finally I got the job done. Doc let go and the student slid the door down as fast as she could. Doc and I just stood there shaking, our adrenaline pumping. We all calmed down and then loaded the deer into the Tufts' van and headed to a remote conservation area in Grafton to let her go.

Carolyn Corsiglia, the clinic coordinator, drove us to the edge of a field and we unloaded the heavy crate. With the students' cameras flashing, Doc lifted the sliding door. It took a little prodding from the opposite end of the crate to persuade her to slowly walk out the front. She gave us no notice, walked a few steps, took a few lofty bounds and then, in horror, we watched her stumble in a tiny depression in the ground. She fell down and then got up and limped a few steps.

Doc grabbed me and said, "Dianne, come with me and the rest of you keep the deer in sight. We'll be right back." We ran to the van and raced back to the clinic.

I followed Doc up to his office and he grabbed two dart pistols and made up two doses of anesthetic drugs. As we headed back ouside, Doc said to put the pistols in my jacket to keep the loaded darts warm. We drove back to the site and there was Carolyn, arguing with a kid about eighteen years old in camouflage clothing. "What's going on?" Doc said.

The young man was a hunter and pointing to the deer—which was partially concealed by heavy brush—said, "That's my deer! I shot it with a bow and arrow up on the hill." He explained he had jumped in his car and drove around where he thought the deer would come out.

"Look at the yellow tag in the deer's ear," Carolyn said. The young man looked; his jaw dropped.

"What's your name?" Doc said with authority.

He cautiously replied, "Steve."

"Well, follow us, Steve." Doc then pushed through the brush slowly. I followed, with Steve right beside me. Doc approached the quietly standing deer and swung his arm around to me without taking his eyes off the animal. I opened my jacket and pulled out the first gun. Steve stepped back a step and his jaw dropped again.

I handed the gun to Doc. As he shot, he exclaimed, "Damn! Missed! Give me the other one!" I pulled the second one out and he shot again. That dart hit its mark right in her hind quarters. She jumped and limped off to the edge of the thick woods.

We checked our watches, stayed back, and let the drug do its work. We had time to talk to Steve and explained we rehabilitated the doe and thought this was a good place to release her. Steve said this was his first time hunting and he was excited to get a chance at his first deer. Ten minutes went by and we approached the deer cautiously. We didn't want her to spook and disappear further into the woods. Doc carefully touched the sleeping deer and said she was down. He checked her vitals and then told Steve to grab a hind quarter. We quietly walked her back to the van, slid her inside, said our goodbyes, and went on our way. Steve was going to have quite a story to tell his hunting buddies and parents.

After X-raying the doe again, we saw she had a hairline fracture on the opposite leg from the original fracture. This time it wasn't that bad, so after a few weeks of healing in the green crates, we moved her into a horse stall at the Hospital for Large Animals. She had this particular barn all to herself, so she could recuperate in private. Every other day, the vet student in charge of her case slowly opened the stall door and shoved hay, water, and grain just inside. The doe jumped off the walls and made an awful racket until the door was pushed closed. Despite the interruptions, she became stronger every day.

One quiet Sunday, I was covering for a student who had another commitment. With no one else around, I slowly opened the door and started shoveling the food in as she bounced around. When I happened to look up, she was in midair, leaping straight toward my exposed body. I had just enough time to dive out of the way and she was out in the corridor. She ran to one end of the barn, turned around and headed back my way. I plastered myself against the wall and studied her stride as she ran by. She was using all four legs perfectly. I ran to the end of the barn and took it upon myself to make a quick decision to let her go! She leaped through the door and made her way down the street and into the pastures and woods that surrounded the back side of the vet hospital campus. I had a lot of explaining to do, but it all worked out in the end.

Years later, she was reported to Fish and Wildlife and identified by her yellow ear tag. She was quite a few towns away from Grafton and had readjusted well to the wild. Another case closed.

I sometimes brought home recuperating patients from work: owls that needed extra care, baby animals, and a peregrine falcon that had to be tube-fed. The peregrine was one of Tom Ricardi's breeding birds. (He was the falconer who rehabilitated the eagle, 91, back in 1985. That bird was released just before my babies were released.)

Carolyn was hand-rearing a baby black bear that someone kidnapped from a den. Becky got to bottle-feed the growing cub one night because I had to bring it home. She was in kindergarten at the time so I brought the curious cub to her class the next morning before bringing him back to work.

Intervention

Once the Massachusetts Fish and Wildlife Department intervened with a pair of peregrine falcons that had set up housekeeping on the outside ledge of a building on the twenty-first floor in Springfield, Massachusetts. The female had laid three eggs in a tray that Fish and Wildlife had provided a month earlier when they noticed the peregrine falcons were looking for a place to nest. The local TV station set up a camera at the nest site and broadcast twenty-four hours a day. Two of the three eggs hatched and the parents were very good at providing fresh kill of many different species of birds for the chicks to feed on.

One day people started calling the TV station and Fish and Wildlife to say that one of the babies looked weak and was not

BECKY FEEDING BABY BLACK BEAR

taking food from the parents. Tom French came to assess the situation through the glass window and agreed that one of the chicks was in trouble. Because the window couldn't be opened to reach the chicks, Tom had to rappel down the outside of the building from the twenty-third floor. It was a good thing that he had done that before when he rappelled down the side of cliffs to band raven chicks in the springtime.

I got a call at ten o'clock at night after my college class ended. It was Dr. Sedgwick asking if I would come to the Wildlife Clinic right away. The babysitter was still at my house so she watched Becky a little longer. Doc and Tom French were standing there looking in a box. I peeked in and saw the cutest little white fluff ball with big black eyes. It was one of the first peregrine falcons to be born in the state, other than in Boston, since DDT wiped out the eastern peregrine back in the 1960s.

Dr. Sedgwick had taken out a piece of meat and sinew that was wrapped around the chick's tongue and lodged in its throat. It made it impossible for the parent to feed the little guy any more meat and it was getting weaker from lack of food. My job was to raise the chick until it had gained its strength and was able to be banded and put back in with its nest mate. Otherwise the sibling would get most of the food because it was stronger. Tom would also band the other chick when he put the chick back.

At home Becky and I fed the young chick "quail in a blender." The mashed-up meal was easy to digest and I could feed it off tweezers. The bird ate it readily when I tapped his beak. He couldn't really focus so I had to be persistent.

He got stronger and as the days went by and I noticed he was bobbing his head and looking up at me. I didn't want him to imprint on me so I decided to make a surrogate mother out of one of Becky's stuffed toys: a twelve-inch standing bald eagle. I took a white sock out of my drawer and grabbed my bird book. I turned to the picture of a peregrine falcon and proceeded to

PEREGRINE CHICK
LOOKING SKEPTICAL
- THATS'S MY MOM?

PEREGRINE CHICK
BEGGING FOR
FOOD

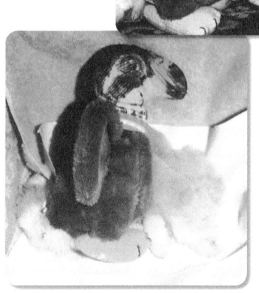

PEREGRINE CHICK BEDTIME -
SNUGGLING UP TO SURROGATE
MOM

draw a peregrine face on the sock, put it over the face of the little stuffed eagle, and placed it in front of him. He just stared at it.

He was hungry and started to paw at the surrogate mother and "food beg." He ate the food readily. After he was full, I laid the "mother" over him and he snuggled up close to it. I had a heating pad under the towels to keep him warm.

The growing chick grew stronger and it was time for Tom French to band it and put it back with its sibling. The two Billys went too. Billy Davis manned the rope that held Tom. He shouted to Tom when he was rappelling down, "How about that raise?"

Billy B. was photographing the event when an angry peregrine parent grabbed his Fish and Wildlife-issued hat off his head and flew out over the city with it. The bird actually brought it back over the roof and dropped it. Tom banded the second screaming baby and got the heck out of there.

The young peregrines dined for a few more weeks and eventually took flight out over the city under the watchful eyes of their parents. The falcons were such celebrities that the local professional hockey team was named the Springfield Falcons.

PEREGRINE CHICK BACK IN THE NEXT

23

Habiba: Super Mom

 IN THE SPRING OF 1986, HABIBA BEGAN TO earn her keep as an employee at Tufts. Two seventeen-day-old balls of fluff, orphaned from a wild nest, were brought into the clinic by Billy B. The high tension tower that held their nest needed work and the angry parents were not letting the workmen near it. The babies would have to be moved. Would Habiba be up for the challenge of raising genuine red-tailed hawk chicks? There was a chance that Habiba would not accept the sudden switch from her warm eggs to active chicks, but it was worth a try.

Two Red-Tailed Hawk Chicks

Habiba, as usual, had pair-bonded with me. She had rebuilt her stick nest on the platform in the mews and had laid two infertile eggs that she was dutifully incubating. I walked up to the nest and distracted Habiba to the front perch. Billy B. shot photos of the delicate operation. I replaced her eggs with the two seventeen-day-old chicks. The ensuing confrontation went as I suspected. The downies were too old to fool her into thinking she had just hatched them out.

She heard the tiny peeps and immediately flew to the nest and tried to attack the chicks. (I had clipped Habiba's talons right before I put the chicks in the nest.) Knowing the attack would probably happen, I put my hand between her and the helpless nestlings. Every time they moved or chirped she would aggressively try to "foot" them with her talons. I started feeding Habiba some meat and then I fed the chicks. All three were hungry and accepted my offerings, but Habiba wanted the intruders out! When I fed one chick, she snuck in and tried to grab the other chick by the head feathers and drag him off the nest. What worried me was the look on her face and the carelessness of how she stepped all over them. The young chicks knew they weren't welcome and one tried to scurry to the corner and hide. They both were panic-stricken. It was frustrating but I knew I had to be patient and persistent.

Habiba was again careless and stepped on their backs as they tried to lay flat and still in the nest. When Habiba raised the broad-wing baby hawk three years earlier, the same aggression came out in her until her maternal instincts kicked in. I knew the next few moments would be crucial for the tiny red-tails. Would she accept them or kill them?

HABIBA ATTACKING CHICK

Then it happened! As I fed Habiba morsels of meat, she accidentally dropped a piece. When she went to retrieve the inviting tidbit, one of the shell-shocked babies snatched the food right out of her beak. Habiba paused and stared at the thief with a puzzled gaze. Her eyes showed an awareness and her body grew less tense. I gave Habiba another piece of food and she leaned toward the baby. The chick quickly grabbed and swallowed that one as well. Habiba responded by immediately lifting her foot so that she wouldn't step on the baby and harm it. She took over the feedings and tore up the food in tiny pieces for them. She made little peeping noises that the birds responded to. Habiba's mannerisms changed completely as she delicately tore pieces that would nourish the new hatchlings.

After the birds' stomachs were satisfied, Habiba opened up her breast feathers and tried to "swallow" the downy chicks up against her warm body. She had a brood patch on her breast area because she had been incubating her infertile eggs, so the skin area was toasty warm. The problem was that the chicks were so big they hardly fit underneath her.

I noticed that the chicks had a large white conspicuous spot on top of their heads and wondered what purpose it served to have evolved so perfectly. When Habiba sat on the chicks it was made absolutely clear to me. The spot on each of their heads looked like a white egg and I'll bet it stimulated the parent to instinctively brood the "egg" when in actuality it was the baby. Even at seventeen days old, the babies responded by nuzzling up tightly against Habiba's body. She took over all the duties of rearing the babies for the next three weeks. She gently preened their soft gray down and gave them a sense of security. I dropped food into the nest remotely and let the babies completely imprint on Habiba. Their feathers burst through their skin like crocuses in spring: fast and all at once. They exercised daily and grew up knowing that they were birds and not people.

As they grew, it was clear that one was a big female and the other was a smaller male. Habiba even tried to lure them out of the nest by taking the food out when they were six weeks of age. The time was coming when the young needed their hunting lessons. I searched for a wild red-tailed hawk's nest that had only one chick. I found one on the cloverleaf of Routes 9 and 495, two busy highways. The nest was hidden in a patch of woods in one of the loops. I asked Billy Byrne to climb the tree and place the big female chick in the nest after I banded it.

The parents were quite upset with the entire disturbance and circled above, screaming. The wild chick was just at fledging age and had probably made his maiden voyage when Billy stuck his head above the nest top. I was worried that I had disturbed them too much and created a problem. We left a token of our appreciation in the form of dead laboratory mice for the two chicks.

I went back the next day and checked on Habiba's chick to see if the other chick had returned to the nest. I had brought Becky with me and many cars stopped because they thought my car was broken down on the highway and we needed help. After waving them off, Becky and I disappeared into the sparsely wooded area.

When I looked up I could see one baby hawk and assumed that it was the chick I had left yesterday. No parents were scolding or circling from above. When I walked

BILL BYRNE PLACING HABIBA'S FOSTER CHICK IN A WILD NEST

around to the other side of the tree and looked through the canopy I saw the chick looking down at me from that side. I was upset because it hadn't worked and I would have to call Billy Byrne up and ask him to climb the tree and retrieve the bird.

All of a sudden it dawned on me that the baby hawk was not walking from one side of the nest to the other to look down at me. There were two birds in there! The wild chick had gone back to the nest. Within seconds I heard unfriendly screams. Becky and I jumped for joy. The parents had returned. We left quickly and I called Billy B. up and asked if he could place the second bird up that day. He did, and the fostering worked. A photograph of the three chicks in the nest appeared in the Boston Globe newspaper. My dream of raising wild orphans without them imprinting on humans was accomplished with Habiba's talents.

Habiba may be imprinted on humans, but she and I know she can raise young of her own kind and be considered an honest-to-goodness red-tailed hawk.

HABIBA FOSTERS CHICKS, FROM *VET WORLD,* SUMMER '86

We Meet Again

One fall day I returned to my old hunting ground with Habiba. I hadn't been there in probably four or five years. I was walking through the old abandoned apple orchard when two boys approached me. I called Habiba down to my glove and one boy punched the other on the arm. It startled Habiba, me and the boy.

He told the friend, who was rubbing his arm, "I told you I saw a lady with a hawk in the woods and you didn't believe me!"

I smiled and commented on how much he had grown. He told me that he was volunteering at a vet hospital and he never forgot the day that I had let Habiba fly down to his gloved fist.

BECKY AND HABIBA

24

Archie, Barnaby and Bullet

 TWO BARRED OWLS LIVED AT THE WILDLIFE Clinic. Because both had injuries that made them non-releasable, they were allowed to live in the animal room and were not confined to cages. They became part of the staff and taught the veterinary students how to care for long-term patients.

Archie was a female that lost an eye in a collision with a vehicle as a youngster. Barnaby, who was a male, had a chronic leg injury, so he had to wear a brace for the rest of his life. It was checked and rewrapped every week to make sure there were no pressure sores.

ARCHIE
THE BARRED OWL

The students loved working with them. How often do you get to work beside owls?

In the mornings, Archie was let out of her nighttime enclosure and flew to the window to sun herself. When the students met to discuss cases with the doctors, someone would get Archie and she would be right in the thick of things and occasionally hoot. She watched us take out and work up different animal patients. We had a kiddy pool near the back door for minnows to feed the fish-eating birds like loons and herons. Archie spent time every day watching the fish like a cat would watch a bird outside a window. Every once in a while Archie dove in, snatched a fish in her talons, flew up to a stool, and left the kill there. She never ate them.

One day we had an osprey that was recuperating from a wing injury. With Archie looking on, we fed him Archie's fish mortalities. Within a day, Archie the fish stealer learned to catch, kill, and eat the shiny minnows. This had to stop because going out to buy a supply of fresh fish was time-consuming and getting a little expensive. A vet student suggested floating a board on top of the water and the problem was solved temporarily. The fish quickly learned to hide under the floating wood as it circled the pool. Archie flew to the stool and tried to peer under the board with her one eye. It didn't take her long to jump on the board scattering the fish so she could stick out a foot and grab one.

Barnaby always stayed up in the stairwell during the day. Archie did not allow him to venture downstairs during the daylight hours while she ruled the animal room. He was content in his day-time quarters on a perch halfway up the stairs. He gave us "looks" every time we passed through his domain bringing an animal upstairs for X-rays or surgeries. He knew we had a patient under those towels because he got a fleeting glimpse of a wing or tail poking through.

At night Barnaby flew down the stairs and into the animal room after Archie retired to her nighttime enclosure with some dead mice. He claimed the area as his own, but only for the night. He was back upstairs by the time we wandered in the next day.

Orphaned Chick

Once we received an "orphaned" baby barred owl. I say "orphaned" because it was a case of someone finding a nestling on the side of the road in the woods and picking it up and bringing it in to us. After examining the brown-eyed baby we deemed it healthy and tried to reach the people who brought it in so they could tell us where they found it. We set it in the animal room for the night. It made a distinctive food-begging noise: "Eeeee!"

I knew that call; it sounds exactly like the baby owl I heard at Quabbin in 1985. I was drawn to the call. Archie was drawn to the call too and flew to the cage and peered in the top slats. We decided to try and see what would happen if we put them together. The baby bobbed his head up and down and sideways and called to Archie, "Eeeee!"

Archie picked up a mouse and fed it to the hungry little cuss. Success!

We kept the downy owlet until the next Monday when we talked to the finders. Norm Smith, director and friend from the Audubon Blue Hills Trailside Museum, happened to be visiting us at the Wildlife Clinic. He is an expert on owls and bands snowy owls in the wintertime at Logan Airport. (It seems the males and juvenile owls leave their summer domain in the Arctic and head south to New England during the winter months. They gravitate to airports, where the hunting areas are flat like their northern home.)

Norm came with the students, the chick, and me to search for the nest. The owl was found next to the road in a deeply forested area, prime barred owl habitat. As we followed the directions the finders gave us, I noticed a big yellow bucket-truck from a utility company just finishing up on a telephone wire on top of a pole.

We took the next turn, and arrived at the area where the chick had been found. As we got out of the car, Norm told us to look for a tree with the top lopped off and to tap on the bark and look up. Finally I noticed a perfect tree with no top. I showed Norm and he nodded to start tapping.

All of a sudden a large head that looked too big to be inside the tree popped out of the top and looked down at us. At the same instant a brown-eyed adult male flew in to the canopy and started hooting excitedly. At that instant I ran to the car and raced back down the street where I had seen the yellow truck. I started babbling about the baby owl in a box that I showed the linemen and pointed to their bucket apparatus. I asked if they could use it to put the baby owl up in a tall tree. They looked at each other and then at me. "Sure," they said, puffing their chests out and rearranging their utility belts. They followed me down the side road and stopped in front of the vet students and Norm.

I jumped out of the car and showed them the tree I wanted them to bucket up to. Then I tore up some dead mice in bite-sized pieces and fed the baby. I thought one of the utility men looked a little sick. Looking at the needle-sharp talons, the men decided the youngest of them would take the bird up and plop it back in the nest. As he neared the hole with thick gloves on, he peered inside, smiled, and said that there were two more babies inside. He gently placed the youngster inside and slowly lowered the bucket. He was the hero of the day. The other men patted him on the back and drove away feeling proud of their good deed.

Barnaby

Back at the Wildlife Clinic that following spring, Barnaby met me at the back door at 8:00 a.m. He was carrying on with hoots, cackles, and head bobbing. Of course I called back and he seemed satisfied. He then went up the stairwell and things were back to normal. The next day he did the same thing: hoots and head-bowing. It got pretty loud as he flew from perch to perch around the animal room with romantic intentions. Was he an imprint? (Archie was still in her nighttime enclosure.)

Then it happened. I bowed to him and made soft hoots and he flew over to me, landed on my head and believed that he was mating with me. It didn't stop there. After about a week of hooting he called me one day from his stairwell with a muffled hoot. Not knowing what to expect this time, I cautiously crept up the winding stairs and there was Barnaby, holding a dead mouse in his beak. He wanted to feed me and the "babies." I smiled and took the dead mouse out of his beak with my hand next to my mouth and pretended to swallow it. All in a day's work!

While working at Tufts I was able to go back and visit the Worcester Science Center, now called the EcoTarium, as a certified wildlife veterinary technician. I had taken classes and attended seminars over the years to become certified.

BARNABY THE
BARRED OWL

I worked side-by-side with Doc Sedgwick and Dr. Pokras who were among the best in wildlife medicine. They taught me so much about the medical aspects while I shared my knowledge of animal care, feeding, and housing. Doc had me teach falconry and rehabilitation skills during the vet students' third-year classes. I was in seventh heaven standing up in front of the curious students with Habiba on my glove. Eventually Tufts chose me as the closing guest speaker in a new program called Adventure in Veterinary Medicine, where older kids and adults spent a week at the veterinary school rotating through the different departments to get a feel for the veterinary profession. They were very enthusiastic students who loved being up close to a wild animal like Habiba.

Every day was a new experience. We once went to a local zoo and treated an old rhinoceros with a nasty foot infection. It was quite an experience to lean under a two-ton rhino to scrub the large wound out as he snorted loudly in his sleep. He sounded like T-Rex in the dinosaur movie, *Jurassic Park*.

Tufts Wildlife Programs

Billy D. and I teamed up doing wildlife programs. We traveled to schools around the state bringing Habiba and a non-releasable bald eagle into the auditoriums. "Bullet" was a beautiful adult nine-pound male eagle that had been shot in Hoonah, Alaska. He was majestic and sat on my glove without fear. We always started off with a slide show on endangered species. Any money made was donated to either the Non-Game and Endangered Species Fund or to the Tufts Wildlife Clinic.

Sometimes I would go down the street and stop in at the Grafton Middle School and bring Bullet into a classroom so the kids could see him up close. I would discuss career opportunities in wildlife and talk about what kids could do as individuals or as a community to help wildlife.

Endangered Species Day

One day Billy and I took Bullet to see Governor William Weld at the state house for Endangered Species Day in Massachusetts. There was a lot of media there so we moved to a larger room and set up behind a long table so that no one could get too close to Bullet. When the governor arrived he asked me where he should stand. I told him I would bring the eagle out on his right side and to remember one thing: don't move!

The next day, in the many newspapers that carried the picture, there was Governor Weld, standing face forward, smiling widely but with his eyes totally focused on Bullet who was looking at him. Billy was also in the background poised to defend the governor if Bullet tried to injure him.

I learned a lot about eagle behavior from Bullet. He would look at the sky and with an extra little stare, see a red-tailed hawk soar by as a speck. I had to wait a bit longer before I could see it. If he sometimes wanted to jump to a perch while I was holding

BULLET, BILLY AND GOVERNOR WELD

LEARNING FROM BULLET

DIANNE WITH BULLET AT TUFTS WILDLIFE CLINIC

him, I would wiggle my fingers in the glove and it would get his attention back to me. He didn't like to eat in the rain. He liked to take the intestines out of a dead rat before he ate it. (Habiba also didn't like the stomach and intestines in mice. She would pull them out and fling them on my clothes!)

When Bullet was relaxed on the glove, his head feathers were fluffed out in contentment. His tongue came out a few times and he swallowed. When he was hot, he pulled his breast feathers up tight to the body so no air was trapped between his feathers. In the winter, he puffed his feathers out to retain heat. He burps. When he was upset at something he tightened up his head feathers and glared.

I was thankful to Tufts for allowing me the time to go into schools between teaching the fourth-year veterinary students and caring for the animals. Billy and I felt strongly that since the eagles were coming back to Massachusetts it was important to educate children about them. Loss of habitat and contaminants in the environment were still issues and always would be. Habiba and Bullet encountered over thirty-thousand adults and students in Massachusetts, and by the children's letters and drawings I think we were getting our message across.

Proposal

I came home from college one day in 1991 and excitedly told Billy that I met with my advisor and that I was going to graduate in the spring of 1992. He smiled and said that we should get married. "What? Why all of a sudden now?" I asked. He told me I had been concentrating on college at night these past five years and now we would be able to concentrate on us as a family. I told him that was not a proper marriage proposal.

Later that week we picked out wedding rings. He drove us to Quabbin and led me to an overlook and said, "With God and Quabbin as my witness, will you marry me and be my wife?"

The answer was "yes" and the next week Becky, Billy and I returned to the Quabbin to relive old memories and prepare to create new ones. We visited the hack site where now nothing remained but the cut-off telephone poles that had supported the eagle tower.

25

The Loss Of Habiba

Tuesday, April 4, 1995

 AFTER A RELATIONSHIP THAT SPANNED eighteen years, the end for Habiba was surprisingly swift. It started with her seasonal moodiness. Every spring she normally became finicky and broody. In 1995, I attributed her lack of appetite to those conditions.

My old friend and companion was already in her nineteenth year and red-tails only live to be about nine to twelve years old in the wild.

I took her to work the next Monday and put her on her outside perch. She had been fussing with sticks on the ground for a month so I expected her to resume housekeeping. It was a warm spring day and I spent the morning outside raking around the Wildlife Clinic. I could see her from a distance and was surprised that she stayed on her perch all day. She usually flew to the ground and looked down the hill through the woods. After eating two mice, she stepped up on my glove and I put her in the mews for the night.

By Tuesday, I was growing concerned because she just wasn't herself and I thought it must be more than spring fever.

I asked Dr. P. K. Robbins, our veterinarian intern, if she would take a look at Habiba. P. K. asked if she could listen to her heart and lungs while Habiba was sitting quietly on my glove. Habiba obliged. Her heart rate was two hundred-twenty and regular, elevated, but still within the normal range. When the student tried to take blood, Habiba suddenly regurgitated some fluid and her breathing became labored from that instant on.

P. K. decided that a blood sample was worth obtaining because she felt Habiba did not expel all the fluid and the onset of her labored breathing was too sudden. She tried to go for a wing vein with little success. The veins were collapsed and she suggested the jugular vein, but after Habiba vomited again, I said I didn't think it was wise to stress her with a jugular stick. P. K. agreed and we decided to let her sit outside for a while so that she could rest and relax. She half-closed her eyes and that was not a good sign either. I tried to block out the grave implications.

After an hour we brought her in for radiographs. By then, Dr. Rose Borkowski, our other veterinarian, heard about Habiba's condition and voiced concern. She was kind enough to help because of the dangers of anesthesia on a compromised bird. Habiba could have complications and easily die.

At this time, P. K. listened to Habiba's chest and said it sounded like the lungs were filled with fluid. I asked to listen. Habiba's lungs sounded moist. I was beginning to understand the reality of what was happening. This was going to be Habiba's last day. After eighteen shared years together, I was going to have to say goodbye.

I gave Habiba anesthesia through a small mask. We took a quick X-ray and obtained a blood sample from her jugular vein. I have radiographed thousands and thousands of birds of every kind, but this day I was struggling to keep my composure. I listened to her lungs again and it sounded like a marble shaking in a tin can. How could she survive this?

Habiba continued breathing laboriously. Every breath was important. An incubator was brought up to surgery so that we could run oxygen in for her. I sat with Habiba but it was painful to see her gasping for air. I silently shed tears of sorrow and pain for there was nothing to do but wait for blood work to come back from the lab. My presence seemed to make her want to softly chirp to me.

I left her alone so she could concentrate on her breathing. Rose and P. K. tried to explain what might be happening: congestive heart failure because of her age, a tumor, or maybe egg yolk peritonitis. What were her options? Tap the fluid out of her abdomen to relieve some pressure on her liver and air sacks? Put her on heart medication to make her comfortable? Possibly take her to surgery if it was a tumor or spay her if the problems were ovary related? We had to wait.

The X-rays came back and they were the worst pictures I had ever seen. Her abdomen was totally white, which meant it was backed up with fluid. Her liver and heart were both enlarged and although her lungs seemed honeycombed, which was good, her air sacks around that area were cloudy and rough in appearance.

Habiba at this time was resting somewhat comfortably in the isolation chamber. The rest of the blood work came back. A normal white blood cell count ruled out peritonitis or infection. Heart failure was looking more and more like the prognosis but they wanted to rule out a tumor.

After looking at the X-ray, I turned to Rose and choked out that if her prognosis was grave, I did not want to prolong her suffering. Rose suggested an ultrasound next, which would be non-invasive, since Habiba could just perch on my glove and have the experts check her out.

We transported Habiba over to the small animal hospital in the isolation chamber and ultrasound personnel and doctors were waiting. The room was small, dark and warm. Habiba's X-rays were available. One student later told me that there were eleven people packed in that tiny room, quietly looking back and forth between the ultrasound images and Habiba, who looked so calm and beautiful.

The abdomen was clearly filled with fluid with no sign of a tumor or ovary problems. Her liver was indeed enlarged and her heart seemed to be fibrillating instead of beating.

Another specialist was called in and took the "driver's seat." He confirmed their findings. Her heart was not functioning normally, which allowed fluid to build up. I watched Habiba who was perched on my glove. She stared straight ahead and concentrated on every breath as they held the probe to her abdomen.

I couldn't comprehend how she could be standing and alive with her heart just fluttering. All the doctors agreed that her condition was quite grave. One doctor wanted to touch Habiba because she had never been that close to a hawk and admired her beauty. I asked her to be gentle and please not to apply any pressure. I then looked at Dr. Gretchen Kaufman, since she worked with exotic, long-lived patients. She said we could tap the belly and start her on heart medicine and that might make her comfortable.

At that moment, Dr. Borkowski dropped her eyes and I turned to look at her. Her face said it all. She agreed that we could make her comfortable for a while but she felt that we should put her down. I thanked everyone in the room and we returned to the Wildlife Clinic.

Rose went in to prepare the drug and anesthetic machine. I had Habiba step gently up on my glove for the very last time. I looked deep into her eyes and told her I was very sorry, kissed her on the beak, and led her into the other room. We closed the door and masked her down with anesthesia one more time so that she could fall asleep first. Rose chose the auxiliary wing vein because we had worked out a good system over the years on critical patients. Habiba's body relaxed and I knew she was gone.

I buried Habiba in my perennial garden. It was Palm Sunday. After digging a hole, Billy D. laid evergreens in the grave for Habiba to lie on. We planted tulips over her.

Goodbye Habiba. Go in peace.

26

Where Are They Now?

IN 1989, THE FIRST WILD EAGLE'S NEST AT Quabbin's northern end was identified. Ross from 1982 and Marjorie from my year were the parents of two chicks. Jack Swedberg's dream of nesting eagles in Massachusetts was becoming a reality.

Also that year, Woodstock paired off with a 1984 bird at Quabbin's south end and had one baby. She was still a vocal bird even as an adult. It seemed fitting that Jack was there when the first chick was lowered to the ground for banding. Jack got to hold it while the press took pictures. (Billy D. had brought the chick away from the nest so that the area would not be disturbed further.) Doc Sedgwick gave the chick a clean bill of health. I took blood and Billy banded three chicks that day while Billy B. documented every trip out with his camera.

I was fortunate to be able to bring veterinary students out to some of the wild nest sites to do a quick physical exam. Holding "the next generation" in my hands was a feeling of satisfaction like I had never experienced before. Here was the result of eight years of work by dozens of people devoting thousands of hours for this single goal: an eagle chick from a wild nest in Massachusetts. I gathered blood samples for a complete blood count and lead and mercury readings. Although the mercury readings were high, the chicks seemed to be healthy.

We were able to foster chicks into wild nests too. Tom Ricardi was breeding non-releasable bald eagles and having success. He let his "eagle parents" raise the young for four to five weeks and then we would foster them into wild nests where there was one baby each.

One year we went to Ross and Marjorie's nest and the baby had somehow gotten his foot caught in the sticks and died from stress, struggling to get free. We fostered a chick into the nest and they raised it as their own. In 1995, Marjorie and Ross had triplets.

Each year more of my baby eagles, who now sported white heads and tails, became parents. Jane raised young with Mr. 01 from the class of 1984 and Attila was on the Connecticut River raising her chicks with a mate from New York State. Their nest had a camera attached to the top of the tree. People from Gill, Massachusetts, could turn on their cable TV and watch the eagle parents raise their young. *People Magazine* had a photo and article on the eagles and their celebrity babies.

Visiting Nests

Each year for the next ten years, the two Billys and I visited eagle nests and banded the chicks.

My sister Janet made the bags we used to lower the eagles to the ground. The sides were medium-weight twill and the bottoms were made of heavy canvas. That way the babies had soft material around their bodies and wings and the canvas protected them from branches on the way down.

Throughout the years we received reports on my babies. Bert was found in a muskrat trap in Maine and had drowned. His silver band number identified him. Ernie was found in an illegal bobcat trap in Maine in 1986. We were told it was only a flesh wound and with care he would be fine. He was transported to Tufts and after X-rays and a bone scan, it was obvious that the lower leg and foot could not be saved, and removing the foot was the only option.

RIGHT: 1989 - FIRST WILD
EAGLE NEST IN
MASSACHUSETTS SINCE
THE TURN OF THE CENTURY

BELOW: FIRST EAGLETS
IN A WILD NEST
IN MASSACHUSETTS

After recovering from surgery, the plan was to release him back at Quabbin. Bald eagles are scavengers as well as fishermen, so Ernie would be better off in the wild with one foot than in captivity.

From the eagle blind in the winters, we learned that Ernie visited the site every February. He waited his turn at the frozen deer meat and inched his way in for a meal.

On one trip, I observed him trying to scratch his head with the leg without a foot. We found out from birders that he spent his summers along the Merrimac River up in New Hampshire near the Manchester town dump. He would sit and watch the herring gulls. If they left the dump with food, he chased them until they dropped the prize. If they didn't drop their catch he chased after the gull itself.

One year Bill D. received a call from Maine's Fish and Wildlife. It seems that L.L. Bean photographers were shooting pictures of kayaks on the Kennebec River for their upcoming catalog. Two adult bald eagles were seen in an aerial battle. They both splashed in the cold water and one lucky bird surfaced and flew away. The distraught kayakers paddled to help the other bird, but it was too late.

They retrieved the eagle from the water and saw that it had only one foot. From its leg band, we knew that it was Ernie. He had lived nine years in the wild; I'm glad he had that many years to live free.

Dick, Snoopy and 91 were the only birds I never heard from again. As of the year 2007, Attila, Marjorie, and Woodstock were still nesting. Jane's territory was sporadic with nesting activities on and off for those years. All in all, forty-one chicks were brought to Massachusetts and released from the hack tower. It is now up to the bald eagle to repopulate the wild habitat and for us to try to keep the environment healthy. We have a long way to go with problems like acid rain, PCBs, mercury contamination, car emissions, habitat loss, and the shooting of bald eagles that still persist today.

ERNIE FLYING WITH ONE LEG

ERNIE MOVING IN TO FEED

Bullet, our eagle, eventually went into Tom Ricardi's breeding program so that he could enjoy a female's company. They were successful in supplying new chicks to be fostered into the wild nests.

An Eagle Eye View

In 1995, I was able to get back in touch with the Quabbin when I took a thrilling helicopter ride to count wintering bald eagles with the two Billys. I had been anticipating this day for years, ever since I had spent that summer of 1985 raising the eight baby eagles. We were about to survey the most important locality for eagles in Massachusetts from a vantage that would forever change my perspective of this wild and isolated place.

The two Billys and I waited at a small, private airport in Sterling, Massachusetts for the helicopter to arrive from its home port in Concord, New Hampshire. As the chopper landed, we went out on the cold windy runway to meet the pilot. He quickly ran to us before we could get too close to the craft. He introduced himself and instructed us on all the safety guidelines that we needed to follow. "Do not go near the back of the helicopter for any reason. If your hat blows off because of the wind, do not attempt to chase it or you will lose your head!" A good point and it got my attention.

He asked if we had any questions and then we cautiously approached the waiting helicopter. I froze momentarily. The excitement of the trip and the whirling of the engine and blades overwhelmed me. I felt a surge of exhilaration that left me lightheaded. *No matter what, don't go back near the tail of the helicopter,* I said to myself as we began to walk.

The pilot shouted out the procedures so that we could hear him over the roar of the engine and moving rotor blades. We all approached the helicopter, stepped up, slid inside and he secured the doors. We found headsets on the seats to wear when we were airborne because the noise was deafening inside and out. They had voice-activated microphones so that when someone talked, we all could hear the conversation.

Billy Davis, now head of the eagle project for the Massachusetts Division of Fisheries and Wildlife, sat up front with the pilot. He was the official eagle counter. Billy Byrne and I were second lookouts in the back seats. As we lifted off and tilted forward, I tightened my seatbelt and gave a big smile to Billy B. We climbed quickly over the leafless trees and headed due west toward Mount Wachusett. We seemed to be going in slow motion over the frozen landscape. Our pilot advised us that we were flying at a cruising speed of sixty miles an hour at an altitude of five hundred feet. To the north was the granite summit of New Hampshire's Mount Monadnock. The morning sun was shining at just the right angle to give the mountain a beautiful glow. Its peak sported the only real snow in the region.

I was awed by the sights. Secluded houses were exposed to our curious eyes. Winding streams and rivers joined frozen ponds and lakes. My eyes moved rapidly to look for anything moving like a deer or coyote. Mount Wachusett was now behind us as we headed for our destination to the west; narrow valleys and steep ridges replaced rolling hills. A linked series of small ponds approached and then the awesome landscape opened up to encompass the main body of Quabbin Reservoir.

Our goal was to scan the tree-lined shore from above, just high enough to spot wintering bald eagles on their favored perches. Every year since 1979, in January bald eagles were counted state by state to chart trends in the wintering population. Eight wandering birds were sighted in Massachusetts that first year. At that time there were no nesting eagles in the state.

Billy D. guided the pilot along the irregular shoreline and major islands. We started our hundred-mile survey route in the northeast section of the reservoir and worked our way south. We discovered a few juvenile bald eagles early on, which made the pilot's day. He had never seen a bald eagle in the wild.

The Massachusetts Electric Company had donated the helicopter flight time and this lucky pilot was given the job of flying it and searching for eagles. We covered the shoreline and twenty islands, counting as precisely as we could. Typically the relaxed eagles would flush from their shoreline perch trees, fly out over the reservoir and then circle back to the shore after the helicopter passed. I was seeing the Quabbin as the soaring eagles saw it, flying low over the tree line and taking in the panoramic scene. After ninety minutes above the reservoir, we jumped over to the Connecticut River for an exciting ride north. The pilot asked if the back seat crew could scan for eagles while Billy D. watched for high tension wires crossing over the wide river. No argument there! We didn't want to crash and be eagle bait. After another hour aloft, we had spotted a total of forty-five adult and immature birds on the reservoir and river combined.

Quabbin Now

Twenty-five years after my summer with the eagle babies, I revisited the site. What a different landscape! Because Quabbin was open to controlled deer hunting in 1991, the population of deer went from sixty deer per square mile to approximately twelve deer. Forest regeneration took off and by 2010 the hack site was totally transformed into a young forest. In response to the new growth, bear, moose, fox, snowshoe hare, and a variety of songbirds have taken advantage of the prime habitat.

The bald eagle was reclassified from an endangered species to threatened status, and in 2007 was completely removed from the federal endangered species list, a tribute to its amazing recovery. Massachusetts, however, still considers it endangered at the state level. As of this writing, over four hundred known baby eagles have been banded in thirty-six natural nests in Massachusetts. Twelve pairs are at Quabbin, nine more along the Connecticut River and multiple nests in Plymouth, Worcester, Essex, Middlesex, Bristol, and Berkshire counties.

For a small state, we are knee-deep in eagles. Eagles with their roots in Massachusetts are now nesting in New York, New Hampshire, Connecticut, Rhode Island and likely other states and they are part of the overall recovery of the species.

Incidentally, the loons finally raised two chicks on Loon Island in 1995. Hallelujah!

27

Making Our Future

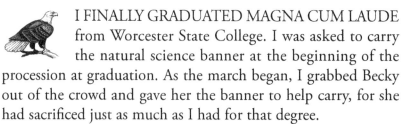 I FINALLY GRADUATED MAGNA CUM LAUDE from Worcester State College. I was asked to carry the natural science banner at the beginning of the procession at graduation. As the march began, I grabbed Becky out of the crowd and gave her the banner to help carry, for she had sacrificed just as much as I had for that degree.

After college, I still gave the last talk of the week for the Adventures in Veterinary Medicine students and their parents. I described the adventures in my life with a slide show of the Science Center, falconry, rehabilitation, the eagle project, and the Wildlife Clinic. I joked that I did it all without a college degree. The parents looked at each other nervously and their smiles faded. I then concluded that when I went for a raise and a promotion, my bosses told me they were sorry, but I didn't have a college degree. After going back to school, I got that degree and my raise and promotion came soon after. I ended my talk with, "So, stay in school!" Then the parents were all smiles.

Blessings

Life was good and in 1993 Billy and I had a son. We named him after our fathers, Richard Benson and Richard Davis. The choice was obvious: Richard Benson Davis. We call him Ben, and Billy swears that's because the letters B-E-N stand for Bald Eagle Nestling. Ben was baptized in the little Methodist church with Wesley and Eleanor Elvidge—in their eighties—looking on.

Billy was promoted and some years later he became the district wildlife manager for all of Worcester County.

When we visit my mother's house in the summer on Cape Cod, a day doesn't go by without an osprey calling over the bay. We watch them dive for fish and bring their catch up to their chicks on a nest pole that Billy put up years earlier. Ben is proud that his father's task back in the 1980s of raising osprey nesting poles could have made such a difference. He stopped putting up nesting poles in 1995 when osprey numbers reached four hundred pairs.

Marjorie Smith

We did an animal program at a private school one day back in the 1980s and Billy and I mentioned that both of us had our interest sparked at an early age by a visiting Audubon instructor.

OSPREY CARRYING A FISH

OSPREY ON A NEST

A teacher rushed up after the program and told me that my Audubon instructor, Marjorie Smith, was alive and well and living in Maine. I gave her my address and later I received a letter from Marjorie. She was happy to hear that I was working with wildlife. We corresponded for twenty-five years. She sent me bald eagle and peregrine falcon articles that she found in the *Portland News,* I sent her articles and updates about our lives.

This inspired me to call Massachusetts Audubon and ask if I could work as a natural history guide during "mother's hours." Now I teach children and adults alike about the natural world and we go on nature hikes on four hundred acres of Audubon property in Worcester. My college days in natural history study paid off. Miss Marjorie Smith sparked my interest back in the fifth grade and now I can return the favor to a new generation of children.

In 2004 it was nice to write to Marjorie about the first wild peregrines ever to nest in downtown Worcester, on the balcony of an office building in a large rec-tangular planter. One parent was previously banded and from a Canadian nest. The mate was also banded and originally hatched in Boston on the Customs Tower They produced four healthy chicks that Tom French banded Billy went out on the ledge to ride shotgun for Tom so that he didn't get attacked by the protective adults. The falcons were screaming the whole time as they dive-bombed the two. Billy B. picked up prey remains including blue jay, oriole, starling, pigeon and woodcock. The peregrines weren't particular about the prey they caught. Billy B. also documented the historic event with his camera. Ben and I tagged along and I remembered again when the librarian in junior high school showed me the book, *Summer of the Falcon.*

A FEMALE PEREGRINE
FALCON SPREADING
HER WINGS

MOTHER FALCON FEEDING HER CHICKS

YOUNG MALE FALCON WITH BANDS

Back To The EcoTarium

I left Tufts in 1998 so that I could stay at home with Becky, now a teenager, and five-year-old Ben. A few years later, when Ben was in school full time, I was ready to go back to work. The museum I worked for in the 1970s, the Worcester Science Center, later renamed the EcoTarium, was looking for a wildlife veterinary technician. They hired me on January 2, 2002, and I have been working there for the past eleven years caring for the animals.

We have all kinds of owls including barn, screech, great horned, and barred, along with a scarlet macaw named O'Hara. We care for snakes, turtles, and lizards, chinchillas, hedgehogs and ferrets. For native wildlife we have opossums, skunks, a porcupine, foxes, and two river otters. (I got to help hand-raise the male otter from a pup.)

Liberty And Justice

We have a pair of bald eagles on display at the EcoTarium, Liberty and Justice, Mr. and Mrs. For-All. They have been nesting

DIANNE TEACHING AT MASS AUDUBON

O'HARA THE MACAW HELPING
DIANNE AT WORK AT THE
ECOTARIUM

GATSBY THE GREAT HORNED OWL

LIBERTY THE EAGLE
AND DIANNE AT THE ECOTARIUM

and laying eggs, but to date the eggs have been infertile. They both have left wing injuries so it may be that the male can't balance on the female's back to mate. Also, the male, who was banded in a wild nest over thirty-eight years ago, could be too old. Every time I walk by them they call to me. I feel like I'm back at Quabbin.

O'Hara The Macaw

I have another love-thing going on at the EcoTarium with O'Hara, a forty-year-old Scarlet Macaw with beautiful feathers of red, blue, and yellow. She thinks a few of the staff are special; all others need to beware of her powerful sharp beak.

Lately she displays herself and waits for me to come over to make mad passionate love. I'm flattered, but would prefer a friendly handshake and have taught her to offer her foot as a sign of affection. When I type the animal reports on the computer, she sits on the back of my chair and slowly inches herself on my arm and tries to "type." She is quite talkative, loves to preen, and enjoys a good laugh. She barks like a dog, clucks like a chicken, and always wants a cracker!

Animal Programs

On Sundays, along with caring for the animals, I do two, sometimes three, programs in the afternoon for the public. One is on reptiles and amphibians. I bring out two mole salamanders, an eastern box turtle, a corn snake, a ball python from Africa, and two lizards: a blue-tongued skink from Australia, and a four-and-a-half-foot tegu from South America. I was bitten by Pablo, the tegu, a week before I finished this book. I went to the hospital, got a prescription for antibiotics and received five stitches for the lacerations and deep puncture wounds. It was my fault for not paying close attention to this big and powerful animal. When I show these animals, I explain to the public that most of the exotic animals we have were pets that people gave up because they got too big or difficult to care for.

I do another program on birds of prey, and bring out a great horned owl named Gatsby and a red-tailed hawk named Jello. I describe their natural history and imitate the calls of a number of owls to end the program.

My day-to-day chores are feeding and cleaning the animals. I monitor their well-being by watching their weights, doing fecals, which is done to check for parasites, and keeping an eye on their diets and health. We receive tremendous help from my old employer, the Tufts Wildlife Clinic. We bring some of our animals to Tufts for their annual physical exams where they are given X-rays, have their teeth cleaned, and blood drawn. Our other animals get their check-ups at the EcoTarium. I love to go to work every day because it is so rewarding, but still, I can't wait to go home to see my family each night.

BEN, BECKY, DIANNE AND BILLY WITH A BANDED EAGLET

Eagle Project's Twenty-Fifth Anniversary

Billy Byrne, Jack Swedberg, his wife, Thelma, and Brad Blodget came to our house one summer to celebrate the twenty-fifth anniversary of the Eagle Project. We laughingly agreed we hadn't aged a bit! It was great to see everyone together.

Jack mentioned that about a year earlier he was up in coastal Maine with Thelma, taking pictures with his Nikon. It seems he fell on some slippery rocks and smashed his expensive camera. He also managed to break two ribs and crack one of his vertebrae. Now in his eighties, he says he's not doing so badly for an old buck.

Brad is retired; pursuing other interests including railroads and railroad history, he remains an avid birder and still shares a wealth of information.

Billy B. and Billy D. have had a close relationship for the past thirty years and are good hunting buddies. Many nights we sit down to dinner after their day in the woods and learn about how many different animals they saw: deer, sometimes a bobcat with kits, and hawks flying through the canopy.

Going digital, Billy Byrne's wildlife pictures are better than ever. At our cookout we reminisced about the good times and how well the eagles are doing today. At the end of the day we took a picture of the "eagle crew." We had taken a picture of ourselves after Hurricane Gloria at the hack site in 1985. We included Brad in our picture this time and I treasure both photographs.

Billy and I are still on our honeymoon. He still calls me his "ravishing creature" and always thanks me for being his wife. We stop each day for a lingering bear hug, count our blessings, and realize how lucky we truly are.

I can't wait to see what tomorrow brings.

EAGLE PROJECT 25TH REUNION GROUP LEFT TO RIGHT:
BILLY BYRNE, BILLY DAVIS, DIANNE, BRAD BLODGETT, JACK SWEDBERG

BILLY AND DIANNE

Epilogue

Billy and I sat on our deck one summer day in 2012 and watched an adult bald eagle fly over the house. It's been twenty-seven years since I spent that summer with the eagle babies. We both looked at each other and smiled. Becky, who was visiting us and was a month away from having her first child with her husband, Matt, looked up. Ben, who was two weeks away from starting college, stepped outside on the deck and also noticed the eagle. Billy looked at our grown children and then at me. He said, "Now that's what it's all about." I turned to him, then our children and the vanishing eagle, smiled and said,

"Yes, that is *exactly* what it's all about!"

Acknowledgements

So many people have had a profound and lasting influence in my life, both personally and professionally.

Marjorie Smith, my fifth grade Audubon teacher, opened my eyes to the wonder of nature and was my friend forty-five years later.

My parents' close friends—the Barrs, Halls, Days, Davises, Thurstons, Currys, Hapgoods and Roger Crearie—who were like an extended family, guiding, friendly and true role models.

My high school agricultural teachers; Mr. Henry Ruba and Mr. Perednia, and my sports coach, Mrs. McKay, who influenced me during those formative years.

The sport of falconry developed my interest in birds of prey thanks to Quinton (Scotty) and his wife, Louise, and Dick Lucius, my sponsor in falconry. Tom Ricardi, Ed Philips (Turtle Man), Mardi Snow, John Tobin, Dick Morrison, Julie Collier and Tom Early all shared my passion for raptors.

The people at the Worcester Science Center/EcoTarium, both from the seventies; Jack Clancy, Richard T. Kleber, Paul Lefrancois, and from the turn of the century; Steve Pitcher, Kathy Kennedy, Lynn Klein, Jen Dobson, Mike and Krystal Hamilton, Nancy

Ramsey and Nicole Auger. To the volunteers who have helped out over the years at the EcoTarium, my utmost appreciation. We couldn't do it without you!

I would like to thank the EcoTarium for allowing me to use the beautiful wildlife pictures taken at the museum.

Those from Massachusetts Fish and Wildlife: Tom French, Richard Cronin, Bill Easte, Jack's friend Roy Lindstrom, Herm Covey, Lee McLaughlin, Mike Ciborowski, Chris Thurlow, and Brandon Kibbe.

Those from MDC: Biologist Dave Small, Officers Richard O'Brien, (O.B.), Sgt. Z., and in memory, Kenny Stolgitis and Ron Gray

Those at the Radio Astronomy Site: Bill Olanyk and Harold Weatherbee.

Special thanks to the Quabbin Visitor Center for all the valuable historical information they provided.

My colleagues at Tufts who included Dr. Charles (Doc) Sedgwick, my mentor, who documented so many cases to help teach eager veterinary students in wildlife medicine, Dr. Mark Pokras, who told me that I need to get my book published, Carolyn Corsiglia, Alison Haskel, Deb Adams, Nancy Sutton, Sue Bennett, and Sandy Oelschlegel at the Tufts library who let me use the then new computers every day at lunch to write a lot of this book, Dr. Rachael Blackmer, Dr. Gretchen Kaufman, and interns: Dr. Janet Martin, Dr. Rose Borkowski and Dr. P. K. Robbins.

My colleagues currently at Tufts: Dr. Flo Tseng, Dr. Maureen Murray, and interns over the years: Dr. Ian Ashpole, Dr. Emily Christiansen, Dr. Sam Young, and Dr. Nicole Rose.

My fellow dedicated educators at Audubon in Worcester, Massachusetts, who include Deb Cary, Donna Williams, Gail

Howe, Ellen Minichiello, Christy Barnes, Kristin Steinmetz, Sheryl Farnam, Martha Gach, Marcia Grenier and Lisa Carlin.

My English teacher at Worcester State College, Professor Charles Wasilko. When I came to him in 1986 at the age of thirty-three, I told him I needed to write this book. He responded that Samuel Clemens didn't write Huck Finn until he was nearly fifty. "Who?" I said. I am now in my late fifties and it's ready to print.

Ed Phillips "Turtle Man." Thanks for your life changing encouragement.

My aunt and uncle, Rauna and Alan Benson. Thanks for making it happen. Carrie too!

To Jack Swedberg, the father of bald eagles nesting in Massachusetts, Billy Byrne whose fantastic pictures grace this book and Brad Blodget who asked me if I would like to see the baby eagles out at Quabbin in 1984, my utmost appreciation. They are also my close friends.

To Emily Eaton who allowed me to use her wonderful loon and peregrine photographs.

I want to thank Gloria Abramoff of Chandler House Press and Mass Audubon, my wonderful editor Margaret LeRoux, and Tom Campbell of King Printing Company for their help and experience in getting this book published.

Finally, the people that matter the most to me: my parents, Dick and Jane Benson, my siblings, Gail, Ronnie, Linda, and Janet, especially my husband and soul mate, Bill Davis, and my wonderful kids, Becky and Ben. The family wouldn't be complete without mentioning my first grandson, Syrus! I love you all.

No list would be complete without the thousands of animals that I have lived and worked with throughout my life.

Photo Credits

We gratefully acknowledge the courtesy of the following individuals and organizations for granting permission to use the photos contained in this book:

PAGE

15	MassWildlife/Bill Davis: Hack tower.
15	MassWildlife/Bill Davis: Eagle with US Fish and Wildlife band, and numbered identification tag.
20	Dianne Davis: School girl photo.
33	Dianne Davis: Nahani the wolf cub.
36	Jack Wilcox: Baby Sasha.
36 & 37	Ecotarium: Ursa.
38 & 39	Jack Wilcox: Sasha, Dianne and Sasha.
41	Dianne Davis: Dianne and Habiba hunting in a winter field.
43	MassWildlife/Bill Byrne: (top) Habiba lining her nest with pine boughs and feathers, (bottom) Habiba attempting to feed the baby chicken.
44	Dianne Davis: Habiba and her full grown rooster.

PAGE

PAGE

Eagle One is an intimate account of a woman's life devoted to family, wildlife, education and the environment. Dianne Davis was part of an ambitious and successful effort to reintroduce the endangered bald eagle, our national symbol, to the skies of Massachusetts. She lived alone in the wilderness of the immense Quabbin reservation for four months, raising eight baby eagles. This life changing experience, combined with years of both learning and sharing the secrets of veterinary medicine and animal behavior, have inspired thousands of people to take a closer look at our natural world.

Reading this book is inspiring. Dianne describes her experiences in ways that will encourage you to think more about your own encounters with nature; her writing and reflections are genuine and heartfelt. This is a book that will make you feel good every time you pick it up.

Deb Cary, Director, Massachusetts Audubon Society, Central Sanctuaries

This book... should be available to any student going into veterinary medicine.
Charles J. Sedgwick, DVM, first director of the Tufts Wildlife Clinic,
Tufts University Cummings School of Veterinary Medicine
Diplomate, ACLM, ACZM

US $24.95   Wildlife/Memoir

ISBN 978-1-886284-80-7

52495 >

9 781886 284807

CHANDLER HOUSE PRESS
EAGLE ONE
Raising Bald Eagles, A Wildlife Memoir
Dianne Benson Davis
Printed in the USA

06/29